The Ne[illegible]d Story

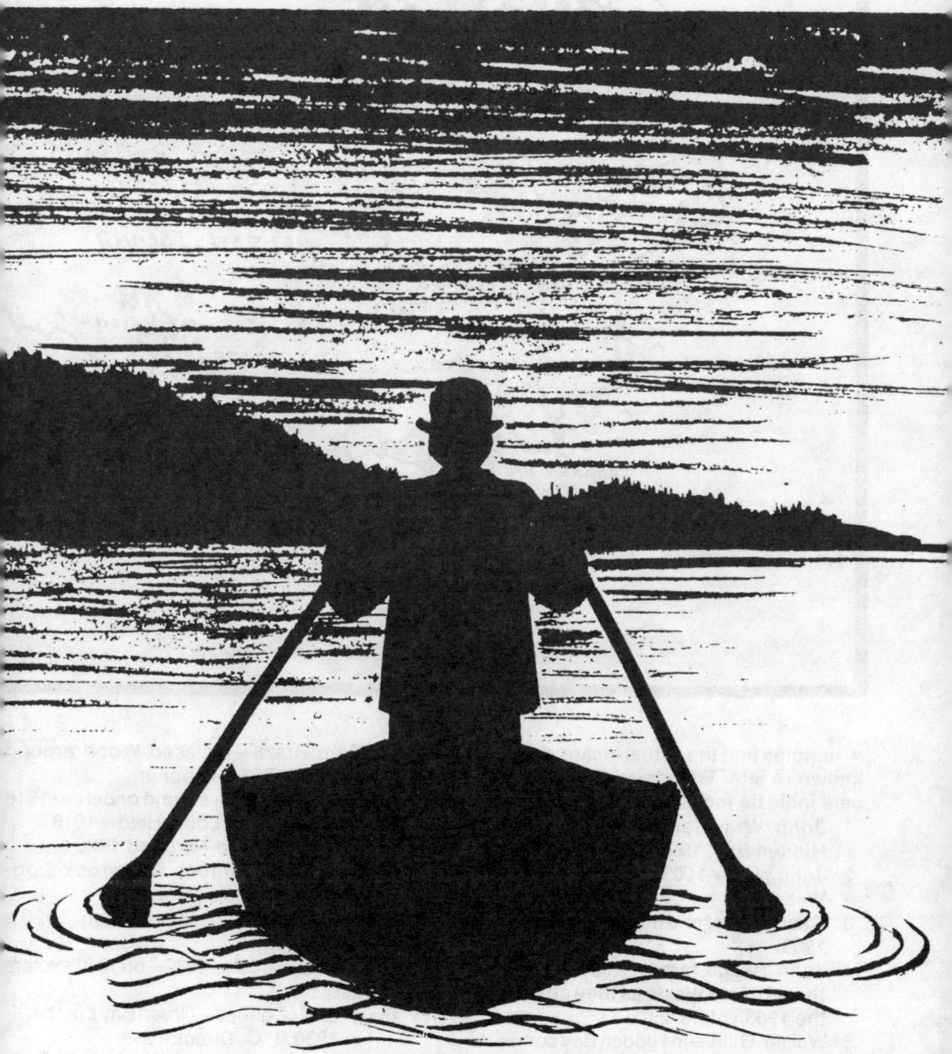

Karen Southern

Tom Brazil Silhouette by Ann Trousdall

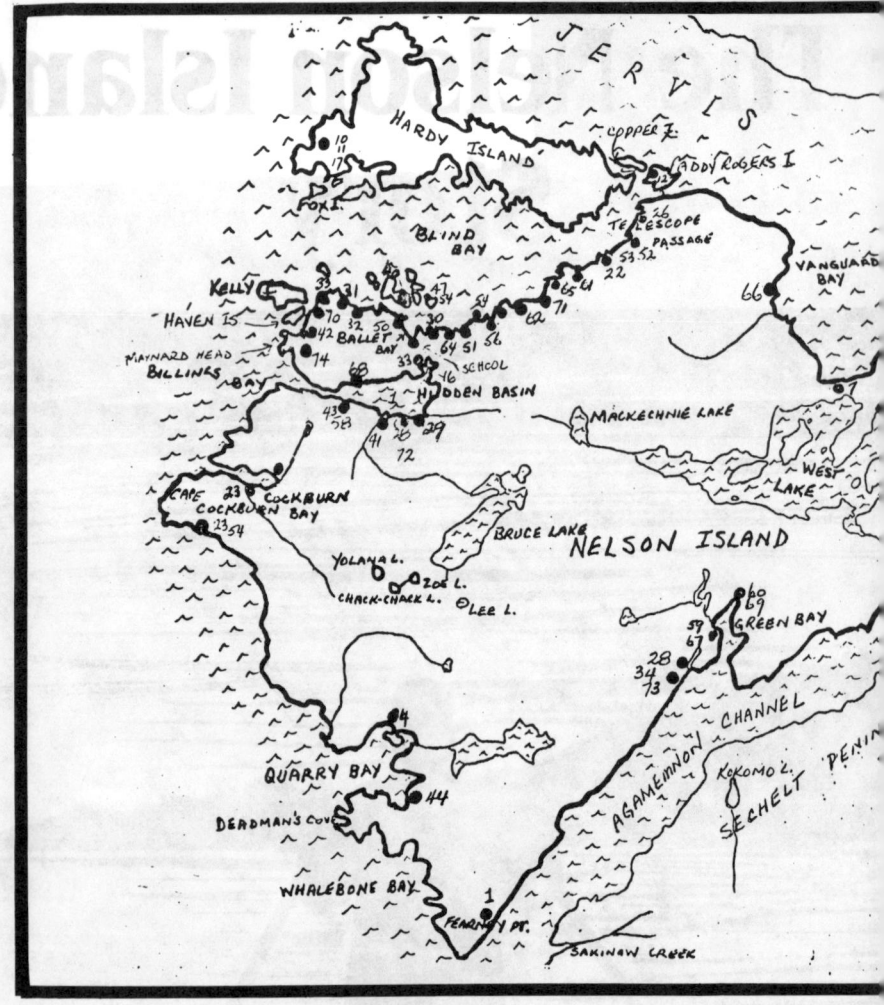

- denotes that the actual location was not known to later islanders; duplicate numbers indicate moves.

1. John Wray family—early 1890s to Hidden Bay, 1906 to Fearney Pt.
2. John West—1903 voters' list as Nelson Westmere
3. George West and mother—also around 1903
4. John Baggs family—may have been there before Wests as they are also on the 1903 voters' list
5. William Gillis—in Hidden Bay sometime before the Hammonds
6. John Hammond family—1907
7. Walter Wray and sisters—1910
8. ● MacKechnie—1913
9. ● G. Y. Smith—may have been in Vanguard Bay before 1914
10. J. M. MacKinnon and caretaker W. Wood
11. Tom Brazil—replaced Wood around 1912 or 1913, or sooner
12. Paddy Rogers—around or before 1918
13. Laughlins and Louis Heid—1918
14. ● Charles Heid—around 1920
15. ● John Shannon, Shamrock Logging—on 1920's voters' list
16. ● Barclay Handbrook—on 1920's voters list
17. L. A. Macomber—1930—on 1920's voters list
18. ● G. McConnell—Green Bay Lumber—in 1930 B. C. Directory
19. ● Jorgenson—sawmill—in 1930 B. C. Directory
20. ● Wm. McDonald—farmer—in 1930 B.C. Directory
21. ● D. Amscold—Shamrock Logging—in 1930 B. C. Directory
22. Forrest (Judd)—Johnstone—1930 caretaking Hardy I., 1931 to Blind Bay

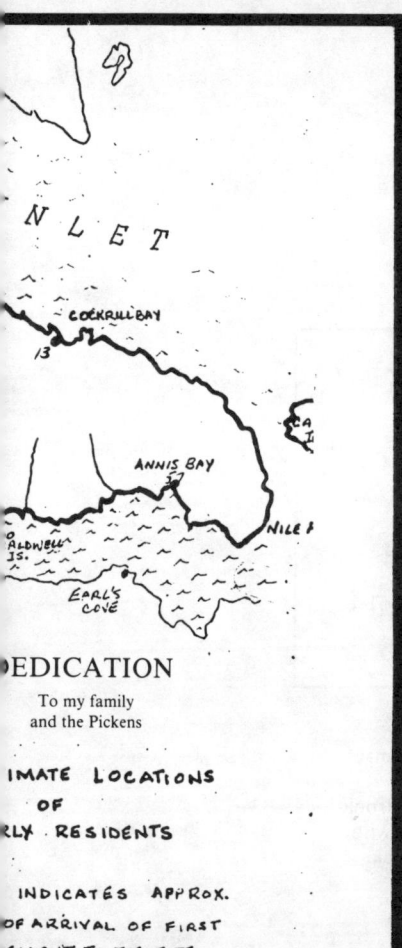

DEDICATION

To my family
and the Pickens

IMATE LOCATIONS
OF
RLY RESIDENTS

• INDICATES APPROX.
OF ARRIVAL OF FIRST
SIDENT TO THE SITE

23. Harry Roberts—1932 to Cockburn Bay; 1937 to Cape Cockburn.
24. • J. McLaughlin—around 1932 or 1933
25. Forester
26. Schutt
27. • Klaussen
28. Ott Heikinnen (Captain Henry)-bought property in Hidden Bay in 1920, but moved there in the 1930s; moved to Green Bay in early 1940s.
29. Harding Brothers—View Point Lodge 1933
30. Paul Harding—number indicates where home was built later
31. Bill Harding—number indicates where home was built later
32. Bert Harding—number indicates where home was built later
33. Art Harding—number indicates where home was built later
34. McNutt Brothers—1934
35. • "Auld Reekie"
36. • Gus Hansen
37. • Delongs—Lim, Robert and S.S.—listed in 1935 Directory
38. • M. Lombnes—caretaker of Vancouver Granite Quarry—1935 B. C. Directory
39. A. Wilson—farmer
40. Hugo Bjorklund—1936 or earlier
41. Jerry Jervis and Margaret McIntyre 1938
42. Lorne and Carole Maynard—1939
43. George and Celia Nuotio—1939
44. Nels Stigson—Quarry Bay—listed in 1940 B.C. Directory
45. • Martin Nynas—logger-listed in 1940 B. C. Directory
46. • Robert Smith—caretaker, Vancouver Granite
47. Tom Hughes
48. • Pete Klein—around 1940
49. Rae Phillips—around 1940
50. Harry Thomas—1941
51. Gordon Deberri
52. Richard Krentz
53. John Vaughn
54. Ann and Jacqueline Pettigrew
55. Lawrence Wray—1944
56. Ed Wehner—1944
57. • Anna in Annis Bay
58. Sandy and Grace Millard—1944
59. Yates and Follets—1944
60. Jim and Lou Read—Green Bay on or before 1944; Caldwell Island—1951-1976
61. Frank Ficek—on or before 1947
62. Geoffrey Partington, Bill Hartley, Robin Partington, and "Smitty" Smith-the "Navy Boys"—1947
63. • Ralph Williams, • Paul Green, and • Art Marshall—around 1947 logged Cockburn Bay
64. Chris Sandvold—possibly earlier
65. Fred Easthope
66. Lewis and John Milligan and families—1949
67. Frank and • Kathleen White—1949-1954
68. Bill and May Westbrook
69. Frasers and Gregorsons—1950 - 1957
70. Allen and Sharie Farrell—1952 - 1957
71. Mike Costello—1954
72. Fredericksons—1956
73. Ken Viitanen
74. Ernie and Nell Christmas

ISBN 0-88839-196-X
Copyright © 1987 Karen Southern

Canadian Cataloging in Publication Data

Southern, Karen, 1943-
　The Nelson Island Story

　Bibliography: p.
　ISBN 0-88839-196-X

1. Nelson Island (B. C.) - History.
I. Title.

FC3845.N4S68 1987　971.1'33　C86-091561-1
F1089.N4S68 1987

All rights reserved. No part of this publication may be reproduced, stored in a retrieval system or transmitted, in any form or by any means, electronic, mechanical, photocopying, recording or otherwise, without the prior written permission of Hancock House Publishers.

Second Printing 1989

First produced and published by
Hancock House Publishers, Surrey, B.C., in 1987

Table of Contents

Preface and Acknowledgments		5
I	**Early Quarry Workers and Pioneers**	9
	"Not Just a Lot of Rock and Christmas Trees"	9
	Twenty-four Quarry Workers Survive Shipwreck	12
	The Granite Quarries	14
	The Wray History	20
	Early Westmere	26
	Arrival of the Hammonds	29
	Hardy Island (1892 - 1951)	36
	To Hal Hammond	39
	Hardy Island School	40
	Macombers Buy from Nobility	41
	Tom Brazil	44
	The Nelson Island School	50
II	**The Loggers and Rum-Runners**	53
	Loggers	53
	The Early Years of Cockrill and Vanguard Bays	55
	Nighttimes	56
	The Twenties	57
	Rum-running Action	60
III	**The Independent Survive the Depression**	63
	Judd Johnston	63
	The Depression Years	72
	The Roberts, Hardings, and McNutts	74
	Harding Bros.	74
	McNutt Bros.	75
	An Ancient Village by Jack Charman (1935)	78
	Sunray	79
	The Lorne Maynard Family	83
	The Forties	89
	Harry and Margery Thomas	90
	Geoffrey Partington	96
	The Community	98
	The Forties in Cockburn Bay	100

IV	**The East Side of Nelson Island**	**104**
	Howard White Remembers Green Bay	104
	The Yates and Follets in Green Bay	123
	The Reads on Caldwell Island	125
	Westmere in the Forties	126
	The Milligans in Vanguard Bay	128
V	**Community Notes**	**134**
	The Place Names and Origins	134
	The Floats and Post Office	137
	The Ballet Bay School	139
	The Fifties	143
	Jottings of the John Antle	151
	The Parties	156
	Boatbuilding	157
	Boats Familiar to Waters of Nelson Island	158
	Storms	164
	The Telephone	166
	The Outhouse, the Backhouse, the Privy	168
	Island Kids	169
	Island Pets	171
	Nelson Island Uniqueness	174
	Stores and Delivery Service	177
	Christmas on Nelson	180
	The Community Dinner	182
	Logging after 1920 on Nelson & Hardy Islands	186
	The Failing of Frank Ficek	189
VI	**After the Exodus**	**191**
	Danger and Death	200
	Sue Milligan Returns	201
	The Sunray Roberts Today	204
	West Lake Today	205
	Conclusion	207
	Epilogue	212
	Bibliography	214

Preface

My interest in Nelson Island and my interest in writing local history began around the same time but through different incidents. In 1976, I met Frances Picken of Nelson Island while we were cooks at our sons' Cub Camp. During that summer a fast friendship was formed between the Southern and Picken families that has outlasted numerous weekend visits with our combined seven children (now seven teenagers).

That same fall, I began an English course at Malaspina College which required a research paper on local history. In uncovering the mystery of what really happened the night the Gulf Stream sank (published in The Powell River News, April, 1977), I found I enjoyed the challenge of recapturing the past.

When the Powell River Historical Research Committee (now the Powell River Heritage Research Association) was formed in January, 1982, to research and write the history of Powell River and surrounding islands, it seemed only natural for me to pick the area of Nelson and Hardy Islands. For over a year, hundreds of cups of coffee and stay-overs have been swapped with John and Frances for tidbits of Nelson lore, addresses of past residents, and boat trips to the islands. Even the trip to the Victoria Archives was shared with the two of them. There, Frances worked as hard as my husband and I did to trace mentions of the islands in obscure, unindexed books. Without their help, all this would not have been possible.

I would also like to acknowledge the New Horizons Program for funding the research; Ann Winberg for her help in typing the manuscript; Ann Trousdell for her drawing of Tom Brazil rowing, and copying over one hundred photos of early Nelson; Carla Mobley for her helpful editing and continuous support; Courtney Cressy for his cartoon of Tom Brazil and illustration of Sunray; Dan Sawatsky for his illustration of the rotten tramway on Granite Island; and Laura Everett for her cartoon of Frank Ficek.

Special thanks to former and present Nelson Islanders who painstakingly answered questionnaires and filled in maps, offered photos, and consented to be taped. They include: Geoffrey and Jacqueline Partington, who were the first. Geoff said at the time, "Why would you want to do a history of Nelson. It's just a lot of rock and Christmas trees." It didn't take long to find out that it was not just a lot of rock and Christmas trees.

Sarah Wray Edmond and daughter Isabel Goodrup, Thelma Deberri and daughter Fran Lambert, Sis Harris, Margaret McIntyre, Joan and Lewis Milligan and daughter Sue, Rowena Underwood (for her father, "Old Mitch") and Evelyn Roberts, for their tapes and interviews.

Howard White and Yolana Roberts Mortenson for all their wonderful reminiscences, Enid Wright and Clara O'Neill for the Hammond history and early Nelson happenings; Agnes Harding, Carole Maynard, Ann Pettigrew, Lawrence Wray, Harry Thomas, Allen Farrell, Florence Frederickson, John West, Ethel McNutt, Harriet Helliar, Wilf Wray, Lorene Yates and daughter Lola, Celia Nuotio, Bunny Loutitt, Florence Wiren (for father A. J. Charman), Dick Hammond (for father Hal), Grace Krentz, and summer residents: Jack Manley, Jim Spilsbury, Dr. J. A. Traynor, and Art Bishop.

I am indebted to Frances Gundry and staff of the B.C. Archives; Brien Brothman, archivist, Federal Archives; the late Golden Stanley, archivist P. R. Museum; Alex Wilcox, research officer Mines and Energy; J. McIntyre, Geographical Names; W. Rogers, Land Title Office; Arthur Thornthwaite, independent researcher; Dave Garling who interpreted legal documents; Bill Weems for his picture of the nutria; and particularly to Lester Peterson who provided almost all of the Sechelt Indian history and offered encouragement and names of former residents. He predicted that uncovering the Nelson Island history would be a "slow clam to open." I am sure that after a year in the steaming, I have only just opened the shell a crack.

Further information will be gratefully accepted by the Powell River Historical Museum, Box 42, Powell River, B.C. V8A 4Z5.

PART I

The Early Quarry Workers and Pioneers

Not "Just a Lot of Rock and Christmas Trees"

What may seem like just a lot of rock and Christmas trees to passing boaters is really a treasure haven of anecdotal history. Every rocky cove has its own story to tell, and although there may be as many versions of the story as there are islanders to tell it, nevertheless, the stories are there, waiting to be recorded in history.

Although Nelson and Hardy Islands are strategically placed at the entrance of the awe-inspiring Jervis Inlet, or possibly because of the grandeur of it, Captain George Vancouver made no mention of seeing them as he sailed past in 1791. The uncharted islands were known only to the Sechelt Indian tribes who summer-camped the area, fishing the plentiful waters, and adding their clam shells to the many middens on the rocky shores.

In the far north of B.C., the Hudson's Bay Company had been making history for almost forty years hustling the furs and Indians, and the sparkle of gold dust had been luring men to the northern mountains before Captain George Richards in the surveying ship, Plumper, sailed around the islands and christened them in 1860.

King George III's navy was well represented in the outcome. The largest island, approximately twelve miles in length, was named for

Rear Admiral Sir Horatio Nelson, the immortal hero of the British Navy, and the next largest was named for his friend, Vice Admiral Sir Thomas Masterman Hardy. Hardy was Lord Nelson's captain on the *Victory* at the battle of Trafalgar and served with Nelson for several years, becoming one of his most trusted officers and a highly valued friend.

The area is speckled with namesakes of flagships and admirals, surgeons and bargemen out of British Naval history. The names Telescope Passage and Blind Bay are from a famous story involving Lord Nelson at the Battle of Copenhagen. When his commander-in-chief gave the signal of recall to Nelson, he lifted his telescope to his blind eye to receive it. When he therefore could not "see" any signal, he continued the battle to victory.

It has been an apt name for the area as many a Nelson Islander has turned a blind eye to a number of commanders-in-chief over the years, ignoring game laws and social codes and obeying the law of necessity in an isolated area.

While gold fever raged, and silver and copper were being coaxed from reluctant ground in other areas of B.C., the less interesting, but more stable granite and lime rock of the islands waited for the B.C. government, still in its infancy, to discover it. And discover it they did. Surveyors measured and charted the finds, the most promising in the province, and newly-formed companies sent men and equipment to quarry the massive blocks to build the first impressive buildings of British Columbia.

Much of the rock of Nelson, Kelly, and Hardy Islands is still standing on the streets of Victoria and Vancouver today, the most well-known being the Parliament Buildings in our capital city. The base of the buildings and the Victoria Harbor sea wall are made of the extremely heavy Nelson granite.

Ironically, though, the first record of Nelson Island was its dealing with the United States. The *Colonist* of June 2, 1894 reports:

(Mistakes in grammar and punctuation have been left as it was reported in The Colonist.).

Nelson I. granite selected by the U.S. Bureau of yards and docks for the Port Orchard dry dock. Mr. R. I. Fox of Seattle contracted for the stone work of the new U.S. dry dock at Port Orchard, Washington has just completed arrangements with Mr. J. C. Preost of the Nelson Island Quarry for all the granite required.

Mr. Fox has secured the exclusive right of the whole output of the quarry and will work it himself putting on immediately a force of some twenty men to begin with.

The new dock, Mr. Fox explained yesterday, is to be over 800 ft.long—largest in the U.S. and with only two bigger ones in the world, the British Columbia granite is the choice of the Bureau of Yards and Docks at Washington. Mr. Fox, when he secured the contract, sent samples of Washington granite as well as several specimens of several B.C. quarries without specifying whence they came. With the result that the bureau pitched upon the Nelson Island stone as being far superior to any other. It weighs 184 pounds to the foot. It is the heaviest granite Mr. Fox has ever met with in his experience. The famous Aberdeen granite and that of Quincy, Massachusetts quarries only weighing seventeen pounds to the foot.

The engineer in charge of the new dock when the Nelson Island stone was submitted to him requested it where upon Mr. Fox sent his samples on to Washington, unnamed with the result already stated. The stone is to be used for the gates only, the body of the dock being built of piling and concrete. Seven thousand feet are to be quarried immediately and the transportation has been arranged for towing the barges to Port Orchard. Mr. Fox states that he will hire all his quarry men in B.C. even though he could get men on the American side for $1.75 a day while he has to pay $2.50 for Canadians. The local men are the best quarry men. Even with the duty of eleven cents a foot on the stone, the Nelson Island quarry can be worked so easily that it is cheaper to use than the inferior American stone.

There is a possibility that the same stone will be used for the building the sea wall of the new canal which is to connect Lake Washington with salt water at Seattle, for the purpose of making a fresh water harbor of the lake. This immense undertaking, which is to cost $7,000,000, is expected to begin in the next two months. The sea wall will reclaim over three miles square of land within the limits of Seattle and the lien which the promoters will have on the reclaimed land will, it is estimated, not only pay for the work but give a surplus of some three and a half million dollars when completed. Nelson Island building stone is not listed in the Minister of Mines yearly reports until 1899, but its earlier existence is alluded to in later reports. The 1904 report states that "Nelson Island, which adjoins Granite Island, formerly supplied the demand for granite, but was abandoned a year ago in favor of the latter island (Granite Island), where the quarries are more easily worked. With the exception of the small amount obtained from boulders, all the granite used on the coast of British Columbia had been quarried from the two islands."

The quarries operated long enough to fill contracts, then shut down. In 1895, the contract for the legislative buildings was filled at Quarry Bay, but unfortunately, the parliament buildings were not to be completed without tragedy.

Twenty-four Quarry Workers Survive Shipwreck

A violent southeaster pounded against the Victoria harbor breakwater. Aboard the tug *Velos*, a worried Captain Anderson gave the word to chief engineer, Arthur Bloor, "Start the engine."

They had postponed leaving for Nelson and Haddington Islands for three hours as the crew rounded up the quarry workers from around town. The storm had increased considerably in that time. It was 9:30 p.m., March 22, 1895, when the little tug *Velos* put out into the lashing blackness, pulling the heavy barge, *Pilot*.

Aboard *Pilot*, twenty-four reluctant quarry workers cursed the madness of leaving in such a gale. As the *Velos* heaved on, Captain Anderson and mate Andrew Christensen could see the senselessness of trying to carry on under such conditions and headed her instead towards Trial Island. "We'll put in at Cadboro Bay until morning," the captain suggested.

Although anxious to reach Nelson to begin filling his granite contract, Frederick Adams agreed to the stopover.

Velos struggled through Enterprise Channel between Oak Bay and Trial Island, dangerously close to the island reefs. With full force, the driving wind threatened to crash *Pilot* into its escort. The odds were too challenging. The March gale forced them to turn back.

As they were angling about, a wave of epic proportions swamped the little tug, smashing her on the reef. Christensen and Duncan, the deck hand, were out on deck. Christensen grabbed the hawser, searing his hands. Somehow he braved the icy water and was pulled to immediate safety by the men on the barge. Duncan, grabbing desperately at the line thrown to him, was swallowed unmercifully by a wave.

Two terrified men, Anderson and Law, gripped the slippery wreck while Bloor and Smith swam into the angry night, intent on shore. They never reached their goal.

With the half-submerged *Velos* acting as an anchor, *Pilot* careened helplessly in the raging surf, now charging towards the tug and the clinging men, now veering sharply away, shuddering against a jagged rock. Agonizing cries came from Law, knuckles white and frozen against *Velos*. From a short distance away Anderson's voice called out above the howling wind. He had swum for land and hit upon a ledge in the channel. Contractor Adams was silent, trapped in *Velos*' galley. Several men on the barge tried to launch the lifeboat to heed the men's cries, but as it hit the water it crashed against the hull of the barge, planks breaking like toothpicks.

As if the watery gods were satisfied with the sacrifice already made, they guided the barge, stern-first, into a tiny cove on Trial

Island into the only spot that would protect her weakened bottom from total destruction on the rocks.

The distraught quarry workers waited anxiously for dawn, their relief at surviving pierced at intervals by the cries of the *Velos'* skipper, Captain Anderson. They shouted back their encouragement. It was all that kept him going, he said later.

Some of the survivors searched the island by lantern light, and found food, clothing, and firewood in a deserted hermit's cabin. A lifeboat from *Velos* was washed up on shore later and patched by the men. A drenched and exhausted Captain Anderson was then rescued and taken ashore, suffering from severe exposure. He was wrapped in blankets and warmed by the fire. When Captain John Irving of the steamer, *Maud*, arrived for the rescue, Anderson was the first to go aboard.

Rumors that contractor Frederick Adams was carrying a large sum of money were refuted by his sons. They offered a $100 reward for the recovery of his body. The Adams family, worried about the safe arrival of the *Velos*, had been sitting out the storm in their drawing room. In the early morning, the dog began to howl. Mrs. Adams gasped, and blurted that something had happened to her husband. Strangely enough, when the bodies were recovered, both of their pocket watches had stopped at 2:00 a.m.

Quarry work was welcomely monotonous after that fearsome night. Blocks of granite were removed without too much incident from the Quarry Bay site, and the construction of the legislative buildings continued.

The Granite Quarries

For eons the rock lay dormant. Eagles soared above it, seals wallowed on it, and the great blue heron gulped his dinner of fingerlings along the shore. Small pieces of rock were of great value to the silent people. They fashioned knives and other tools, and used it to heat the water to boil the salmon. Even the mighty cedar was felled by placing hot stones around the roots to gradually burn into the soft wood and topple the tree.

They watched, puzzled, as the white men moved in with derricks and steam hoists, stripped away the sea blush and the blue-eyed

Marys, and drilled holes in the solid rock. They saw them put something in these holes and move quickly away. Then suddenly the seagulls cried, mergansers dove out of sight, and seals flopped noisily into the protective waters, as the strange ones brought thunder on clear days. With wedges, the white men released the massive blocks of stone and dangled them on overhead tramways. Then they loaded the hunting grounds of the silent people, piece by piece onto the scows and carried them to the waiting province.

Jock MacKay watched the Indians flee the waters around Quarry Bay in their cedar dugouts. He was glad to see them go, although they hadn't really bothered him in his short time in Canada. He'd heard stories of scalpings though, and he didn't want them around the boarding shacks.

This was an amazing country, he thought again, everything bigger and better. Take this rock—he had worked the famous Aberdeen granite, but it didn't compare to what was standing here before him. The grain was so uniform he couldn't detect a vein or knotlet in the entire sheet. Not even a slight discoloration. The whole point between Dead Man's Cove and the rest of Quarry Bay was the same. Before they were through, they'd quarry most of it, between what they needed for the Victoria graving dock and the New Westminster bridge.

He'd overheard Robert Armstrong, president of the Vancouver Granite Company, talking of cutting into the 300-foot shelf in Deadman's Cove, as well as the point jutting into the bay here.

By the time Jock MacKay had worked his way up the quarry ladder of success, he'd seen several outfits come and go, although the main contractors were still the Vancouver Granite Company. Hugh E. Keefer was the secretary-treasurer for them. Morris and Abel took paving blocks from the east side of Quarry Bay for a fee of eight cents a stone. The nine-inch by four and one-half-inch blocks were valued at $2 per square yard. By July, 1916, 40,000 to 50,000 blocks were on hand, representing quite a bundle in those days. Each quarry often had an independent mill operating on their property with the purpose of cutting and finishing the quarried blocks. Keast and Allen was one of the firms that built a 100-foot by 50-foot mill. As well as their own derrick crane and compressor, they were equipped with a double-blade saw, a large lathe, planers, and surfacers. Another outfit, J. McDairmid and Co., had a mill and two surfacers.

A new method of quarrying was used by most contractors by 1911, using compressed air. When the granite had no rift or direction of ready cleavage, a hole was drilled the desired depth, and a small charge of dynamite exploded at the bottom of it, which formed a cavity in which a small charge of powder was then exploded, causing a crack or crevice parallel to the surface of the rock. The workers then inserted a pipe, sealed it off, and blew compressed air through it. The gradually increasing pressure extended the cavity made by the gun powder blasts. They were getting pretty sophisticated then. When compressed air wasn't available, they used water under pressure, and small powder charges exploded at intervals of a few days.

Prices varied. Quarry blocks from Granite Island (later Kelly Island) were quoted at 50-55 cents per cubic foot loaded at the Nelson Island plant. If over eight-feet long, or over 150 cubic feet in volume, they were valued at sixty cents, even more in special cases. The production in 1915 was 25,000 cubic feet. Small quantities were shipped to Australia and Honolulu.

Before concrete became so widely used, the base of all the better buildings of the coast used the superior stone. In Vancouver alone were the Merchants Bank, Granville and Pender; Bank of Commerce, Main and Pender; the Court House; the Hudson Bay Company; and the Credit Foncier Building.

A darker granite, more suited for monumental work, was found half a mile southwest of Billings Bay. The firm of Alexander MacLennon and James Craig applied to lease the granite property in 1915. Most of the notable people of B.C., as well as a number of the notorious, were buried beneath tombstones of Nelson granite, according to the government yearly reports.

Until 1903, when the Granite Island quarry began working, the quarry at Quarry Bay supplied almost all the granite used on the coast of British Columbia. Granite Island, Kelly Island, is just off Nelson, about a mile long and a quarter of a mile wide; it is composed entirely of massive gray granite. It was usually easily worked, as the cooling fractures were generally vertical, and allowed massive blocks to be removed. The main working face was on the south end of the island 80 to 100 feet above the sea. An inclined tramway from this working face was used to load the stone on the scows. The Bank of Montreal in Victoria and the Federal Buildings in Seattle, Washington, as well as the new Post Office in

Quarry Bay granite showing size of the sheets. Report of the Building and Ornamental Stone Canada, 1917

The B. C. Parliament Buildings in 1917 with the Victoria Sea Wall in foreground. Base of buildings and all of sea wall is Nelson Island granite. Report of the Building and Ornamental Stone Canada, 1917

Bank of Montreal in Victoria is one of numerous early B.C. buildings built of Nelson or Granite island granite.
Report of the Building and Ornamental Stone Canada, 1917

The Winch Building and Post Office in Vancouver built of Fox and Granite island granites, 1917. Report of the Building and Ornamental Stone Canada, 1917

Vancouver in 1908, used rock from this source. The Quarry Bay operation was abandoned in favor of this more easily worked one. Messrs. Kelly and Murray of Vancouver owned the quarries.

In 1908, the Ellis Granite Company of Seattle reopened the Quarry Bay site, with the total production being supplied to Seattle. The working face was almost 100 feet longer than the Granite Island site, but only 30 feet high.

Another small quarry opened on the south side of Hardy with its total output going to the breakwater in Vancouver, according to the 1917 Building Stone government report.

Many more streets were cobbled with blocks from Granite Island and Fox Island. The Winch Building in Vancouver was also built with stone from the small Fox Island quarry. West Coast Granite Company had taken over from Kelly and Murray to supply this production and paid their workers $4.25 per day. Even then, the men were given time and a half for overtime and double scale for Sundays and holidays. Work seemed to peak in the early twenties when an average of fifteen men worked ten months annually, closing at Christmas and reopening when the weather improved. Until 1926, the quarry averaged 50,000 cubic feet per year, totalling 150,000 tons or 500 scowloads.

The Dominion government drydock at Esquimalt and the new UBC buildings at Point Grey took the bulk of the shipments, with the United States taking most of the rock sold for monumental trade. The Fordney tariff, the U.S. import duty, was increased five times, from three cents to fifteen cents, showing the superior quality of the granite.

Statues of Nelson Island granite, and war memorials for the men who didn't return from the Great War, were erected at Convent, Sacred Heart, Point Grey; Harding Memorial, Stanley Park; as well as cities such as Victoria; Vancouver; Chilliwack; Nanaimo; Kamloops; Calgary; Boise, Idaho; and McMinnville, Oregon.

Over the next thirty-six years, little is noted in the government reports. Work was intermittent and only when there was a demand for stone. Twelve men worked in 1935. Fewer men, an average of eight, were employed by the Vancouver Granite Company in the fifties when poor quality stone was sold for jetty rock and rubble. During 1961 and 1962, B.C. Slate Company worked the quarry, taking quarry rubble to produce split-face granite for building finish veneers.

Considering the dangerous materials involved in quarrying, there were surprisingly few accidents noted. In 1935, Magnus Lombes was killed instantly when he was crushed by 400-500 pounds of falling rock. An ex-islander confided that this, or another early accident, was really a murder that had been covered up. Supposedly, it was committed by a relief man from the peninsula during the depression. "The things they used to do and get away with!" she exclaimed. "Lots of accidents weren't really accidents."

Wilf (Tiff) Wray, whose father, Charles, ran the boat at the quarry, drilled, and did some blasting at the time the accident happened, said he remembers his father saying that it was just that, an accident. He was lifting some hooks with "tongs" and the rock came loose and crushed him. There was no murder involved. Lombes was taken to the Powell River General Hospital where Dr. Henderson was coroner. There was no blame attached.

Years later, Tiff himself was a quarry worker like his dad, who had worked from 1923 to 1940. He made much better than the $5 a day Charles did, but like him he learned to tell the difference between "hard" rock and "soft" rock. He would look for a seam or grain of the rock, much like a piece of cedar. When they found the grain, they drilled holes five or six inches deep and about the same apart, and used plugs and feathers (two pieces of iron with hooks on them), then tapped in the plug with a hammer until the rock just split. They were working for Bordignon Masonry Ltd. who barged the blocks to Vancouver for shipment to Japan for headstones.

An Italian crew were loading the large blocks for the Japanese market when an accident occured involving the powder man. The men heard the blast and looked up to see a piece of rock buckle him up as it hit his chest. He had used too short a wire, thinking he could outrun the blast. After the inquest, the same slab of rock that had killed him was sent with him to Italy to be his gravemarker.

The Wray History

John Wray heard of the railroad coming through to Bute Inlet in the early 1890s. He wanted to be in on this development that never materialized. He and his wife, Sarah, loaded their five children and their belongings into an old halibut dory and rowed out of Vancouver, catching what breeze they could with a small sail. After fifty miles, he pulled into Hidden Bay. It was as far as he got.

North of the Quarry Bay quarries, Nelson Island remained virginal. Long dug-out canoes brought the Coast Salish Indians from Sechelt to the beaches they had claimed for centuries. They built fish traps around Hardy and Clio Islands, and left their mark in red ocher on the rock face of Telescope Pass across from the island in the entrance.

Numerous middens on the island concealed discarded arrowheads and implements, now precious artifacts. The Wray family settled close to one of these middens and farmed the Hidden Bay site. They were there until Mr. Wray came back from getting the mail one day and found his wife with everything packed. "I want to get out of here, right now!" she told him.

He could feel the determination in her voice, and heeded her wish. She was a tiny woman, just five feet and a hundred pounds, and was doing her best in this strange new world. But each time she hit something or bumped anything, it echoed and reechoed across the bay, and she could take it no longer. She was a city woman from England and had been to the seashore only twice in her life before coming to the island. As well, her oldest three children, John, Harold, and Charles, were boys and more help to their father than to her. The young girls, Emily and Ruth, still needed constant attention. And, of course, she hadn't a convenience in the world.

The Wray's next home was Quarry Bay. Here their daughter Harriet was born in 1895, the first white baby born on Nelson Island. John worked at the quarry for a while before moving to Pender Harbour where little Sarah and Walter were born in 1897 and 1900. For the two years they lived there, Mrs. Wray never saw another white woman. Only four bachelors lived in Pender Harbour permanently, Charlie Irvine, George Tough, Harry Tegg, and a man by the name of Pritchard. John Lyle, a trapper, and Jack Vickers, a beachcomber, came occasionally to the area.

It was all wilderness. At that time there was a boat every two weeks. If there was a passenger arriving at Irvine's Landing, the *Comox*, would stop on the way up to the coastal camps. If not, it would only stop on the return trip. The Wrays had no way of knowing before the steamer came. It took six hours to get to Vancouver from Pender Harbour then.

John and Sarah Wray in the orchard. S. Edmond

The Wray family in 1902. Left to right: Harold; John, Jr. (Jack); John, Sr., holding Walter; Sarah; Charles; Emily; Ruth, and Harriet. Sarah, Jr., ran out of the picture.
S. Edmond

Jack Wray, John's oldest son, home from the hunt around 1902. S. Edmond

John Wray with 450-pound shark caught off Pender Harbour. Harriet made more with this photo than John did selling the shark oil. H. Helliar

Tugboats coming into the logging camp at the head of the harbor used to bring in newspapers and books. Engineers on the *Comox*, Chris Dragovitch and George Miller, would bring John a bundle of newspapers and magazines nearly every run. A magazine couldn't be bought on Nelson or in Pender Harbour. Sarah remembers her father sitting by the hour and reading the paper.

After a short stay in Egmont, they moved permanently to Nelson Island in 1906. John Wray applied for an original Crown grant and preempted the 160-acre property near Fearney Point in Agamemnon Channel.

Wray's early life on Nelson was primitive. Their three-bedroom home of cedar slabs was comfortable but not luxurious. A large verandah shaded the house in summer. Kerosene lamps lit up the home-made furniture and hand-filled feather beds. The plumbing was outside in the yard with the feed sheds.

It took a lot of hard work to maintain an existence. John, who was a professor, taught his family at home, both book learning and how to survive in isolation. With their mother's help, the children became adept at gardening, salting, smoking, and canning, and learned early to sew their own clothes. What they bought, they purchased in bulk.

During the summer all hands were up at 4 o'clock to pick the gooseberries, raspberries, and currants from plants Sarah had planted. The Empress Jam Factory supplied the twenty-eight pound tubs which they filled and rowed to the steamer at Irvine's Landing, for same-day delivery service to Brackman-Kerr Milling Co. in Vancouver.

Sarah had chickens and sold both eggs and hens, while John fished for the family. During the hunting season, Wrays could sell deer meat, as they had a Free Farmer's License. The game laws of 1895 allowed farmers to kill, at any time, deer who were "depasturing" their fields. Resident farmers, free miners actively working, and Indians, were exempt from the prohibitive game laws if game was used for their own consumption. The curator of the Provincial Museum and his aides were also allowed to hunt if they were collecting specimens of natural history.

Outside the closed season, farmers in unorganized districts could legally sell game for a period of five days after shooting, if they could prove their time of killing. It is interesting to note that the hunting license at this time to people not "domiciled" to the province or serving in Queen Victoria's army and navy, was $50! It was often cheaper to purchase land with a house on it and become "domiciled" than to buy a hunting license.

The Wrays found selling the deer was a helpful way of supplementing their meager income.

The monotony of the constant work load was occasionally broken by a visit from the Hammonds, after their arrival. The Hammonds would leave Hidden Bay on the early slack tide and return by the late slack, giving them six hours for their visit and journey around the island. On Sundays Mrs. Wray enjoyed a weekly visit with Mrs. West at Westmere. These welcome respites made the isolated living more bearable.

In 1910, John's brother Walter and his sisters moved to the island from England. Harriet remembers him telling them that a war was coming. He warned them of the immense army that was gathering forces in Germany.

The Wray children all grew up on Nelson, safe from the furor in Europe. They all read a lot, the girls crocheted, and they attended dances in Pender Harbour when they were older. Most of them left when they went to work or married.

Harriet returned with her husband, Fred Helliar, when he logged Quarry Bay years later. She had a reputation for being a good hunter, although she denies it. She admits to shooting the hawks before they got the chickens, but a better story is told of her deer hunting. Apparently the men would organize a hunt with great preparation, and go off into the hills for miles. After they were gone, she would silently tread 200 yards from the house, kill a deer, and have it dressed and hanging in the shed before the men were back—skunked.

There are no Wrays on Nelson now. The eight Wrays visited with their children into the early forties when John died at the age of eighty-five. The grandchildren share happy memories of summers near Fearney Point.

Early Westmere

John West, his brother George, and their mother arrived in Irvine's Landing at the turn of the century. Mrs. West was a school teacher from England who, when widowed, had put her sons through college. At the time of her arrival, she was the second white woman in the area. They had spent some time in Los Angeles and Vancouver before coming to this out-of-the-way fur-trading post, a world away from bustling England. Charlie Irvine was itching to go to the Klondike and the Wests arrived in time to mind the shop while he tried his luck at prospecting.

After Charlie's disgruntled return, the Wests settled on Nelson Island. Their property sided on beautiful West Lake and fronted on the fish-rich ocean. George took up residence across the lake with his mother, while John built on the sea side. It must have seemed an ideal spot for a hotel as he set to work to build Westmere.

The coast in this area was so sparsely settled and so infrequently visited that different men warned John of his folly. "It's too big. It will be too cold. It will be too hard to heat. No one will come," they all said. "There's already a hotel at Irvine's Landing."

But he built it anyway—a seventeen room hotel with a store and post office. But it was too cold. And it was too hard to heat. And almost no one came. So after a while he took a crosscut saw and sawed it in half, boarded up the end, and burned the other half for firewood.

John West, Jr., says his "Pappy's hotel was 100 years ahead of its time—opening day, there was only one couple."

To supplement the hotel revenue, John, Sr., did some handlogging. He brought a bride out from England and started a family. John, Jr., was born in 1913; Robin and Pansy were born later, all in Vancouver. John, Sr., acquired a steam donkey for his logging operation but during the first war, the market for fir and cedar dropped drastically. As the island didn't grow the required spruce for airplane building, he lost everything. He remained on Nelson until he died, in the forties.

George West was presumed drowned when his overturned canoe was found in the lake earlier.

Westmere attracted a few more visitors over the years. The people who came were loyal, often sons and daughters and grandchildren of the original guests.

The original hotel at Westmere, built by John West, Sr., was later cut in half to use for firewood.　L. Wray

Isabel and Ivy (Sarah Jr.'s daughters) and Jimmy and Ron (Walter's sons) were some of the Wray grandchildren who enjoyed Nelson Island summers.
S. Edmond

John, Jr., fished commercially for forty years. He remembers clearly the market falling in the thirties when a white spring salmon sold for one cent a pound, pink spring and ling cod for two cents, and red spring for three. The local fishermen competed with the Japanese whom the canneries had brought in earlier in the century. A resentment grew. John says, "young Japanese storekeepers in Egmont boasted of what they would do when they took over Canada." The older generation remained quiet. John, like others of his day, felt the government was justified in interning the Canadian-Japanese.

The 1903 voters' roll (in which Nelson Island was listed in the Richmond electoral district), gives the name of one of West's and Wray's neighbors as John Baggs, a cattle rancher. "Neighbor" is used loosely as the Baggs family lived in what is now referred to as Baggs' Bay, part of the larger Quarry Bay. He had a ranch and some cattle, but unfortunately for the Wrays, his cattle preferred Wray's seaside meadow, and his bull, their cows—which could only be reached by trampling down Mrs. Wray's flower garden. It put a strain on the neighborly relationship.

The Baggs had eight children, and from all reports, found life very difficult. He planted an orchard on an old beaver meadow, but the ranch and orchard weren't enough to sustain them. "They were poor," said a much later resident, "which must have meant dirt-poor, as no one in those days had very much, and worked hard to get that." Mrs. Baggs died young, around 1910, leaving her large family without a mother.

A summer neighbor of the West's was Harry Senkler. Land was easy to obtain in the early 1900s. It seemed to be there for the asking. Manzanita, or Senkler Island as it is generally known, was just one example. John West was in Vancouver to do some business and was looking for a lawyer along Hastings Street. He liked the firm name: "Buell and Senkler," on a window and went in. He met Harry Senkler, the junior partner and suggested he drop in to Westmere anytime he was in the vicinity.

Harry's wife, Margaret, happened to be cruising in the area a short time later, and stopped to visit with John West and his wife at Westmere. John took them for a row to one of the islands on the lake and suggested that it would make a nice summer house for the Senklers. It was a beautiful clear day and Margaret was enthralled. She and Harry later returned and purchased a larger island with a good building site on it. A profuse growth of Manzanita bushes gave the name to the island, but it was and is still known as Senkler's Island.

John West was to get another "neighbor" in 1907. John Hammond had been timber cruising with his brother Fred in the early 1900s, and sized up the rich stands of Douglas fir and cedar in Hidden Bay. He took out two preemptions in the area. Preparations were made to move his family from their home in Gillies Bay, Texada, to this secluded lagoon.

Arrival of the Hammonds

If there had been anyone around to see the arrival of John Latimer Hammond and his wife Mary (May) and family, to Nelson Island, they would have been amused to see the floating contingent. Young heads bobbed about the pleasure boat, *Lady May*, as it pulled a raft into the lagoon with two scared horses, several wide-eyed pigs, and a flock of clucking chickens. There was bedlam as they all had to swim ashore. The chickens got such a fright that they took to the woods for a week.

May and her new baby made their way carefully, while eight other children eagerly explored their new surroundings. One-year-old Coral kept coming back to Mama's skirts while May viewed the beautiful secluded 320-acre crown-grant area that was to be their home for most of the next thirteen years. White capped mountains of the Coast Range formed the backdrop to the cedar forests below them.

During the first year they all lived in a raft house in the bay while Jack built their house ashore. A team of oxen was brought in to help with the logging, and farm equipment was utilized to tame the area that was to be known as "the ranch." Mary (Minnie) was the oldest at fourteen, and Cliff and Hal were twelve and ten respectively. Besides Isabel and Coral, the two babies, there were Enid, three, Doris, four, Henrietta, six, and Barbara, seven. Life was to be a great challenge to the Hammonds in this isolated area.

There was enough to do to just keep a large family fed and many hours were spent tending the garden, and canning and pickling the harvest. Venison and fish were salted in crocks, or canned. Water was often a problem in the early years when their well, which was fed mostly by surface water, would go dry each summer. To alleviate the shortage, they piped water from the stream flowing into the bight between the house and Jimmy's Point.

Getting jars enough for the preserving was always a problem, especially when the fruit trees they planted a mile inland began bearing. The orchard supplied them with apples, cherries, butternuts, plums, pears, Italian prunes, and quinces. Some of the apples grown there have names no longer known: Wismer's Dessert, Twenty-ounce Pippens, Wolf River, Lord Suffield, and Russet. More well-known ones were Duchess, King, Gravenstein, Winesap, and Yellow Transparent. One particularly fruitful year, May and Enid gathered the whiskey bottles left by the thirsty loggers when the Rat Portage Logging closed shop. The now collectables were filled with stewed raspberries and blackberries through a funnel, then a cork was set in, and the bottles dipped in liquid resin from the fir and spruce to make a complete seal.

With Jack busy logging and building, as well as farming, May and the boys often did the hunting for the family. Hal hunted at a very early age, shooting his first deer at eleven. He became quick too, once bagging fourteen wild geese at an outing.

At first May dressed as a proper lady for her hunting excursions, with long skirt and hat, but as she headed for the hills, her heavy serge skirt became soaked and weighed a ton. Common sense soon prevailed and trousers became her hunting apparel. Clara thinks she may have been the first woman in B.C. to wear a pair of men's pants. She became quite a hunter; a carcass of deer was always hanging in the shed.

The need for medical help could sometimes pose a problem for these early islanders. Most of the time they stayed healthy. With Dr. Burnett, the family doctor, living in Vancouver, *May Hammond* had to be equal to any emergency. She kept her shelves stocked with such things as castor oil, epsom salts, painkillers, and bromoquinine. One time though, three-year-old Coral was in danger of suffocating from her badly swollen tonsils and adenoids. There was a south-east gale whipping at the Malaspina Straits that day when May and Coral were rowed out to the Santa Maria. Coral was literally thrown into Captain Lawrey's arms. May inched her way up a cold metal ladder as the waves lapped at her ankles, and was

Four of the Hammond sisters, in the wilderness, in floppy sunhats which required starching and ironing. M. Hammond

Hammond's log house, built in 1909, with Hal's launch in foreground. M. Hammond

Jack Hammond with ox team on Texada Island, before coming to Nelson Island in 1907. M. Hammond

Rita and Barbara Hammond in Hidden Bay, 1912.
M. Hammond

May Hammond hunting in hat and long skirt. M. Hammond

Clara as a baby in May Hammond's arms, 1914.
M. Hammond

May Hammond in the potatoes at the ranch in 1916. M. Hammond

helped aboard by two deck hands. Coral was safely delivered to Dr. Burnett and relieved of her miserable tonsils before returning to Hidden Bay.

Three more children were born to May during her stay on Nelson, all without any more help than that of a friend. Nelson was born in 1909, Phyllis in 1911, and Clara in 1914. Mrs. G. Y. Smith of Vanguard Bay was midwife on occasion. Clara was May's thirteenth baby. Her first son, Bertram (Bertie), had drowned when just three years old. She survived through more than most pioneer women, and still seemed to thrive.

The 'flu epidemic of 1918 was just another pioneer challenge to her. Twenty million people perished around the world in the most destructive epidemic in history, and fifty times that number were affected. When it hit the islands in the fall, Hal was away working and picked up the highly contagious bug. He was a pretty sick young man when he arrived home in his launch. May quarantined him in the big house by the water and sent the rest of the family up to the ranch to camp out for several weeks. She cured Hal by giving him one tablespoon of milk every four hours, and putting poultices of raw onions on his feet! She managed to keep all the others free from the dreaded disease.

May was a wonder. When the four oldest children were small she helped educate them, giving them the only education they obtained. She kept a wonderful garden, transplanting her sweet briar rose from Ireland to all of her Canadian homes, and tending her red peonies. She recorded the Hammond memories on film, even developing some of the photographs herself. She saved her young daughters from pursuing pigs. She hunted, cooked, baked, preserved, and with the help of Enid and Barbara, even lined the big house with salvaged wood, and laid new floors in the main part of the house, as well as the porches and sheds. She kept shop and fed numerous visitors, providing them with free lodging and hunting guides. She even starched and ironed the girl's sun hats away up there in the wilderness. Of course, none of this could be accomplished without a great deal of help and cooperation from the rest of the family. May's ability to supervise may have been her greatest asset.

Wilderness or no, Enid says, "Mother couldn't face life without reading *The Province*, or *The Vancouver Daily World* then, of course," and welcoming her visitors from outside. Many boats anchored or tied up at their little quay—fishing boats, tugboats, launches, sloops, schooners, and luxury yachts. Some of the captains of these boats came into the bay on a flood tide and then had to wait until slack tide in the treacherous tidal falls as the "basin" filled or emptied.

The novelist, Bertrand W. Sinclair, was a friend who often dropped anchor. On one of his visits to the bay he dreamed up a novel dealing with Chinese smugglers and set it in this secluded area. Sinclair was a novelist of Canadian fame who was receiving a $2,000 down payment for a novel manuscript and $1,000 for a novella, in 1920. He wrote many books set both in Canadian and American (Montana) locales, and perfected the "cowboy" story before Zane Grey became popular. Some of his B.C. books included *Big Timber, Poor Man's Rock, Hidden Places*, and *North of 53*. *The Bank Trollers* was a popular west coast poem of his.

Other guests of the Hammonds included Victor Spencer of Spencer's Department Store, the forerunner of Eaton's; Billy Woodward, of Woodwards Department Store; E. K. Debeck, a lawyer and Clerk of the House for years; South American Ambassador, Rogers; and the Cloughs, father and son who traveled extensively around the world and sent many postcards.

Guests closer to home included residents of Granite Island where the quarry was a thriving industry for many years. The Andersons, Lewises, Beatons, and Hugh Campbells came often to Hidden Bay. The veterans from the soldier settlement, Jim Young, Charlie Robinson, Sam Slaven, Guy Buchanen, and Bill Smith were all good friends as were Martha and Martin Warnock who lived for a short time in a raft house in Hidden Bay.

Music was a happy part of the Hammond life. May brought an antique organ with bellows, with her from Texada Island. Then, around 1912 or '13, a more modern one was acquired to provide the chords for the singing. Both Hal and May played the accordion as well, and visiting violinists always carried their instruments with them. Occasionally, friends on yachts and launches would bring their wind-ups, complete with horns. At those times, classical records and some, "well otherwise" as Enid puts it, would keep them entertained. I can't help but wonder if anyone brought May the record or music for *My Wild Irish Rose* that became popular in 1900 or *When Irish Eyes are Smiling*, that beautiful song of 1912.

Jack Hammond continued his logging, taking time to do some fur trapping and farming and even some boat building over the years. His health was bad though, and in 1914, according to his daughter Clara, the doctor ordered him to a warmer climate for a couple of years. He left for the Fiji Islands, traveling on the *Niagara*.

He left May and the family with little or no income. Clifford enlisted in the 72nd Highlanders some time the next year and Hal, whom May had exempted, became more or less sole support of the family. He was working for C. T. R. Nixon at the quarry on Hardy Island. The store that she opened in her home helped considerably, but she finally had to sell the property on Texada Island to buy the necessities. Although it was a thin time for the family, they don't recall ever going hungry.

Hardy Island (1892 to 1951)

Hardy Island was for years a forested gem at the entrance to Jervis Inlet, almost two thousand acres of virgin timber, and hundreds of acres of shoreline, rich with native clams and imported Japanese oysters.

In its ninety years of recorded history, the four district lots have changed hands fourteen times, but only one man, Tom Brazil, ever lived on the island year 'round for any length of time, and he was never an owner.

On December 17, 1892, Alexander Grant and Harry Tegg were crown granted one lot apiece for the exorbitant price of $1 per acre. The former paid $723 for Lot 1487 and the latter $884 for Lot 1488. The next year, Tegg added the 185-acre Lot 1489 to his ownership and in 1894, Grant purchased Lot 1486 for $207.

Harry Tegg was remembered as one of the remittance men who came out to Canada in the early days, the black sheep of a prominent English family. He was a character who lived at Irvine's Landing in the late nineteenth and early twentieth century. Nothing is remembered of Alexander Grant, but in December, 1903, both Grant and Tegg forfeited their land to the crown for arrears of taxes, although Tegg managed to keep his eastern property, Lot 1489. The three forfeited lots were sold to John McLelland MacKinnon in 1906 for a total of $267.17, a real bargain for the canny Scotsman.

All four lots were transferred to James S. Emerson, and then back

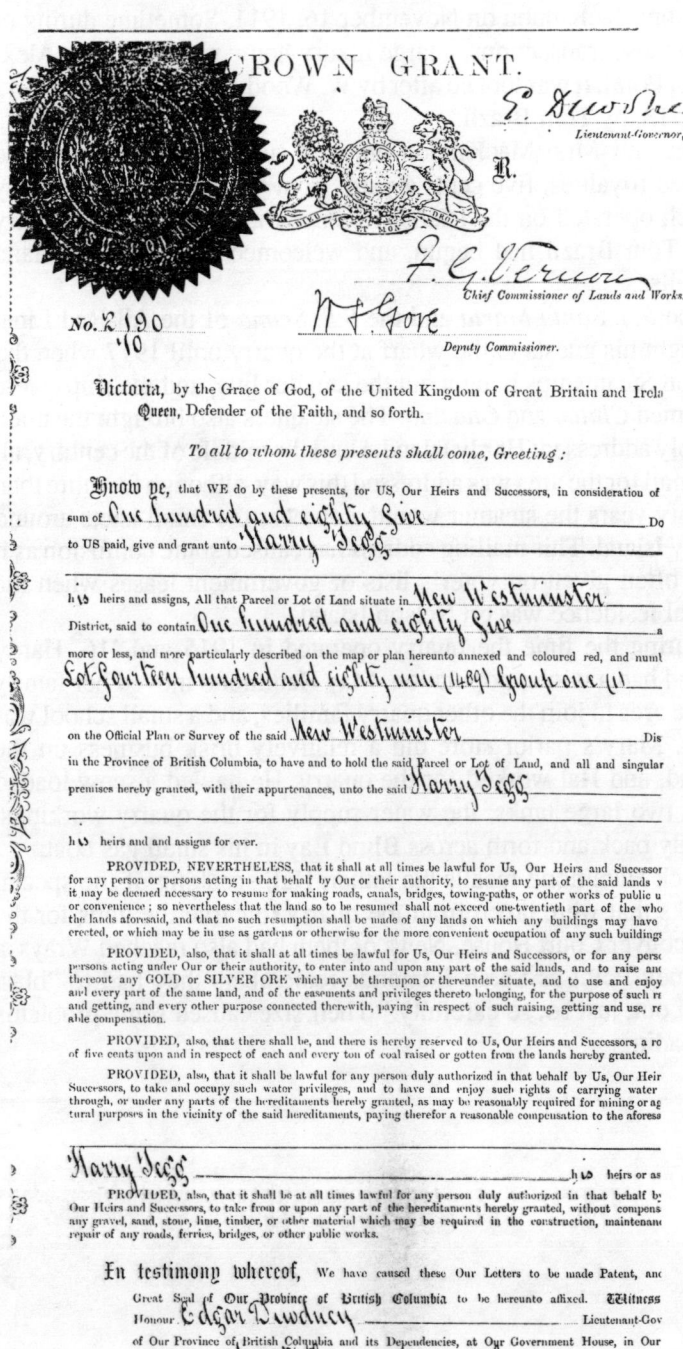

CROWN GRANT.

E. Dewdney
Lieutenant-Governor

F. G. Vernon
Chief Commissioner of Lands and Works.

W. S. Gore
Deputy Commissioner.

No. 2190/10

Victoria, by the Grace of God, of the United Kingdom of Great Britain and Ireland, Queen, Defender of the Faith, and so forth.

To all to whom these presents shall come, Greeting:

Know ye, that WE do by these presents, for US, Our Heirs and Successors, in consideration of the sum of One hundred and eighty five Do[llars] to US paid, give and grant unto Harry Tegg _____ his heirs and assigns, All that Parcel or Lot of Land situate in New Westminster District, said to contain One hundred and eighty five a[cres] more or less, and more particularly described on the map or plan hereunto annexed and coloured red, and numb[ered] Lot Fourteen hundred and eighty nine (1489) Group one (1) _____ on the Official Plan or Survey of the said New Westminster _____ Dis[trict] in the Province of British Columbia, to have and to hold the said Parcel or Lot of Land, and all and singular the premises hereby granted, with their appurtenances, unto the said Harry Tegg _____ his heirs and and assigns for ever.

PROVIDED, NEVERTHELESS, that it shall at all times be lawful for Us, Our Heirs and Successors, for any person or persons acting in that behalf by Our or their authority, to resume any part of the said lands w[hich] it may be deemed necessary to resume for making roads, canals, bridges, towing-paths, or other works of public u[se] or convenience; so nevertheless that the land so to be resumed shall not exceed one-twentieth part of the who[le of] the lands aforesaid, and that no such resumption shall be made of any lands on which any buildings may have [been] erected, or which may be in use as gardens or otherwise for the more convenient occupation of any such buildings.

PROVIDED, also, that it shall at all times be lawful for Us, Our Heirs and Successors, or for any perso[n or] persons acting under Our or their authority, to enter into and upon any part of the said lands, and to raise an[d take] thereout any GOLD or SILVER ORE which may be thereupon or thereunder situate, and to use and enjoy an[y] and every part of the same land, and of the easements and privileges thereto belonging, for the purpose of such ra[ising] and getting, and every other purpose connected therewith, paying in respect of such raising, getting and use, re[ason-] able compensation.

PROVIDED, also, that there shall be, and there is hereby reserved to Us, Our Heirs and Successors, a ro[yalty] of five cents upon and in respect of each and every ton of coal raised or gotten from the lands hereby granted.

PROVIDED, also, that it shall be lawful for any person duly authorized in that behalf by Us, Our Heir[s and] Successors, to take and occupy such water privileges, and to have and enjoy such rights of carrying water [to and] through, or under any parts of the hereditaments hereby granted, as may be reasonably required for mining or ag[ricul-] tural purposes in the vicinity of the said hereditaments, paying therefor a reasonable compensation to the aforesa[id]

Harry Tegg _____ his heirs or as[signs]

PROVIDED, also, that it shall be at all times lawful for any person duly authorized in that behalf by Our Heirs and Successors, to take from or upon any part of the hereditaments hereby granted, without compens[ation] any gravel, sand, stone, lime, timber, or other material which may be required in the construction, maintenan[ce or] repair of any roads, ferries, bridges, or other public works.

In testimony whereof, We have caused these Our Letters to be made Patent, and [the] Great Seal of Our Province of British Columbia to be hereunto affixed. **Witness** [His] Honour Edgar Dewdney _____ Lieutenant-Gov[ernor] of Our Province of British Columbia and its Dependencies, at Our Government House, in Our [City] of Victoria, this Twentieth _____ day of July _____ i[n]

This is a copy of Harry Tegg's crown grant, signed by Edgar Dewdney, lieutenant governor. Powell River Museum

to John MacKinnon on November 16, 1911. Sometime during or after these transactions, a large luxury home was built near Alexander Point. It was looked after by W. Wood, and later, around 1912 or 1913, by Tom Brazil.

Mr. and Mrs. MacKinnon enjoyed summers in the area and reaped royalties, five cents a yard, from C. T. R. Nixon's quarry which operated on the island. He encouraged the deer sanctuary that Tom Brazil had begun, and welcomed guests to his island paradise.

The *S.S. Santa Maria* and the *S.S. Selma* of the All-Red Line, brought his guests to the wharf at the quarry until 1917 when the Union Steamships bought out the smaller line, and the ships were renamed *Chilco* and *Chasina*. The steamers also brought the mail, simply addressed: Hardy Island. Until the middle of the century, all the mail for the area was addressed this way, although for more than twenty years the steamer would stop near the small islets around Kelly Island. This mailing address has caused some confusion as it was often given on voter's lists or government leases when the actual residence was on Nelson Island.

During the time the quarry operated in 1915 and '16, Hardy Island had a winter population. May Hammond moved her family to the area to join the other quarry families, and a small school was built. Mary's parlor store did a relatively brisk business on the island, and Hal worked for the quarry. He hauled a scow loaded with two large tanks, the water supply for the quarry workings, slowly back and forth across Blind Bay in his small gas boat.

Dick Hammond recalls his father, Hal, speaking of the special blocks that were taken from the quarry to carve the lions for the Vancouver Court House. News of them had also reached Wrays at Fearney Point as Sarah Edmonds remembers they had to "blast them out, just so, so carefully." Their size caused some problems in loading.

To Hal Hammond
(Unsung Hero of W.W. I Days)

Through the haze I see him coming
    Inching o'er the churning water

Skirting past the hidden reef there
    Rolling in the morning swell

Carries tanks with pure clear water

    To fill the boiler at the quarry
    To pump the pistons of the engine
    To turn the wheels of the tramway
    To load the scows that take the granite
    To the builders of the province

Back and forth he paces water
    Lonely in his constant vigil

Till the evening drawing nearer
    Rides him higher in the ocean

Pocket heavy with his pay lot

    To feed the family at the quarry
    To work the garden for their mother
    To pack the jars with golden bounty
    To fill the cellar for the winter
    To shape the settlers of the island

Just eighteen, he shares a burden
    That would tax a man of thirty

But he shoulders it with courage
    Plays a father to his sisters

Even helps to build the school

    To educate the younger children
    To a better way of living
    To a life thus filled with knowledge
    To avoid the pain of warring
    To then build a better country

*When Cliff Hammond joined the 72nd Highlanders in 1915, and May had Hal exempted, he was was more or less sole support of the family, his mother, eight sisters and one brother.

Hardy Island School

While Hal was working for the quarry, his younger brothers and sisters were attending school for the first time. The four oldest Hammonds had been taught at home by their parents, never ever seeing a school. These younger ones had been given a start at home and were experiencing a "real" teacher for the first time.

The teacher, Clarence J. Frederickson, a young seventeen-year-old, was experiencing his first class. He had twelve pupils in this "rural and assisted school" as it was listed in the Public Schools Report, half of them Hammonds. Nelson Hammond, who spent most of his school years with just his sisters for company, had three other boys in the class this first year, 1915-16.

They were all very shy and solemn on opening day, and Enid felt the teacher was too. The tarpaper over shiplap schoolhouse rested on large logs set on boulders right at the very rim of the ocean. On this first day, the tide had been high, and the teacher could see it ebb from the little window. Enid remembers that, "Suddenly the floor began to slant seaward; there was a tearing sound and screaming of nails being drawn from timbers. What a surprise! The wall parted from the floor. The roof began to have a rakish look. I have never forgotten the look on the young teacher's face. `Outside!' he yelled, dragging out the smallest students. The little building actually collapsed as in an earthquake."

The school operated until the quarry contract was completed. The regular school year was 206 days, and Hardy Island School was open only ninety-nine-and-a-half of the 123 prescribed days. During the following school year however, the school operated for all but three days. Ruth Smith was the teacher for the 1916-17 year. The number of students had dropped to eight, six girls and two boys. Three of the early students included Mary Secco, Jack McDonald, and Ken Campbell. Miss Smith sent home a total of seventy-seven reports during the year and made welcome twenty-three visitors, nine trustees and fourteen others, as well as teaching several grades of work. It is interesting to note that the school opened and closed with *The Lord's Prayer*.

Macomber Buys from Nobility

While the quarry was still operating and the first school term was well under way, Jean MacKinnon, to whom her husband had transferred the property, sold the island to Christopher John Leyland, of Beal, Northumberlandshire, England. He owned Hardy until 1927. On his death, it was transferred to John Murray Naylor and Christopher Digby Leyland. The younger Mr. Leyland, a retired captain of the British Army, was the owner of Haggerston Castle, Beal, Montgomeryshire, England, and John Naylor was from Leighton Hall, Welshpool, England. The changing market value of land is always of interest. When this once-beautiful piece of real estate sold to C. J. Leyland in 1915, the price was $32,000. At that time, the quarry was still being leased to Sechelt Granite Quarries and MacKinnon held the remainder of the $50,000 mortgage for the company. Leyland took over the mortgage and became entitled to interest and royalties. When the land was transferred in 1927, the market value was listed as $11,930, but when Le Roy A. Macomber, a wealthy lawyer and financier from Seattle, purchased the island three years later, the value had fallen to $10,000.

Nobody remembers now whether the nobility from England ever visited Hardy, but Le Roy and Marion Macomber and their family were frequent summer visitors. He legalized the game preserve that Tom Brazil had begun and hired Judd Johnstone to help Tom in his caretaking duties. The houses of the quarry workers were all falling down and old tin cans were rusting away when the Johnstone girls first visited Hardy. The tumble-down shacks were quite a contrast to Macomber's "mansion," as Evelyn Roberts remembered it. Macomber's home had the most beautiful skins all over the floors—lion and tiger and zebra—trophies of Mr. Macomber's brother, it's believed. Big photo albums of the hunts were passed around to company to view beneath the crystal chandelier, which reflected off the windows across the front of the house.

For a time Pansy West cooked for Macombers, their daughter Marjorie, and Marion's three grown children and friends, in this wonderful retreat.

A large boat shed by the harbor housed several canoes which were still there in 1949, recalls Joan Milligan. A trail led from the harbor where the *Principia*, Macomber's yacht, was moored, to the

The *Principia*, Macomber's yacht at Hardy Island float in the early forties. Powell River Museum

May Hammond seeing relatives off on the *Santa Maria* at Hardy Island wharf. M. Hammond

Granite quarry of the Sechelt Co., Hardy Island, which was purchased by C. J. Leyland in 1915. Government Building Stone Report 1917

house where an outside fireplace warmed their guests on cool summer evenings. An imported eucalyptus tree, famous along the coast, shimmered in the off-shore breeze. On the northwest side of the island a salt-water swimming pool with snake-like railings provided barnacle-free swimming, and anywhere on the island, Tom's deer provided them with entertainment. It was fun to watch a boater try to escape from them with an armload of damsun plums. By the time he fed each nuzzling freeloader along the path, he was lucky to be left with a handful.

Tom Brazil, their keeper, entertained them as well. Guests often puzzled over the booby trap along the trail. A large pile of old deer bones could be seen beneath a snare. "That's what happened to the last person who tried to hurt one of my deer," he warned ominously.

Judd Johnstone guided Mr. Macomber on big game hunting trips, and became a confidant of his. Amid the splendor of Lowe Inlet in Grenville Channel, Macomber would admit he was always wondering how to make his next million. He envied Judd's easy existence, his acceptance of the riches around him, his never needing the monetary kind.

Macomber contemplated selling the island around 1936 or '37, says Jim Spilsbury, owner of a rather dilapidated sign, on which cement has been mixed. It reads: FOR SALE, HARDY ISLAND $14,000. He would have liked to have bought it but didn't have that kind of money then. He remembers Slim Deberri trying to put a deal together to buy it as well as Bat McIntyre of the Rodmay Hotel in Powell River.

Macomber's didn't come up to visit much after 1940. Le Roy died of a heart attack in 1946 at a relatively young age of fifty-six. He had added two more offshore islands to his possessions which he left to his wife.

Polish Count Markowski and his wealthy American wife leased Hardy for six months in 1948. Agnes Harding's daughter Dorothy, then sixteen, cared for their two small children. But Hardy Island wasn't warm enough for them year 'round. They lived in California.

Three years later, Marion Macomber, chatelaine of Hardy Island for twenty-one years, transferred the property to E. R. Gibson, retired, of Sechelt, and R. R. Howay, a civil servant of New Westminster. Still more lots had been added to the Macomber lands—Fox Island and another small island off Hardy's shores.

Hardy Island was never to be the same again. The timber was too valuable to be left untouched forever, and Tom Brazil was too old to keep up the game sanctuary.

Tom Brazil

For nearly fifty years Tom Brazil, gamekeeper and caretaker of Hardy Island, could be seen rowing his boat in the water around Hardy and Nelson. He always stood up to row, pushing instead of pulling his oar. A felt bowler hat was pulled down over his head rain or shine, summer or winter, and a well-worn sports jacket bagged about his wiry frame. He made quite a picture heading towards Hardy Island in the setting sun.

He was the longest staying resident on these islands next to Harry Roberts, and Hardy can't be mentioned without speaking of Tom—he's legend now. Everyone has a kind word and a good story to tell of him, but little of his early history was actually known to many. He was born in 1867, the year Canada was born, and like Canada, his life touched the shores of the Pacific and Atlantic. It isn't known just when he came from Prince Edward Island on the far east coast, to Port Renfrew, Vancouver Island, on the far west coast. He worked as a wireless operator and caretaker for a hotel there before coming to Hardy to caretake the luxury home of J. M. MacKinnon, replacing W. Wood. He was middle-aged by then, but he cleared the land and planted a small orchard. To stave off loneliness, he made friends with the deer that abounded on this natural ranch.

He knew most of the islanders as they came and went over the years. In 1915 the children of the Hardy Island quarry workers made friends with his deer and watched as Tom put out piles of oatmeal, "shorts" as he called them, to feed the sleek animals.

When Le Roy Macomber, a lawyer and financier from Seattle, bought the island from Leyland, he legalized the deer sanctuary that Tom had started and hired him as gamekeeper.

Forrest (Judd) Johnstone came to Hardy around 1930 when Tom would be past sixty. He looked after caretaking the upper half of the island while Tom looked after the lower half. Macomber had bought the rights to the beaches and the caretakers were paid to keep the clam diggers and oyster hunters away. It was felt that the sight of the plentiful deer would entice would-be hunters, or a careless match would burn the valuable timber.

When Macombers visited though, the home was filled with friends and great gaiety. Visiting boats tied to the dock and the boaters were invited to walk through the cool forested trails which Tom kept swept like the paths of Stanley Park.

Some of Tom's deer become as well-known as old Tom. "Billy," a young buck in the 1930s, would regularly awaken visiting tourists who were docked at Hardy Island by pawing the sides of the boats with a forehoof. The daily handouts he received were his and his alone. In fact, he let no other deer even stroll down the float. He was only one of the 200 or more deer on the island at that time, but was a special pet of Macombers. He had taught himself to manipulate the latch on the front door and often walked in unannounced.

The deer would nudge visitors and poke their noses into their pockets and were known to eat ice cream, leaves, potatoes, meats, and bread crusts—even cigarettes and straw hats. Salt was their favorite treat, but used with discretion. Tom himself fed them troughs of bran or generous portions of oats each morning and evening. "Come away, come away," he called to his charges.

Only once that anyone remembers did Tom have any real trouble with a deer—a strange buck put him up a tree. It had probably come from Nelson Island as there were no fences on this successful sanctuary. They were always free to swim Telescope Passage to Nelson Island or across to the mainland.

Although most are familiar with Tom's success with deer, fewer know about the pheasants which he raised from eggs. A few shrill whistles would have them about his feet like barnyard chickens. A story is even told of his calling them from the deck of a tugboat when a captain had commented that it would be nice to knock down "one of those babies" that were flying overhead. "Watch this," Tom said, and had three of his pets leave the flock, and with stiffened wings land almost at his feet. It was said that he had the signature of the captain to verify this story.

Tom's old felt hat stood for several jobs over his lifetime—caretaker, gamekeeper, "postmaster," he looked after the mailbag for many years; and telegraphist during World War II.

He thoroughly enjoyed his drink and often made the rounds of his friends in the bay. Dora Johnstone kept a watchful eye on him but

Tom Brazil holding Clara, with Phyllis around 1918. M. Hammond

The Hammond girls in the Hardy Island School, 1915-1916, with teacher Ruth Smith. Missing from the photo are Mary Secco, Jack McDonald, and Ken Campbell. M. Hammond

Seven of Tom's deer show up for treats when he entertains a guest. Powell River Museum

Many people enjoyed feeding the deer on Hardy Island during the thirties. The Macomber home is in the background.
A. Harding

Hardy Island was under the Naylor-Leyland coat of arms during the time that nobility owned the island.

View Point Lodge guests picnicking in front of Macomber's home.   A. Harding

Tom Brazil, August 1953.

Tom Brazil   Courtney Cressy

it was really his parrot, "Barbara," that kept him in line. She would fly at him and peck him, "beat him up" said Thelma, Dora's daughter, if she smelled any liquor on his breath. He had a soft spot for his pet anyway, and kept the coal oil lamp burning for her while he was away.

His drinking was the subject of a couple of stories about Tom, and to be fair, the fog entered into one of them. He had rowed to Pender Harbour for supplies and while there, had visited the bar, filling his belly with gin. The fog had crept in around the islands when Tom started out for home, but he left anyway. He rowed the familiar route, hour after hour, with only the splash of his oar pushing the water ahead of him and the honk of the distant foghorns for company. His friends said with affection that only the oars held him up. Finally he felt the thud-thud of the boat on rock and pulled it up on the land. When Judd Johnstone found him the next morning he discovered the island he'd landed on was Texada!

Perhaps Tom was best remembered for his practical jokes like his paper mache spider the size of a dinner plate. He liked to fool his guests, and as he pulled a string in another room, this spider crawled up the wall in front of them.

The "electric eels" that he kept along the path on Hardy was another story. Frank Jenkinson, Tom's friend from Saltery Bay, tells of the thin curving pieces of driftwood with eyes painted on them that were strategically placed along the trail. A short way along was a light bulb hung from the trees. When his unsuspecting visitor asked whether it worked, Tom would say, "Oh yes."

When it became apparent there were no wires or generator close by, Tom would tell him it was what he used the electric eels for, at which point the visitor realized he'd been taken.

A variation to this story is the string of light bulbs along the straight stretch in the path—for racing his jack rabbits at night. Tom also had a large glass bullfrog which he claimed he used as a decoy.

"Oh?" guests would say, "to catch what?"

"Bullfrogs."

"What do you do with them?"

"When I get enough of them, I sell their hops to a brewery."

A favorite story is of Tom rowing to Pender Harbour when a gas boat came abreast of him. The owner called out, "Tom, would you like a tow?"

To which Tom replied, "No thanks, I'm in a hurry."

That story in itself said much about him. Another side of Tom was his interest in the daily papers. The telephone, that God-send to islanders, kept him in nightly touch with John Wray at Fearney Point. The lines were particularly hot during the British elections. He had an interesting way of speaking and voiced his opinion on politicians or any person who didn't know much about what they were doing by saying, "He doesn't know any more about politics or ... than a pig does about a pocketbook."

He missed John and their telephone conversations when Mr. Wray passed away in the forties.

His deer were still a comfort and he fed them faithfully. Jim Spilsbury remembers stopping in at Tom's one very cold day in 1941 to find Tom had apples out on saucers for his pets. He coached Jim's small son to hold out apples for the deer. They stayed two days while the bay was frozen over. Guests were infrequent in the winter and he enjoyed their company.

Tom was quite an age before he thought of applying for his old-age pension. He showed Agnes Harding a list of his family in Prince Edward Island and told her they were Roman Catholic. Agnes corresponded with a niece, and records were located which showed Tom already in his eighties.

He was beginning to fail then and soon needed more medical attention. He spent some time with Cherry Sandvold, but his last days were spent in a nursing home in Vancouver helping others weaker than himself and having a cheery word for everyone. He was eighty-eight when he died in the mid-fifties, at a time the community itself was dying. Enid Hammond Wright remembers Tom as a "special type of person. One of the best."

The Nelson Island School

When the quarry on Hardy Island closed, the Hammonds returned to Hidden Bay. For the next three years, the school consisted of only the Hammond family. A number of teachers came and left, staying only one term. "They weren't the nature-loving sort, and couldn't endure isolation," one of the Hammond girls remembers.

Lilian Wheeler and Claire Prepontaine shared teaching responsi-

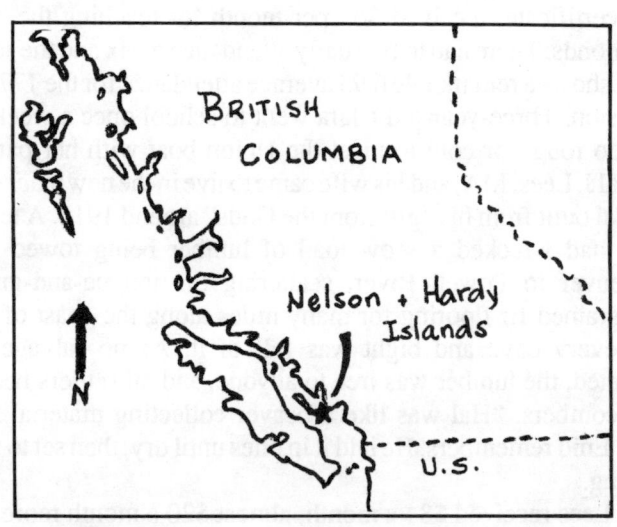

Edith Tarbuck, teacher, and group of Hammonds, 1915. M. Hammond

bilities the first year in the bay. Miss Prepontaine with her third class certificate, received $65 per month for teaching the seven Hammonds. There had to be a daily attendance of six and the school report shows a remarkable 6.95 average attendance for the 177 days in session. Three-year-old Clara went to school once a week if it was too rough or cold to meet the Union boat with her parents. Samual J. Lees, MA, and his wife came to live in the new teacherage that Hal built from his "gift from the Gods" around 1918. A terrific storm had wrecked a scow load of lumber being towed from Vancouver to Powell River, scattering the tongue-and-groove edge-grained fir flooring for many miles along the coast of Nelson—every cove and bight was full of it. As no salvage was attempted, the lumber was free to anyone, and all settlers became beachcombers. "Hal was like a beaver collecting material for a dam," Enid remembers. He laid it in piles until dry, then set to work building.

Mr. Lees received $84 a month, almost $20 a month more than the teacher before. The Hammond children had lost their solemn shyness with the teacher by this time and Clara even admits to stealing a blueberry pie from Mrs. Lees. With her co-conspirator, Phyllis, they tasted the tempting pastry, found it fell far short of their mother's culinary arts, and fed it to the dog. She says, "The worst part was, Mother made us go and apologize."

When the new teacher was hired for the 1919-20 term, she was paid a whopping $96 per month. A Miss A. S. Grant, second class certificate, taught the spring term that year. Other teachers in the Hidden Bay school were Edith Tarbuck, Grace Smith, and Agnes Dainard. The school closed in 1920 when the Hammonds moved to Sechelt. It was to be thirty years before the next school on Nelson was opened.

PART II

Loggers and Rum-Runners

Logging

The earliest loggers to Nelson Island were the old time handloggers who never saw a power tool but used two of the mightiest powers known to man—gravity and the tides. The size of the first growth timber needed all the natural power they could find. It would sometimes take six days to fall a single tree and keep it moving to the water. They chopped limbs, jacked it out of soft ground, and trimmed the top off over and over to keep it on the skids and in motion. This was the size of tree they'd yell "Timber" for, one that would give them 8,000 board feet of lumber from its 138-foot length.

With a handlogger's license, thought to be $10 in the early 1900s, $25 in 1916; calked boots; springboards; long handled falling axes; a slim eight-inch falling saw and a thicker bucking saw; as well as a claim from a forest ranger for a year; a man was in business. The ranger would assign the area and mark it with cloth flags at its limits. One mile for one year, on a hillside where no animals, or later steam engines, could operate.

Using selective cutting, he would fall his boomsticks, slim straight spruce logs, as long as possible, 125 feet or so, and bore four-inch holes in the end to couple them with heavy boom chains. With steel cables these boomsticks would be anchored in a protected bay where the logger would fill them with logs for the outside market. The handlogger knew every log in his boom.

One good-size tree would be worth a dozen smaller ones, called "pike poles or hammer handles"—the kind he yelled "brush" for. If the logger could float a big one in one day he had something to brag about, but if it took a week, he still made money.

In 1903, Peter Moran listed himself as a logger on Nelson, and Samuel J. McAllister, a woodman. A woodman cut wood for the boilers of the steamers and tugboats on the coast.

With the help of animals, loggers could take timber from the flatter areas. Between 1907 and 1914, Jack McConville logged with oxen at the head of Hidden Bay and around and out of West Lake as well. Jack Hammond built portions of his logging road which is still visible — built without spikes.

John Turner was another logger in 1907 and George T. Clarke on the Agamemnon side came in 1910. The 1912 voter's list gives seven names of men working for the Rat Portage Logging Company whose manager was W. Burdon: John D. Jeffrey, Alexander Mathew, James McDade, James McDonald, James William McDonald, Reginald Vass and Michael Sweeny. As Sweeny was listed as engineer, this outfit worked with a steam donkey engine, a further advancement in the logging business.

They logged out of Bruce Lake through one side of the Hammond farm. Their cookhouse was built on a float on the lake, the remains of which were still there just a few years ago according to Dick Hammond, Jack's grandson. In the next few years they logged into Bagg's Bay.

Paddy Rogers was a handlogger in Blind Bay, coming sometime before 1918, when Laughlin and Heid arrived to log the east side of the island around Cockrill Bay, and later the top of Vanguard.

Over the years many outfits came for awhile, took what they wanted and left.

The Early Years of Cockrill
and Vanguard Bay

A few years before the Green Bay shingle mill opened, before the armistice of 1918, the Laughlin family moved to Cockrill Bay. Laughlin's oldest daughter Pearl, had just married Louie Heid, and she was anxious to keep him out of the war. As a logger he was exempt.

Mr. Laughlin and Louie logged at Cod Reef. They had a chute for the logs, and horses to help with the heavy work, one step removed from handlogging. Once a week the Union Steamships, the *Chilco* or *Chasina*, would come in to their float at the camp to off-load groceries, boomchains and any other equipment needed.

They logged a few years there, then came out to the point of Vanguard. Mr. Laughlin left then, selling his horses to McRae at McRae's Cove. A steam donkey was purchased for the operations to continue. Sis (Clara) Harris, then young Sis Laughlin, remembers how much nicer this was as she didn't have to haul hay for it. The job of cutting wood to feed the donkey was taken on by Walter Wray, John's brother, who lived in Vanguard Bay with their two sisters, Amelia Wray and Mrs. Francis Smith.

Walter Wray was the magistrate for the area, an Englishman who looked like King Edward but who fell under his sister's reign. Amelia was the oldest, the matriarch of the family. Walter documented the birth certificates for the local people, sometime later doing all the Johnstone children.

They raised chickens and kept a large garden from which they sold produce and poultry to the mill site in Powell River for a time. In later years he would often act as caretaker to some of the homes on West Lake where he kept a dug-out canoe. Betty Wray remembers this canoe as taking half an hour to start and half an hour to stop.

There were very few people in the area then. On Nelson the Amscold family who had two boys around the age of Sis, lived 'down' from them, and as well as the Wrays in Vanguard, there was another couple, Mr. and Mrs. G. Y. (George Yarnold) Smith. Mr. Smith was remembered by one of the Hammond girls as the caretaker for a slate quarry that had operated in Vanguard around 1910. There is some confusion here as no record exists of this quarry. He may have been in charge of the vacated workings at

Deserted Bay, much farther up Jervis Inlet, at one time, or it is possible that a quarry did exist here and records have been lost.

G. Y. Smith had a garden and fruit trees behind the island in Vanguard and often gave dances. Sis recalls one time Mrs. Smith had a big surprise for them, "she was going to be a fairy! She was a little bit of a woman, around seventy then. Everybody clapped and clapped, and she bowed and bowed. She loved it." The only other "neighbors" included Paddy Rogers, the handlogger in Blind Bay who married a woman with three or four children; Mr. Linber, Mr. McClinic, Mr. Baker and the Hiltzes and their grandchildren up in Hotham Sound.

Life was much different for Sis and her brother on the island. She had lived on the Coast Meridian Road halfway between White Rock and Cloverdale and had attended school there to grade four, but she had no schooling on Nelson. What else she learned came from the many books she read.

They worked hard all week, and on Sunday they would row to Blind Bay where they would picnic on clams and fresh baked bread.

The fishing was wonderful then. Sis' grandfather would go out with a rod and pole, a worm and bobber and get ten or fifteen fish, enough for a couple of days. Sis and her brother used to lay on their stomachs trying to get a tommy cod, their favorite. "You could get a fish them days with just a piece of lead with a hook on it," Sis remembers. And the water was so clear they could watch the fish on the bottom. Her brother liked to hunt too, and often shot squirrels with his .22 which Sis and he skinned for their mother to cook. Ducks too, were fair game for a meal. For fun they made stilts and walked about the uneven shores, and at night they would sometimes play cards.

But more often than not, they worked. The young Laughlin boy often greased the log chute with skid oil. When their mother and father separated, Sis remained with her sister. At twelve she was doing more than most full-grown women. After her sister underwent a serious operation, she took care of her, as well as cooking for the men in camp. Besides her father and brother-in-law, there was an engineer in the crew and three men who came from Pender Harbour each Sunday and worked through to Saturday night. One of these three men was Henry Harris, a young fifteen-year-old who worked right along with the older men.

Sis stayed with her sister until she married this hard-working young logger a few years later. After logging a spell in Hotham sound, Sis and Henry moved to Vanguard where, in 1926, the men logged right up on top of the hill. Henry was still working for Louie Heid who also had his brother Charlie Heid and Henry Smith with him then. Sis would often go up and blow the whistle if they needed a whistle punk. It was something she'd done since she was a kid, when a pile of coats was needed on her small shoulders to protect them from the heavy line and pulley she carried to string around the trees for the steam whistle.

They left Vanguard to take up permanent residence in Pender Harbour shortly afterwards.

The Twenties

Before the twenties began to roar and the flappers danced the Charleston, thousands of Europeans fled their war-ravished home towns and the resultant high taxes, to come to our fresh new country. With returning soldiers ready to marry and start families, as well as the increase in immigrants, a demand was created for housing, and in turn, cedar.

For the last two years of the war, Canadian loggers had been falling spruce for airplane lumber, and cut cedar had decreased to a minimum. After the long duration of the war, the roofs of the nation needed repairing and returned carpenters ordered cedar shingles by the truckloads. Small mills sprang up along the coast working day and night. The cannery in Green's Bay (as it was known then) was converted to a shingle mill in 1921. Cedar meant money—on the stump, in the log, or in the finished product.

The Union Steamships carried shiploads of new Canadians to the logging camps up and down the coast, and Nelson Island camp boats went out to meet the steamers. The shingle mill in Green's Bay took on reinforcements.

This three-machine mill was larger than the cannery had been. A forty-foot by sixty-foot addition sat mainly over the water at the lagoon end of the cannery building. It was only equipped to handle shingle bolts and with the short supply, very quickly ran out of them, putting the mill on part time.

A larger supply of bolts was soon found on Friel Lake which is situated on the low mountain between Hotham Sound and Jervis Inlet. They set up a camp there, and built a flume to take the bolts to salt water. Ian McKechnie recalled the problem they had with the flume in the 1973 *Peninsula Voice*:

> To lessen the speed at which the bolts traveled, the flume was set at an angle down the hillside. At one place there had to be a sharp curve and this was the nemesis of the Green Bay Shingle Company. Try as they did to prevent the bolts from breaking out the side of the flume, which allowed dozens of cords to go hurtling through the gap and down the side of the mountain, they did not seem to be able to overcome the trouble. They even installed a telephone from the intake of the flume to a small island a few hundred yards offshore where a lookout was posted. If a break occurred, he would phone the top to stop the supply. I am sure that if they had had more money they would have eventually overcome the trouble. But finances ran out and they were forced into bankruptcy.

At that time, Ian was employed at a sawmill at False Creek which was heavily owned by his father, a medical doctor. As president of the outfit, he poured his energy into becoming a great lumber tycoon. Sawmills then worked ten hours a day, six days a week, and paid their workers the munificent sum of thirty-one cents an hour. "It did not take long for the illusion on coming greatness in the world's forest industry to dissipate; a combination of sweat, sawdust and aching arms and back did not seem to enhance my potential. I longed for greatness in an easier environment."

When George McConnell, a friend and millwright at the False Creek mill, suggested they take over the mill at Green Bay that he'd heard about. "Green inveigled George into thinking that if he, Green, was paid part of his interest in the bankruptcy, the mill could be opened up and operated. As George was not a business man, he believed it all." With a saw filer by the name of Sansen, Ian joined

George McConnell in his new, but doomed project.

Despite the setbacks, sawmilling was much more profitable on Nelson Island than farming. A government scheme of the time placed veterans into a farming settlement on the island but the impossible rain forest conditions kept them from making their fortune in agriculture.

Some of the men who tried their luck with shovel and hoe included Jim Young, Charlie Robinson, Sam Slaven, Guy Buchanen, and Bill Smith. They were all friends of the Hammond family. Hammonds themselves had moved to Sechelt shortly after the men came to the project.

Among the veterans were men who tried to forget the horrors of the war. Some were scarred badly or missing an eye. Some shrank from the gaze of strangers on the street and their own reflection in the mirror. Nelson Island offered refuge to these men, a place where they could face humanity in small doses, where the beauty and solitude of nature could ease their handicaps. With the snowfall each winter the farmers and loggers left the area to await reopening of camp in the early spring.

Nightime Invaders

It was during the winter of 1920 that the oldest Hammond sister, Minnie Ritenhaus, was alone on the island with her infant daughter while her husband was at work in Union Bay. It was an extremely cold winter with lots of snow and the lagoon frozen over. At another time she would have enjoyed the silent beauty, the jelly fish, like wooly stars beneath the feathery patterns on the ice and the heavily laden boughs sparkling in the moonlight. But this time she was terrified.

During the night the wolves came right down to her porch. They howled all night and scratched on the door. She paced the floor in terror. All night they howled, and all night she paced. When daylight arrived and the wolves left, she hurriedly warmed rocks in the oven and made a bed in a box for her baby, lining it with the heated stones. She threw some clothes into a bag for the two of them and bundled them against the cold.

Her hands froze as she untied the cold slippery ropes on the boat and tucked her small charge in beside her. She knelt in the bow smashing the ice as she went. It was hard exhausting work and it took some time to clear a path to the open water. At last she had placed enough distance between her and the wolves and was able to catch the steamer to safety.

The steamer represented safety in other ways. Often the women of the isolated areas would take the boat to Vancouver and have their babies in the hospital. Around 1920, Sarah (Wray) Edmond accompanied her sister-in-law, Mrs. Charles Wray, to Vancouver on the Chilco when baby Leonard was born aboard ship, with Sarah assisting at the birth. Captain Lawrey and mate Jim Fletcher, who no doubt had ordered boiled water, became good friends of the Wrays and Edmonds.

Rum-Running Action

The secret coves of Hidden Basin and Cockburn Bay played a minor part in the dramatic decade that followed the quiet years after World War I. When the Volstad Act in the United States made prohibition national law on January 16, 1920, a few Nelson Island men began setting up stills to get in on the action that was beginning to take place. Unlit boats darted out of the shadows laden with illegal contraband, always watching, always wary. Every craft was suspect, for even more dreaded than the Coast Guard was the hijacker.

For eight years, the rum-running filled pockets, and kept conversation humming in the hidden bays. As long as it was not home-brewed moonshine, it was not illegal in Canada to procure liquor for resale to the U.S. In fact, the Canadian government even charged a $20 per case duty on the bonded products and so made a handsome profit on Carrie Nation's "successful" cause. Most of the larger ships made trips to California with their contraband, such as the *Quadra*, *Malahat*, and *Coal Harbour*, that sailed out of "Rum Row" in Vancouver with papers for Mexico. The government didn't charge duty for Mexican-bound liquor and the Mexican officials cooperated with the runners by supplying false Mexican papers. In return they took a share of the profits. This fifty-cent per case share was called "mordita," which means "little bite." After a few years, the law was changed to charge $10 per gallon for all destinations and the Mexicans no longer got their cut.

The runners in the Nelson Island waters never used these false Mexican papers. More often than not, their liquor was illegal moonshine. They operated out of smaller craft and made shorter jaunts to the Puget Sound area on the Washington coast. These boats often trawled innocently under the watchful eyes of the Coast Guard. They waited for nightfall to transfer their load to the speedy craft that darted out to them, relieved to meet their buyer before the pirate ships could interfere. William J. Gillis and his son were former Nelson Island people to make a quick buck in the prohibition game. Theirs was just a small business; they didn't have the sophisticated protection on the Beryl G that others had—no armored plating or automatic weapons. They didn't even keep a close watch for the feared pirates.

They were just preparing dinner when the hijackers boarded. The unsuspecting pair fought them off with their bare hands but they were outnumbered. Cruelly, the three intruders murdered the seventeen-year-old boy and his father, cut the bodies into strips to make them sink better, and dropped them overboard.

The grizzly 1926 murders were the only known ones committed in B.C. waters during the dramatic rum-running days. The successful capture of the murderers by Inspector Forbes Cruikshank of the B.C. Police, who infiltrated the hangouts of the hijackers on the Washington waterfront, is a story in itself. The men were arrested and tried within a year and a half of the crime. Two of them were hung in Oakalla, the third was sentenced to death but was later given life imprisonment. It was a sad end to the man who had planted the asparagus beds in Hidden Bay in the early part of the century.

The gruesome incident made many a small operator more wary. The Coast Guard Detachment was made larger and more effective about the time of the trial, and rum-running began to lose its adventure. By 1929, there was very little action in the coastal waters of America. An old house at the head of Cockburn Bay hints at its part in rum-running. It has a cement cellar and is located on the south side of the creek. An upstairs window looks right out of the bay, giving full view of secret signals of approaching boats. Faint names and dates on the walls of the canyons are reputed to belong to these rum smugglers.

A decade or more after the action had quieted, Yolana, Lee, and Zoe Roberts found some old five-gallon ceramic jugs concealed in the woods back of the cabin, but no portion of the large cache of rum, reported to be buried in the area. The jugs and the old-timer's stories are the only evidence left of Nelson Island's rum-running days. If the cache is still there, that rum should be really good now.

PART 3

The Independent Survive The Depression

Judd Johnstone

In 1930, Tom Brazil's caretaking duties were lightened when Judd Johnstone was hired to watch the upper half of Hardy Island. Judd was almost forty then, and already steeped in pioneer legend. Because most of Judd's colorful life takes place in Jervis Inlet, whose waters wash the shore of Nelson and Hardy Islands, and because his background greatly influenced his later life on Nelson, more of his story is told than others.

Judd was a great story teller and liked to tell the story of his beginnings. His Kentuckian father, Charles Roscoe Johnstone, rode into a small Colorado town, romanced and wed the Scottish schoolmarm, Dora Ida Hanna, and rode out four days later, his bride behind him on his saddle. Judd was born Forrest Johnstone to this frontier couple on June 30, 1891, in Kendell, Kansas, but was known to his family and friends as Judd. He was born into a time that was immortalized by Hollywood—the days of Billy the Kid and Wyatt Earp. His early life was spent in the Colorado Hills, and Wyoming and Montana territories. His father operated a placer mine on the Rouge River where Judd learned to swim in the swift current.

But the Rouge didn't produce what Canada was reputed to—nuggets as big as hen's eggs. Charlie Johnstone packed his family into a covered wagon and headed west. He was unusually tall for a man, around 6-feet 5-inches. He had a unique way of financing his journey. In each town he would eye the horses tied to the rail outside the saloon, and would pick out the sleekest, fastest-looking one, then go inside to the bar. It wouldn't take long before this giant stranger had everyone's attention. He'd then bet all present that he could outrun this horse in a hundred yards.

All takers lined up outside on the main street while Charlie and his competition took their mark. At the sound of the gun, both raced toward the finish. From the first, Charlie's enormous strides outpaced the sleek animal. Smiles disappeared from the crowd and heads shook as they prepared to pay off.

Judd's dad grinned as he hitched up for the last lap of his trip with his new provisions; the knowledge that a horse could never get up enough speed in the short distance of a hundred yards to outrace a fast man, his meal ticket to the gold fields.

Sometime after the death of their little son, Patrick, in 1900 in Libby, Montana, they arrived at the port of Seattle. Judd's third daughter tells the story of her grandfather selling his wagon and buying a four-masted schooner from an old sea captain. He gave him a few lessons in sailing and although he could neither read nor write, drew him a map of the coast so accurate that Charlie had no trouble finding his way to Earl's Cove. Here, shingle bolts, not nuggets, kept him occupied. He was known as Buccaneer Johnstone, or Timber-line, to those on the peninsula.

He built a home for Dora Ida and their sons, Judd, Frank, and Steve, and their daughter Ruth. The split cedar-boards he used for their one-room cabin were shaved smooth with a draw knife.

Earl's Cove was to be the stopover to earn the means to travel north to the golden nuggets, but their plans never materialized. Charlie did take his family to Alaska, but it wasn't until after the war was over many years later, when logging and trapping took the place of the proposed prospecting.

His son Judd remembered a past so alien to our life today that paddlewheelers traveled the coast. *The Mermaid*, a sidewheel paddle steamer used to dock at Pender Harbour once a month then. Woodcutters cut and piled cords of wood at different wood stations—Gibson's Landing, Lund, Rock Bay, Alert Bay, and Shoal

Bay. They sold for $2 a cord while whiskey sold for ten cents a shot at the local saloon.

The John Wray family was in Egmont at this time, a storekeeper was in Irvine's Landing and John West was on Nelson Island. They were the only other white people in the area. It was a country for hunters, trappers, and fishermen and a time when rules and regulations were unheard of. It was a free land, no police, no game wardens, no fisheries department, no logging restrictions, no licenses for anything. Their schoolmarm mother taught them to read and write, for there were no schools then either. Most of their time was spent hunting.

Deer hides averaged seventy-five cents a piece. With hard work they could get a scow load in two days although two skins a day gave them a good income. Bear hides too, brought good money and ducks were hunted for the outside market. The boys and Ruth became good hunters, using both the heavy old .44 buffalo guns and bows and arrows. The Indians became their friends, and like them, they often preferred the silent weapon. It was cheaper, recoverable, and undisturbing to the animals. It was also much lighter than the guns the young boys used. One of these was originally a muzzle-loader but had been bored out and made into a single-shot breech-loader. The .45 calibre gun was complete with a foot-long bayonet. Tales of shooting grizzly bear and cougar abounded among the young Johnstone boys. Frank at eight, shot an eleven and a half foot cougar just outside the cabin, to protect his mother and sister.

The Johnstone hunters moved to Jervis Inlet, an even more game-filled area, when the cedar market slumped. The steamer trip to the logging camp stood out in Judd's mind for his lifetime, particularly the stops they made for fir bark for firing fuel and water for the boiler. After Charlie and his boys learned the logging business, they formed their own outfit. Each summer their boom of logs was sold to a broker in Vancouver. Once they lost their boom—their whole year's work—to a crooked broker.

The handloggers always had plenty of time to hone their hunting skills. To prove to Daddy, as they called him, that they were hunters of great prowess, they used to go on "wild man" hunts above the snowline on the mountains. With just ammunition, matches, and a bit of salt, they would camp out for a week at a time. At first they shared their game, then later they toughened the rules. Each had to shoot his own meat, and couldn't carry anything with him when he moved on. They wore only a pair of overalls and an undershirt and half a light blanket was allowed, but no shoes or jacket. There was snow on the ground for the last of their forays.

Judd's mother had three more sons and one daughter after coming to Canada. Jack was born in the fall of 1903 while they were living on the Agamemnon Channel, Ivan was born in Vancouver Bay April 24, 1905, the first white baby born in this remote area of Jervis. Bruce and Catherine (Kate) were born in Deserted Bay in 1909 and 1913 respectively. Her husband, if he was home, was the only midwife she had. Without another woman for company, she made a home for her growing family in Deserted Bay, and later, after Jack was born, in awe-inspiring Princess Louisa Inlet. She made bread and biscuits from the sourdough bucket she kept bubbling on a shelf and sewed clothing from flour sacks. Her home was a one-room shake cabin with an open fire in the center and a double bed in one corner. The house had a double shake roof to release the smoke. The children slept on benches around the walls, with the youngest in a small bed which pushed beneath the larger one during the day. Dora chopped wood and carried water to her primitive dwelling on the only bit of level ground in the inlet.

The inlet is almost five miles long and half a mile wide, with mountains rising from the sea to heights of 5,000 to 8,400 feet. The beautiful secluded area was sixty miles from the nearest white man then, and separated from Jervis by a narrow twisting entrance with tidal rapids of nine knots. It was in this mountainous region that Judd and his brothers did their wildman hunts.

Judd's father spoke Chinook well and was a kind man. The Indians at the head of Jervis often came to him for advice. He was generous to a fault, a trait Judd inherited, and shared or gave away whatever he had.

When they weren't logging or hunting, they tried prospecting, but it was really the hunt that they thrived on. Daddy never used a repeating rifle then, one shot was almost always enough. If not, he carried cartridges between the fingers of his left hand and was reputed to shoot as fast as a man with lever action.

The family moved to Alaska after the war when a logging camp moved into Deserted Bay seven miles away. It was said that Daddy felt cramped and decided to move to a more isolated area. Kate was added to the family in Alaska. As a beautiful young girl of fourteen, she followed family tradition by shooting her first bear.

Judd's family, from left to right: Grace and Dora in back, Evelyn, Alice, Thelma, Frank, and Bob at quarry home in Blind Bay.
Powell River Museum

Thelma and Judd Johnstone's wife, Dora, holding Grace. Photo was taken in 1924 or 1925. T. Deberri

Forrest (Judd) Johnstone in American Army, 1915. T. Deberri

Sunray, the fairytale cottage. M. McIntyre

The Sunray guest home. M. McIntyre

His sons, Judd and Frank, joined the American army at the onset of World War I. Army life must have been a brand new world to them. Judd's logging experiences earned him the position of supervisor in a cypress camp in Washington.

Judd moved to Alaska with his family after the war, but one of his brothers was left permanently in Jervis Inlet. Ivan died of the 1918 'flu and was buried where the Malibu Club is today. Frank was one of the fatalities of the war. Judd felt ready to settle down, and Dora Ellen Jeffries from Pender Harbour had taken his fancy. In the coldest part of winter he made his way down coast in a small boat, married Dora and took her back to Alaska. His bride preferred Jervis Inlet, and after a few years they returned.

Judd and Dora's first four children were girls, Thelma, Grace, Evelyn, and Alice. Thelma and Grace were born in Alaska where the family lived for awhile in a tent. Aunt Ruth (Jackson), Judd's sister, told a story to Dora's grandchildren years later in Blind Bay, about the wolves coming up to the tent. Ruth and Dora had a frightening time trying to keep the two babies quiet. They could hear the wolves sniffing about just outside the frail walls. Judd and the men were away hunting at the time.

Jervis Inlet was warmer than Alaska, although for two months of the year the impressive mountains would keep all sunshine from the Malibu. As the inlet would freeze over, they had to drag their dugout canoe over the ice to the open water.

The mail boat came once a year to the inlet. Unless the police boat or timber ranger were coming in they saw no one else. If there was any business to be done, Judd would row from Jervis to the justice of the peace at Pender Harbour. He would stop long enough to see him, then head for home again. Thelma remembers going along on one trip with her dad and Grace, but can't remember arriving home. Judd had probably rowed into the night when the girls had fallen asleep. He had a sail that he put up to catch the wind and aid in his rowing the long round trip—well over 100 miles.

Power boats were still rare on the coast. Thelma remembers the first one they saw. They all stood around and watched the man with the two-cycle. He may as well have had two heads, the sight was just as strange.

The excursion boat that went up Jervis was another wonder to Judd's small fry. They would run to the point and marvel at it. They were still used to an age in which people they knew would *row to*

Alaska. The men fished along the way to earn a living and holed up in fishermen's shacks during a storm. They made these hovels of driftwood stacked against a tree or other protection.

They would row during the late spring and summer, fishing along the way. In the fall they would make their way back, trapping as they came. "It was the way it was, the style of the coast," said Evelyn, one of Judd's daughters.

Thelma, Grace, Evelyn, and Alice attended school in Egmont for three years before the move to Nelson Island. Around 1931, Dora expressed a wish to build a home in Blind Bay. They lived at the quarry for a few years before their beautiful big home was built. Frank and Bob were added to the family while they lived at the Malibu and Chris was born in Blind Bay. Later on, Grandma Johnstone joined them for awhile, and Grandma Jeffries came to live with them in the fifties.

Judd was kept busy by Le Roy Macomber, building rock cairns to keep the starfish from eating his newly imported oysters which Judd had planted for him. Several years after his coming to Hardy, a deer epidemic hit the area. The island was just too small to support the large population that had built up on the game preserve. Judd, the hunter, had to lift his gun to a different kind of killing. Soft faces that once nuzzled him for a piece of fruit were pitifully drawn. Weak bodies wracked with infection staggered about. While once a scow load of deer skins was a happy sight, a good two or three days work, now the sight of the many bodies of the inflicted deer sickened him.

With Judd away at work, Dora kept busy. The hard-working woman was as likely to be on the roof repairing shakes or doing odd carpentry jobs as she was to be in the kitchen baking bread or washing clothes. She had very few niceties, but among them was her good dress with a design of sequins.

One night, when the children were all asleep, she took the little row boat and went out to jig for cod for the next day's supper. When she returned a while later, she discovered Thelma, very much awake and looking very guilty. She tried to hide something which Dora recognized at once as her good dress—full of holes. Beside Thelma was a pair of scissors and a pile of shiny sequins.

As the girls got a little older, they liked to row across to what is now the Saltery Bay picnic site, to pick the juicy blackberries that covered the shores. The day after one of their trips in 1933 or '34, they heard a thunderous noise from the direction of this spot. They rowed over to investigate but couldn't get near the area for floating debris. Huge uprooted trees, large limbs, and smaller branches covered the muddied water. The patch where they had picked berries the day before was now under the remains of a mountainside that had slid down and filled in the deep bay. The area had been recently logged off, leaving the unprotected banks to the mercy of the elements.

Judd was too proud to go on relief during the Depression. His meager $20 a month from Macomber wasn't much, but enough to keep his family fed. It even bought Grandma Jeffries a bag of flour each payday. But unless you went to the relief camp with your family, the government wouldn't provide schooling. Although correspondence was free to children under fifteen, the textbooks were expensive and Judd wasn't convinced that formal education was really necessary. His brothers and sisters had done well without it. It's possible too, that Judd misunderstood the new law, passed in 1931, that charged children over fifteen, $5 per course for their correspondence courses. Instead, Dora did her best around the old oak kitchen table. Frank learned numbers quickly, but writing words baffled him. He never thought it mattered much as he never had any trouble finding work. In fact, he had his first job at four. Judd had a trapline on the shore and Frank's job was to keep the dug-out canoe off the rocks while Judd set his traps.

At six, he was fishing with the family during the old bluebacking days when Judd and many other men along the coast took their whole families to their yearly fishing grounds. Judd's spot was across from the light on Quadra Island. Many set up protection from the elements in little hovels along the beach.

It was here that Frank caught his first big fish. When the cannery boat came over to buy Judd's catch, Frank held up his beauty. "What would you like, boy," the cannery buyer asked, "money or a can of peaches?" It's not hard to guess what a young boy would choose. He shared the single can with his parents, brothers and four sisters.

When he later went to work for pay—$7.50 a day at the Fairview Logging Camp—big money for a youth of fourteen in 1942, he still shared with his family. Dora made use of every paycheck to run the home and feed and clothe the growing family.

Judd's ability to live off the land helped tremendously. He knew all the edible plants and mushrooms and taught his children to distinguish them from the poisonous ones. He trapped and fished, did anything to help out.

Entertainment was cheap. Judd was a wonderful storyteller, a delight to meet. Family and guests alike enjoyed his stories of growing up in the Jervis Inlet, walking through to the Interior of B.C. and hunting the wild animals with his brothers on their "wild man" hunts. Like all good storytellers he embellished a little, and some of his stories became tall tales. Most knew the difference and enjoyed them for the telling.

On one of his treks into the mountains of Jervis Inlet, Judd found a crystal mine. Beautiful chunks of hard prism-like quartz, which could cut glass, were part of his find. Another time he told of finding jade, thought to be from a cache hidden by the Indians of the Interior who came down to trade with the coastal tribes.

One of Judd's grandchildren remembers him as "the oldest hippy" she knew. But he'd be sixty-five when she was twelve, and entitled to slow down a bit. Seems he never believed in working too hard, though, and never let a catastrophe like a tree falling on his house upset him much. He'd just saw away at it as he needed the firewood.

The Depression Years

During the thirties, several families moved to Nelson Island. Land was cheap, loggers could still find virgin timber, there was still a small market for salmon, and a few jobs were available at the quarries which paid a substantial forty cents an hour. Even the nose of a seal produced a $2.50 bounty and paid for many a family's bare necessities.

Food was no object. Clams were plentiful, deer were there for the taking, a fish could be caught in fifteen minutes, and there was plenty of free seaweed to fertilize a garden.

The Judd Johnstone family were glad to have neighbors move in down the bay in those early years. First to come were the McLaughlins in Ballet Bay. The Forresters were next, then the Schutts, and the Klaussens with their large family, followed.

The John McLaughlins lived on their boat with just a storage shed and washing facilities on land. The others built houses in the bay. Pansy West and her brothers John and Robin moved around from West Lake to the Blind Bay area and worked at the camp. They built a little shack into which Hugo Bjorklund and his new wife later moved. The house, which burned while Bjorklunds were there, was built on the little island which adjoins the property which Easthope later owned. Fire was a very real danger to islanders with wood stoves and wet weather. The family wash was often hung around the fire to dry, resulting in more than one disaster. Klaussens lost their home this way. When Bjorklunds shack burned, Bea panicked, then grabbed the coal oil lamp and ran out. Hugo was upset when he found she hadn't picked up his tobacco as well. The Johnstones could feed them, he said, but none of them smoked.

The Roberts, Hardings, and McNutts

Harry Roberts and Cherry arrived at Cape Cockburn in November, 1932, in his sailboat *Chack-Chack*. They settled in Chack-Chack Cove, built a dock for the boat, and began building the small house and barn. It was a busy time getting the ground tilled for the garden, and planting the orchard. As it took priority to the house building, they were still living aboard the *Chack-Chack* when Yolana was born the following October in St. Mary's Hospital in Pender Harbour.

The proud parents, new baby, and nurse Mable Johnstone, sailed home to the cape, the most western part of Nelson Island. To the south of them was a beautiful gravel beach and to the north was Cockburn Bay, a sheltered boat harbor which they called Chack-Chack Cove or The Cove. Their land was mostly rocky hills with "the draws" filled with large trees and woods. Before their coming, someone had logged part of this, leaving behind two skid roads, one where the little creek comes out halfway down the cove and the other coming out at the far end of the beach. They used this as a trail from the cove to the beach in those early years, and later built a road in the same place.

B.C. was still young and British Columbians in these isolated spots were still pioneering. Harry was well experienced in this area.

After his mother died at the turn of the century, his father and family came from England to Roberts Creek where Harry's uncle had settled. He was just sixteen at the time and completely alien to this Canadian wilderness. Before he left Roberts Creek though, he'd built a sawmill, store, and post office, and his sailboat, as well as his house that was locally known as "the castle."

He met Cherry in Vancouver where she was working at the time. They had both been married before. Harold, Cherry's son, was staying with an aunt while he went to school. As Cherry was from a large family in Kamloops where her dad had a cattle ranch, she was well used to the outdoor life.

Harry kept a journal of these early years. On October 28, 1934, he wrote: "Yo becomes a 'land-lubber' for she goes to live in a cottage. Her old home *Chack-Chack* is sold, so the crew moves ashore into the cottage built right against the rock bluff. With a new big cook stove and a good fire going in the fireplace, the place is as warm as old *Chack-Chack*, and oh so much more room for little feet which are just beginning to feel their way around."

Although the islanders admired Harry's skills and craftsmanship, they found him a little eccentric. He was very devout, and seemed quite taken with Brother Twelve who had established The Aquarian Foundation, a semi-religious sect that settled on Vancouver Island in 1927, and the next year on Valdes and de Courcy Islands in the Gulf Islands. After Brother Twelve was involved in a scandal and absconded with jars of gold donated by his faithful followers, Harry was given more than a curious glance when he joked about starting his own colony.

The Harding Brothers

The same year Yo was born, the Harding brothers moved into Hidden Bay, to the northeast of Cockburn. Their father, Paul Sr., a veteran, had taken out a 96-acre preemption for them. While Ernie, Art, Bill, and Paul, Jr., "proved up on the property," Bert worked for Ott Heikinnen. The brothers cleared five acres and built the View Point Lodge of hand-hewn logs.

The Hardings were all single then, hard working, good-looking young men who could fall a fir tree eight feet in diameter, do heavy quarry work, or hook a rug and bake bread. Money and jobs were scarce while the lodge was being built, and a rowing trip to Pender Harbour was made to collect $18 welfare. It was a big help in the dirty thirties when a can of corn beef cost eleven cents, bread was seven cents, butter was twenty-five cents and canned milk, an island staple, was six cents for a small tin.

The Granite Island quarry offered work to the Harding Brothers, but the work only lasted until the contract was filled.

The McNutt Brothers

On the east side of the island, the *Lady Peggy*, a private craft, brought the McNutt brothers to the discarded cannery houses in 1934. They were laying people off jobs in Vancouver and Roger Green hired the McNutt brothers, Dave, Fred and Jack, to log off his timber in Green Bay. Ethel McNutt was from the city and wasn't quite prepared for what greeted her. There were no windows or doors in the cabin into which she and her husband Dave, and two children had moved, and that first afternoon her husband had to go back to Pender Harbour for more supplies, leaving them alone in the growing darkness. When the kerosene lamp was lit, their first visitors arrived. Bats! Terrified, she climbed into her daughter's bed and pulled the covers completely over her to block out the strange sounds. It seemed an eternity until her husband arrived.

After a while windows and doors replaced the constant fresh air, and the visitors became welcome ones—loggers and fishermen mostly, but best of all came occasional visits from family in Vancouver. Ethel and her sisters-in-law very seldom saw any women between trips to Irvine's Landing where the "Gonzalves and Dames" ran the hotel with its store and post office. They would load their supplies, then round out their outing by watching the Union Steamship come in.

Boat Day was the coast's saving grace. Whether it was meeting the steamer out in the bay or rowing to the docks at Stillwater or Irvine's Landing, it was the highlight of the week.

There was much excitement as all the residents of the area from babies to grandparents gathered on the wharf and watched for the red funnels to appear around the bend. Dogs howled at the sound of the ship's whistle, a long blast, two short toots and another long blast. The postmaster hurried to the dock with the outgoing mail, and people talked eagerly to friends they hadn't seen since the *Comox* or the *Chilco* made its last run from the coastal camps. There was a saying on the coast, "You could tell the population of the area by counting the people on the dock on boat day."

They watched as the steamer landed. They could tell which captain was on the bridge by the distinctive landing he made. When the gangplank was lowered they were once again linked to the outside world. The rasping winch released the mail bag while the passengers made their way down the creaking, narrow gangplank. Freight was off-loaded to the freight carts which ka-thumped along the wide planks of the dock. Cardboard cartons looking very much the size of small battery-packed radios and marked RCA Victor or DeForest Crossley, were perched atop the freight many times during the twenties and thirties. Those that could afford a radio and the $2 license, if they bothered, and very few bothered to "legally" listen to their radios, found it a great comfort through those lean years.

Thelma Deberri, nee Johnstone, laughs when she remembers her dad's first radio, which the Union steamer brought. Judd had more fear of it than he had of meeting a wild animal on his path without a shotgun. He sent all of his family out on the porch in case it exploded and gingerly approached the strange object. It had two rolling dials on it and Judd carefully hooked it to the battery, turned it on and rolled the dials. He rolled and rolled and still couldn't pick up anything. It wasn't until he lifted his hand from rolling that he accidentally stopped at a station and heard an announcer's voice. Then after a decent interval during which no explosion took place, the rest of the family were called to listen.

Many an evening was spent listening to Jack Benny, Kate Smith, Fibber McGee and Molly, and Fred Allen. "They were good clean programs," Ethel McNutt remebers, and as they sat they "visualized what was taking place." After a hard day logging, or cooking for hungry loggers, it was a great way to relax their tired muscles.

Although the Johnstones, McNutts, and Roberts shared the same island and probably enjoyed the same radio programs in the evening, the long distance between their bays kept them separated.

Only a major event, like the news of a baby born on the island would find its way from cove to cove. "Home-babies" were few on the island. Lee Roberts was one of them on January 4, 1935. As if anxious to see his new home, he appeared before Harry could get his wife to the hospital. Afterward Harry rowed to Hardy Island to use the telephone to bring the doctor. Mother and babe were then bundled off to the hospital for a few days. Chris Johnstone was another native Nelson Islander who was born at the quarry, to Judd and Dora. These two boys were the first native Nelson Islanders since the birth of Clara Hammond in 1914. Over the years there have been fewer than a dozen babies actually born on the island.

In the spring of that year Harry logged another entry: "First run with the new boat, *Leyo*. This morning being fine, we got things aboard and set off for our first big out. We ran as far as AJC's Island (Charman's Island) where we saw Jack and his boy watching us from the shore. We dropped hook, had lunch, then with the others we set off fore a sail with very little wind. We found our boat very good against the wind."

A. J. Charman, who was said to have descended from Charlemange, was a pioneer of the Sunshine Coast area, a philosopher, writer, and gardener who spent holidays with his family on Haven Island, or Charman's Island, as the islanders called it. Jack, in one of his columns for *The Coast News*, wrote: "The greatest gift of our island to visitors is the detachment it gives from those things that are too much with us. The walls of the mental rut that is a danger common to all, break down in a fresh environment—the mind is set free and the mind is man."

It was said that he had found the answer to real living, this man who had gone to sea at fourteen, a mere boy. He wrote for both *The Province* and the *Coast News* with a touch of mysticism infused into nature. The following article was dated October 30, 1935, and ties in with what Lester Peterson tells of SKWALT, the Cape Cockburn Indian Village that was raided by a northern renegade tribe who had come into contact with liquor and guns. Many villagers were killed in the raid.

An Ancient Village

By Jack Charman of Gibsons, October 30, 1935
(contributed by Yolana Roberts and
printed with permission from his family)

The Skipper led us through the unspoiled woods of Nelson Island and out to as fine a stretch of beach as the lower mainland coast can show. Two miles or so above Quarry Bay, the shoreline of the island sweeps southward with the curve of the new moon, out to the bold head land of Cape Cockburn, and in the height of the curve is a beach of rounded pebbles. Behind a gravel bar above high water line there is a level grassy tract of land extending inland to the foot of steep rock bluffs, evidently a filled-in lagoon—a formation common hereabouts—and the bar itself is grass-grown, shaded here with a few old sentinel trees, half hidden there with evergreen thickets, the whole making as charming a spot down coast to Welcome Pass as the heart could desire.

Down at the water's edge a family from a nearby reserve was pushing off for the homeward run after a visit to the beach. "They still come to the old spot," chuckled the Skipper. "There was an Indian village here once. Look this way—along the surface of the ground—and tell me what you see." We gazed along the shore in the direction indicated; from previous conversations on the subject we knew what to expect, yet at first we could see nothing but the wiry seashore grass, bending in the wind. Then suddenly a row of shallow depressions became visible, and so plainly that one wonders why they had not been seen at a glance.

A village stood there once, so long ago that diligent enquiries by the skipper, up and down the coast, and among the old folks of the reserve, have failed to find a surviving memory or even legend of it. As shown by the grassy hollow the lodges stood in a row along the shore with the largest, probably the chief's—in the center, those on either side decreasing regularly in size. They are near the margin now, for the bay is being eaten away by the tides, but in old times the lodges were probably separated from the sea by a wide strip of gravelly land—and the former lagoon, behind them, would have been a convenient harbor for the red cedar canoes. An interesting spot and one that might repay competent exploration—or would it not be more seemly to leave that ancient homeplace of those who were before us in this land to the song of wind and sea and the sea birds calling?

The Skipper told us he had found a number of blocks of granite, roughly square and still showing marks of fire, at a place where the seaward bank was crumbling to the wash of the tides. "Remains of an Indian fireplace belonging to one of the lodges, I expect," he said and suggested that we go to see them. He had left the rocks as he found them but when we reached the spot they were built up to form a little camp fireplace, not carelessly thrown together but placed so that each blackened side, scarred by the household fires so long ago, forced inward as it had formerly.

People of the reserve down the coast still come to this open stretch of beach, and though all knowledge of a village of their ancestors has passed from them, a ready explanation was at hand—otherwise one might have imagined that some restless spirit had returned from the happy hunting grounds to rebuild the ancient hearths of the tribes.

Sunray

Cherry Roberts heard a shocked cry, and looked up to see her husband falling helplessly from the roof of their new home. "Oh no," she cried, holding her swollen stomach, and running to him. She turned him over expecting the worst, but he was all right, at least alive. She could hear him moaning.

"Get help," he managed to say. Cherry looked wildly about, hoping to see a boater miraculously passing their isolated cape, but there was no one but their two small children. Her fear chilled her more than the late fall dampness. She took off her coat and wrapped it about Harry's shoulders, then felt the bones of his arms and legs quickly to see if there were any obvious breaks. Satisfied that there wasn't, she ran down to the rowboat.

"Yolana, Lee, come with Mommy," she called in the direction of the beach, and they scrambled to see where they were going, puzzled to be getting a boatride again so soon. Cherry scraped the boat over the rocks, and hurriedly lifted the kids in, giving the boat a push as she awkwardly maneuvered herself into the middle seat.

A swell from the west made it hard to get around the cape, but Cherry rowed valiantly, fighting both her condition and a head tide. It seemed hours until she could find help, but finally she spotted a power boat with two men aboard. She waved frantically as they came near. The two of them helped her and the children into their craft, and tied her rowboat behind while they listened to her story that came out in short breaths.

The power boat rushed to cover the route to Cape Cockburn where the men carried Harry to the rowboat, then again lifted his badly bruised and painful body to the larger vessel. As there was too much risk involved in losing both time, or the precious rowboat if they towed it behind, Harry had to wait for help while they returned it to the cove and tied it to the float.

They set out into the swell, right into thick fog. The older of the two men cut the motor, called out, then listened, trying to get their bearings. They were lost. They drifted aimlessly for awhile, then finally recognized a landmark. As they pulled into the St. Mary's hospital float at Pender Harbour, Harry looked up at the ramp, standing almost on end at low tide.

Nothing about this trip was going to be easy, he thought as he clung to the sides of the stretcher, struggling to keep from falling off head first and cringing at the pain. He stayed ten days at "the little white house," but it was many more before he was able to return to work.

The house that had almost finished Harry, was completed in 1937. It was a fairy tale home, made entirely from logs towed from Texada Island and the far side of the cove. Except for the roof, which Jack Charman helped him with after the fall, he did it all himself, with an adz and crosscut saw. It had sixteen outside walls, and seventeen windows made like sunrays out of cedar strips and cut glass. The floors were cement, painted over, and the roof was split cedar shakes. Every piece of furniture was made by Harry as well, even the four-poster bed and dining nook. The living room had a stone fireplace with two bottles set into the stone to reflect the sunlight. A log staircase led to a loft where the young Roberts slept. Cherry planted roses and honeysuckle that crept around the front door, and Harry built an arbor that adjoined the house. The picturesque home has became more well-known on the coast over the years than "the castle" that he built at Roberts Creek.

Harry wasn't the only Nelson Islander to suffer in 1936. The

Harry Roberts lived in Cockburn Bay (Chack-Chack Cove) before moving to Cape Cockburn. Both Hidden Basin and the cove were the scene of rumrunning action in the twenties. M. McIntyre

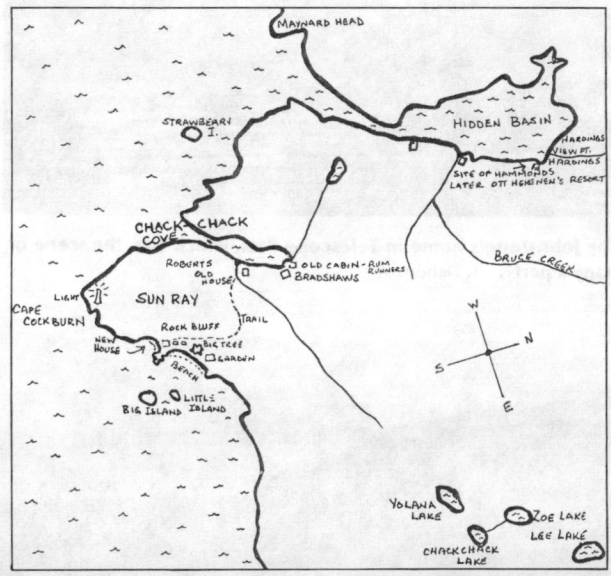

Harry Roberts under bower at Sunray. M. McIntyre

The Johnstone's home in Telescope Pass, which was the scene of many a party. T. Deberri

CPR excursion boat which visited Jervis Inlet. T. Deberri

Blind Bay quarry filled its lime rock contract with the sulphite mill of the B.C. Pulp and Paper Company at Woodfibre, and closed its doors after seven years in operation, laying off all its workers. Paul Harding died that year as well, before he could see his boys complete the View Point Lodge.

Luck was as changeable as the tides. The next year was more promising for the Roberts. More sunshine was added to Sunray with the birth of Zoe on April 4, 1937.

The Lorne Maynard Family

Carole Maynard remembers her initiation to the island clearly. She believes that experience is the best teacher anywhere, and on an island where weather plays a major part in what you do and when you do it, it is invaluable. Being able to read the water and heed the signs of change takes time for the uninitiated. She learned her lesson well.

She and Lorne moved permanently to Cockburn Bay, Nelson Island, in 1939, although Lorne's boat, the *Therma*, was already familiar to the islanders as he made his living chartering out to the provincial boiler inspector. It was while he was away on one of these trips into all the out-of-the-way logging camps, that Carole began to wonder about his return. As she had a couple visiting, she decided to go to Pender Harbour for the mail. They set out in the 14-foot *Sea Wave*, making good time on the trip down.

After getting her mail and ten cents worth of potatoes, they headed out of the harbor. Not too far out, a southeaster began to blow up. They bounced up and down in the ground swell, which before long showed angry white hoods. The spray came over the gunnels. The boat was tossed on the ever-enlarging waves, now and then taking on green water. They were nearing Nelson and bailing as fast as they could, but the idea to go ashore and wait for calmer water was appealing to all of them.

They pulled the boat up on to the gravel beach and propped it above the tide line. After a few hours it became apparent that the sea wasn't going to get any better, and preparations were made for a longer stay. They combed the beach for planks to lean against an alder tree for protection, and threw a tarp over the engine. A dig for clams produced no more than a dozen during the afternoon, but the potatoes saved the day. As the June rain played havoc with their fire, they took turns on fire watch and prepared to stay the night. Once, when it was Carole's turn, a plank fell from their shelter, hit her on the temple, and knocked her out. This was turning into more of an adventure than she had anticipated. Sore, but recovered from the blow, she waited out the night with the others.

The weather had seemed to change overnight, but she had been on Nelson long enough to know that a southeaster lasts for two or three days, but it is often quiet in the morning. They launched the boat as soon as the sea settled enough, and headed for Cockburn Point. Unknown to them, a worried Harry Roberts had set out earlier to find the overdue boat, as he had seen them pass his house the preceding morning. Quarry workers had reported seeing people on the beach near Quarry Bay, and he headed for the protected site. While Harry was searching in the bay, Carole and her friends were passing the entrance having just come short of the quarry area on their landing the day before.

Harry came out to meet them and asked wryly, "Just how long does it take to go to Pender Harbour and back?"

After a lesson from him in types of seas and what speed to travel in each, he followed them safely home. It made her sympathetic towards anyone in trouble and wary of "those mirror-calm days that are always weather-breeders."

At least the days afforded sight to would-be rescuers. At night on the water, a boat was no better off than the driftwood. It was at night, though, that Carole once chanced to aid a rescue. She was all set to turn in, just making a last trip to the outhouse, when she thought she heard something off Maynard Head. "Lorne, I think I hear something on the water," she called out.

"I'll go out and investigate." Lorne grabbed his jacket and pushed his way through the stormy night. A fierce westerly was pounding the shore throwing his little skiff back to him each time he tried to launch it. Finally he managed to get it into the water, but failed to see anything on the first trip around. As he made his way back, he heard a voice calling,"Help!" He strained to see, barely making out the outline of a boat against the islet off shore. As he came closer he could see the prow lodged against the rock and a single occupant. The waves bounced off the islet and doused the men with water as

Harding brothers felled trees with falling saw in 1936. Shown here with Lyn Delong, left, are Paul, Bill, and Bert. A. Harding

Looking down on Hidden Bay and Ott Heikennin's (Captain Henry's) boat. M. McIntyre

Waiting for the rapids to become slack are Jerry Jervis, Margaret McIntyre, Margaret's brother and sister-in-law, and the Hardings. M. McIntyre

Ott Heikennin's (Captain Henry) lodge. The Hidden Bay Ranch Resort in the thirties. M. McIntyre

a line was thrown to Lorne by a very relieved man. They freed the boat from the rocks and Lorne towed it around the island, often seeing it hurled towards him by the waves. It was easier to get the boat in than to launch it—it was just a matter of how far up the rocks it would be thrown. The stormy fall night chilled them as they secured the vessels. Lorne removed the distributor from his tow to dry it out.

Carole had bacon and eggs on for the cold and wet boater when they came in, and offered him dry clothing. He identified himself as Jim Williams, but it wasn't until they sat down to eat that they discovered he was the Indian Chief from Sliammon. "Dropped son off at Vancouver hospital," he told them between bitefuls. "It's been a bad day. Someone stole my battery and a couple of other things, out of the boat, then a 10-foot wave broke over the windshield and killed the engine. I was heading up the outside of Texada at the time.

Remembered my father telling me about how it was protected in here." He stopped to take another mouthful, then continued, "Managed to get up on the bow and guide myself in with oar. Headed for the first bit of land I could see. Lucky you heard me, I was getting damn cold."

The Maynards put their unexpected guest up for the night and Lorne fixed his engine the next day. They had lots of company in their guest house over the years, but this man's arrival had been the most unusual.

The Maynards were friendly with another fellow who was later to become well-known in the Nelson area, Jim Spilsbury. He was the local radio expert, who had started a traveling repair service in 1931. He sold radios and did repairs out of his boat, the *Five B R*. Jim was established by the Depression. As very few people could afford new radio equipment, he kept the old functioning.

The Nelson Islanders didn't fare as well in the Depression.

Nobody starved, but no one made a fortune either. The rival lodges in Hidden Bay—Harding's View Point Lodge and Ott Heikennin's—did a modest business, but depended heavily on big gardens and fresh fish. Most were happy to live simply, away from the hell that Hitler was creating in Europe and the unrest that was settling over the rest of the world.

Two women who moved into Hidden Bay were actually more newsworthy locally than was the political scene. It was still rare for women to be living on their own unless widowed or stranded, and neighbors watched from a distance while Margaret McIntyre and Jerry Jervis made a valiant effort to pioneer in a man's world. Armed with a good sense of humor and a lot of determination, they built a log home with much help from Allen, Margaret's brother, and the Harding brothers, who put on the rafters. They earned the respect of all when they split 2,000 shakes themselves, all except Ott Heikennin, that is, who insisted "it be falling down."

They battled regularly with Ott Heikennin, the granddaddy of male chauvinists, who didn't like women and insisted these two couldn't live life the "simple way" with their good furniture and four dogs. Ott, who used the name Henry, the English version of Heikennin, was dubbed "Captain" one day by the girls, and was often referred to after that as Captain Henry. He owned the Hidden Bay Ranch Resort, an unusual building with arches from the roof in an odd fashion. Captain Henry resented the Harding Brothers having a competitive lodge in the bay and took great care to keep their guests and their luggage separate from his when they met the steamer. Most of the time he was successful, but some remember the uproar when they got mixed. George and Celia Nuotio and young son Allan moved to Billings Bay in May of 1939. Their first home was a tent until George could get the cabin built on their 345 acres of land. He was away fishing from June to September, but returned in time to get their cabin winterized before the first frosts.

The Depression bred crime, but most was never recorded as newspapers were no closer than the peninsula or Powell River. A "Gas-boat Bandit" struck Vanguard Bay in February of 1935, when Ivor Jorgenson was victimized. The bandit tied Jorgenson to his bed while he did the robbery, untying his hands when he left, according to the *The Powell River News*. His booty also had a depression ring to it—sixty-five cents, some carpenter's tools, gas, oil and a bit of oatmeal.

On September 8, 1938, an unusual find was made on Nelson Island suggesting a possible crime, but no follow-up story was given. A skiff, a cluster of bones including a human skull, and bundle of blankets were found by an unnamed prospector. Two brothers, John and Donald Clu of Vancouver were missing and an investigation was underway to link the boys to the find.

Most crime was petty, illegal pitlamping, or operating a still, but occasionally it was more serious like log rustling. It all seemed petty compared to the killing and destruction that was to take place at the close of the decade. In September, 1939, Canada declared war with Germany. Nelson Islanders viewed European strangers with suspicion. There were whispered rumors that Hitler had men hiding in the hills of Gibsons and isolated islands, ready for the takeover when Europe fell.

That winter on Nelson, islanders fought only the elements. They thawed pipes, plugged draughts, chopped wood and kept floats in repair. Harry Roberts made a note in his journal at Christmas: "Our first meal in the place I built for meals in this home, Sunray, and what a meal! A dozen people, all told, and more good things than we could eat. Some of the people had not eaten very much for weeks, for they just had not got it to eat. So this Christmas was one in which we happened to be able to share with others in need."

The Forties

The forties were ushered in to total blackness along the B.C. coast. Gun shots in Hidden Bay proclaimed the New Year and the new decade. Art Harding, Fred Schutt of Blind Bay, and Cherry's boy, Harold Arnold, went overseas and the war touched Nelson Island. Lorne Greene, "The Voice of Doom," brought news of the front on "The National" but life carried on as usual for most islanders.

Only Judd's daughter Thelma, the new Mrs. Ben King, came as close to the action as the boys did. She and Ben were ocean trolling in the far north by Calvert Island when a submarine almost sunk them. Oil from an enemy submarine which had been torpedoed was still bubbling up around them when they accidentally got between the corvettes. The suction was powerful. "We weren't supposed to be there. I was crying, I held on to the mats but couldn't stay on. It was terrible. They had an enemy sub there. Did we ever get into trouble, the fellows bawled us out." More than forty years later, Thelma can still recall the terror she felt.

Shipbuilding was stepped up for the war effort and George Nuotio worked in the shipyards of Vancouver while his wife Celia cared for his young son Allan and the Hidden Basin property.

The war also changed Tom Brazil's lifestyle when he took on a government job with the army. He spotted aircraft as they flew over Cockburn, a navigational reference point. Tom Hughes, who was much younger and more able to distinguish the different aircraft, often helped him out, thinking that Tom Brazil was no better than the post mistresses and storekeeper's wives along the coast, who kept government single channel transmitters for reporting enemy plane sightings.

Jim Spilsbury, who twenty years later was to call Nelson Island his second home, maintained this "flock" of radios that were called the Aircraft Detection Corps network. He did this first by boat, then by plane, a four seat waco biplane which he bought in 1942. It provided him with many a colorful adventure over the years.

Harry and Margery Thomas

The 36-foot diesel cruiser, *Istomina*, brought Harry and Margery Thomas to the Blind Bay-Billings Bay area in 1941. They had purchased McLaughlin's property which "Midge" christened Ballet Bay in honor of their daughter, Audree, who at fourteen had joined the Russian Russe de Monte Carlo ballet troupe.

Harry was a W. W. I vet who had lost one arm in the service, but it didn't seem to hold him back any. He often fished with two rods, using a hook for a second hand, and became proficient at shucking oysters with the aid of his foot.

Small Fry, his very reliable clinker with an Easthope engine, was often called upon for ferrying people in emergencies. Harry's straight-back profile could be seen going out to the steamer in all weather, in winds "so fierce they would drive your whiskers in backwards," as he would say. He handled the open mail bag for several years, relieving Tom Brazil of one of his duties.

They lived aboard the *Istomina*, (again named for his daughter who had been given the Russian stage name, Anna Istomina), for four and a half years before their house ashore was built. It was exciting, and tricky, to finally move their piano into their new home. It was the second on the island; Laurie Wray at Westmere had the other.

Harry used to say, "When the tide is out, the table is set." The Thomases joined the other islanders in their harvesting and canning or salting of all the sea and shores had to offer—oysters, clams, cockles, muscles, cod, herring, and salmon. They raised their own rabbits and chickens and shot grouse and deer. Venison was often canned on their kitchen wood-burner, fired by the "best wood to burn." Lots of bark was available for kindling.

The problems of finding food and heating their homes was easier and cheaper to solve than that of surveying the land. As it was expensive to bring surveyors up from Vancouver, it was often done by the islanders themselves. Harry once helped Lorne Maynard survey a piece of property he'd purchased next to his place. Lorne had brought an old friend of his up from town to do the job, and this friend had brought an old crony with him to help. The two went around the piece of land during the day, and sat down in the evening to go over the survey. Try as they did, they couldn't close their line. Each blamed the other. "You are so damned deaf you can't hear," one said.

"Yes, and you are so damned short-sighted you couldn't see what you were writing down."

Lorne quieted them down, and decided he would enlist Harry's help. The next day they covered the ground again. This time when the survey was drawn up, the lines closed perfectly. Lorne commented that it was the only piece of land surveyed by four men—one with a wooden leg, one with only one arm, one near deaf, and one near blind! Ott Heikennin did his own surveying too. When he sold part of his land to Margaret McIntyre and Jerry Jervis, Margaret remembers he "measured the land by striding about in his oversize rubber boots without the faintest idea of what he was doing." He said there was no hurry to have it properly surveyed as long as they paid their share of the taxes, which he claimed was twenty dollars. As taxes in those days were dirt cheap, twenty dollars would have been enough to cover the whole fifty acres that he owned. Their part should only have been about two dollars.

He refused to take their two dollars and insisted now that they get it properly surveyed. To avoid the expensive business of bringing in a surveyor, they discussed it with their lawyer who, on the advice of a surveyor and the tax assessor, agreed that two dollars was reasonable. "Ott wouldn't hear of it," Margaret said, and cut their water pipe out of the dam on the lake.

As the women were both in the army at this time and didn't really have time to bother with all of this, they sent a surveyor up to do the job properly. He came back roaring with laughter, saying that Heikennin's agreement of sale to them had included the lake, the dam and all the water—he had no water rights at all!

Determined to get even, Heikennin then said, "that the agreement was to be measured from high water mark and at low tide we had no rights to walk on his beach at all."

By this time "Jerry was a major in the army and carried some weight. She and the lawyer and tax assessor got together and they phoned Heikennin and really talked turkey to him. He gave in grudgingly and we were very magnanimous and said we had no objections to him using the lake, the dam and all the water he wanted. That didn't satisfy him. It had to be his water, his lake and his dam, so he loaded his house, his livestock and everything but an old barn, and towed the whole works out of the lagoon to Green Bay, which he promptly christened "Hidden Bay" in memory of the old one, and refused to allow anyone to use the name on their letters. They did of course, and I believe the confusion and row that resulted was really something.

"By that time we were totally disinterested. We sold the place to an Australian called Talbot-Lehmann." He had also bought the Heikennin piece,"So after all the jiggery-pokery, the place became what it was originally—one piece of rocky land."

Arguments over water rights on the island were as common as clams and still continue although no one has matched Heikennin's reaction to date. One of the islanders even volunteered a title for this history, *The Isle of Disputes*.

During the forties though, the community grew in an enviable state of cooperation. Problems were shared and help was always at hand when needed. Several weddings took place in the early part of the decade and new babies began to appear with regularity. Homes sprang up in every sheltered bay.

The Hardings built large wonderful homes from lumber ordered from Eaton's, it was said. With the whole dripping rain forest in their back yards, they ordered the wood, which came all the way from the Eaton's warehouse in Winnipeg, where it had probably been shipped from the Vancouver sawmills, where it had probably been cut from logs boomed from Nelson Island. And, they added, just as if they had ordered a tin of tobacco—it came "no charge for delivery."

Jerry Jervis and Margaret McIntyre look out the turret of "The Castle" built by Harry Roberts before he moved to the island in 1932. M. McIntyre

George and Celia Nuotio and son Allan, in 1940, at the lake above Hidden Bay. C. Nuotio

Yolana Roberts at Sunray. M. McIntyre

This story is part of the Nelson Island lore now, but Agnes Harding tells the true version: The Harding men logged their own trees, towed them to Pender Harbour to the sawmill and brought the lumber back to the island. Of course it makes more sense but doesn't make nearly as good a story. Bachelors added spice (and more) to the community life. Frank Ficek, a donkey engineer, barbered for the local men, but was most noted for his powerful home brew and his never ending quest for a housekeeper. Gus Hanson, the caretaker of first the Quarry Bay site, and then the Granite Island quarry, used to tease the Roberts girls at Sunray. He would get out of his boat and roar from the depths of his 300-pound frame, "I've come to get a housekeeper!" He had as much success as Frank Ficek.

Hugo Bjorklund, a one-eyed "Swede-Finn" also was single, but had been married in the thirties. He was a handlogger who worked quite a lot with Frank Ficek in those days. He built three or four log homes on Nelson and did odd jobs for Captain Wehner and Judd Johnstone. He earned himself a reputation with his axe. He could fix anything with it—even his alarm clock.

Tom Hughes was a fisherman who lived on his boat for many years until Pete Klein of Pender Harbour gave him a house on a float. Hardings helped him apply for a Home-Site Lease for an island out from their home.

The Home-Site Lease was being offered to fishermen as a priority at that time and Tom was one of the few to take advantage of it. It consisted of locating the land, in this case a small island of less than eight acres. Papers were procured from the forestry at Pender Harbour and an agreement was signed which stated that the leaseholder would pay the lease and the taxes, make improvements and live on the land for six months of every year. At the end of the twenty-one years, or in Tom's case, ten, because of the smaller size, the leaseholder paid to have the acreage surveyed, costing anywhere from five to twenty dollars. If he or she had lived up to all the conditions, the land was his, or hers, as it turned out to be in Tom's case, as he died a year before the lease was due. He had willed the land to Ann Pettigrew who fulfilled the conditions for the final year.

Hugo had also leased an island, now known as Clio Island, before selling his home on Nelson to Fred Easthope.

Fred Easthope was another old character, one who survived on gingersnaps and lived to be ninety. Many wondered how it was possible as he always kept his chain saw behind the wood stove, and started the stove with gas or kerosene. One time Harry Roberts was with him and questioned the act. "Oh, the Lord will look after me," Fred, a devout Christian, assured him.

"Well, I'll wait outside," Harry replied, "I'm not in his good books."

Draughts were a constant worry to Fred. He hung strings in the doorways of his home and spent hours studying the direction of them, and plugging the cracks. He bathed daily in the ocean year-round, and had an interesting hobby, that of collecting rare books. He attended the Shaughnessy Estate sales and brought many collector's items back to the island. He kept a case of white kid gloves on hand for guests to use when they looked at the books. They had to be quick though, as he was reputed to only allow people a fifteen minute visit.

He was rumoured to be the black sheep of the Easthope family who made the very reliable Easthope engine that bedecked many an Islander's boat. His own boat, the *Triton*, sported another make. His well-known boat with the four or five-foot addition to the stern, survived many a run-in with rocky shoals around the island. He wasn't known for his navigational skills—but then he didn't need to be—the Lord looked after him.

In return for the Lord's services, old Fred paid for a one-line ad in the *Vancouver Sun* for twenty or thirty years. It was at the end of the boats and engines column and read: *Jesus saves*.

Captain Edward Wehner arrived in Blind Bay in 1944 on his way up the coast in a fish boat. He was looking for a piece of land for his retirement, which presented a problem because as an alien he was not eligible for a Home Site Lease. With a cosigner by the name of Fitzgerald, who occasionally visited, he was able to obtain a piece of property, or at least live on it, making the necessary improvements. His Bavarian wife, Lotte, had not accompanied him on his first trip as she was running a boarding house in Vancouver. At one time, though, she had been an opera singer and was known then, and still by the islanders, as Madam Wehner.

Had Wehner not been German, the couple would still have made waves in the Bay, as they did not fit any of the required molds. She was very much older than he was and each had separate living quarters. He also wrote articles for a Vancouver newspaper. Some thought him a clever con artist.

In those anti-German war days, a German newcomer to the area was naturally viewed with suspicion by the islanders. Captain Wehner was viewed with suspicion by the police as well. They tore their home apart at onetime—stripped wallpaper from the walls, ripped open the mattress and even went through their shortening looking for subversive evidence. He must have passed inspection as he lived in the area for many years. In fact, he himself claimed to have worked for the British Secret Service in North Africa in the early part of W. W. II and did not approve of either Hitler or the Nazi cause.

He had been a resident of Brazil for a number of years before living in Africa and after the war, often promoted expeditions to the Amazon. The first one was quite large, involving a boat called the *Orion* and a number of people, but it apparently fizzled out.

Geoffrey Partington was intrigued with Captain Wehner's expeditions to the lost mine, which some said held gold, some diamonds, and joined him on one of them. The two set off in a smaller boat than the *Orion*, the *Halfmoon*. All went well until Wehner fell ill in Trinidad. Geoffrey met two fellows there who were interested in the expedition and they continued on without Wehner in an even smaller boat. One of this trio was a flamboyant adventurer, writer by the name of Dod Osborne, the other a handsome English entrepreneur, John Hoskins.

With spirits high, they set off, their sense of adventure whetted. As they got closer it was adventure they got, but unfortunately it was in the form of a shipwreck which ended all hope of finding the lost mine.

There was never a lack of after dinner conversation in the forties as long as Nelson and Hardy Islands had their bachelors or Captain Wehner around. Their adventures were always food to fuel the Islander's favorite game of speculation.

Geoffrey Partington

Geoff Partington's arrival to Nelson Island three years earlier had also been something of an adventure. He and Bill Hartley had been in the navy and had traveled into some of the inlets on the coast looking for acreage to lease. The weather was bad in 1947, when they first came into Blind Bay in their 18-foot boat, powered by a 6-hp Briggs and Straton, one of the last of the Linton boats built in Coal Harbour. They put into Captain Wehner's who suggested a small bay near him for their lease.

With the land papers procured, and lumber enough for a 12-foot by 12-foot shack bought from Baker's sawmill in Pender, they started off. They had purchased an old shoot-the-chute barge from the exhibition grounds in Vancouver and had made one trip with what they would need for homesteading, as well as roofing, windows, and stove. This second trip was presenting more difficulty. As they crossed the mouth of Agamemnon Channel they ran into a little bit of slop. It was "kind of a stupid thing to do—greenhorn kids—we could defeat the world," Geoff says now.

There was no freeboard on the barge and it filled with water.

Suddenly lumber started to drift away towards the beach where the creek comes out of Sakinaw Lake. Geoff jumped over the side and started to swim around to gather up the carefully calculated wood. Bill stayed with the boat gathering up the pieces that had drifted further away, and was soon around the corner out of sight. "Of course we had no life jackets, we didn't worry about those things in those days," Geoff recalls.

He had a rope with him and wrapped the lumber with it. The water was getting colder and there was just half an hour of daylight left that chilly fall day. He made it ashore and climbed up on the rocky bluffs looking for Bill. A while later, Bill came by towing the lumber and the unreliable barge. He scanned the shore, circled around, and took off. Too late, Geoff realized that Bill hadn't seen him and was heading to Pender Harbour for help. He was soaking wet and icy cold when Bill returned an hour later. After the rescue, they took stock of the lumber and accounted for every single piece of it before starting off again.

With just a jug of fresh water, they towed all night. In the morning a westerly blew up and kept them from getting around Cape Cockburn. They put into Harry Robert's place at the cape and he put them up for a couple of days.

Captain Wehner was in a pretty bad state wondering what had happened when the young guys finally showed up. "This was my introduction to Blind Bay," Geoff says, "and it's been much of the same since."

Geoff's brother Robin, and another fellow by the name of Smith joined them. They bought a small gill-net boat which eventually progressed into two landing barges, and beachcombed the area together for the next four years. Then with different ideas for the future, they went their separate ways.

The Community

By the time the "navy boys," as their neighbors called Geoffrey Partington and the other young men, made their first appearance in Blind Bay, the community was going strong. The older Johnstone girls had all married. Thelma had been cruelly widowed at nineteen and had remarried. She and Slim (Gordon) Deberri, a fisherman of the area, lived in a float house with their daughter Franny. Grace had married Richard Krentz and had two small children, Dorothy and Richard; and Evelyn and John Vaughn were the proud parents of young Gary. The Maynards had two sons, John and Royal, and Nuotio's second son, James, was born. The Hardings, too, were getting in on the Nelson Island baby boom. Agnes had met and married Paul after she and her daughter, Dorothy, from a previous marriage, had visited the View Point Lodge as guests. Robert and Mary were the children of their union. Ernie and Bert married girls from their Vancouver home area. Four children: Barbara, Beverly, David, and Jimmy were born to Bert and Daphne; and Art and Lynne were beginning their family of five: Margaret, Arlene, June, Steven, and Joann.

In 1945, almost every family had a two-year-old. Judd and Dora Johnstone's three grandchildren were all doing what the "terrible twos" do—island style. With Franny on a float house, although neatly fenced, it must have been fun. Royal Maynard was this same delightful age when he swallowed an open safety pin, during a southeast gale.

The water around Cape Cockburn looked black and ominous as Carole held her frightened son, and Paul Harding headed the *Agnes H* into the heavy sea. St. Mary's Hospital seemed a long way off at that point. The boat heaved and pounded against the waves and the sea spray beat against the windshield obstructing their vision. At last the little white hospital came into unfocused view.

Harry Roberts' son, Lee, early 1950s.
M. McIntyre

Dora Johnstone and her grandchildren in the mid-forties. In the front are Franny Deberri, Dorothy Krentz, and Gary Vaughn. Dora is holding Richard Krentz. T. Deberri

The Deberri float home in Blind Bay. It is now on land owned by Tait. It was towed from Seymour Narrows. T. Deberri

The nurses prepared for an emergency operation, as the doctor examined Royal on his arrival. He was soon under the anesthetic. It was the first of two operations in the next few weeks to locate the dangerous pin. Carole stayed at Al and Queenie Lloyd's in Pender Harbour until Royal was fit to go home more than six weeks after the event.

The other youngsters fared better than him, except possibly one of Art and Lynne Harding's babies who began her life on the water. Lynne was a war bride from England whose parents worried continually about Lynne expecting her baby in Hidden Basin. Stories of rapids and six-hour waits for slack tide were naturally cause for great concern to the prospective grandparents who had visions of a baby born amidst gas-streaked water and fish scales in the bottom of the boat. Lynne assured them she would leave for Pender Harbour in plenty of time and had every intention of doing so. Baby had other ideas. When it announced its arrival early, it was between slack tides, and Lynne had to be carried through the trail by Paul, to Art's waiting boat. In spite of their haste, Grandma's visions were prophetic and outside Pender Harbour Baby was born in the boat. Lynne was intent on keeping her parents from finding out about their grandaughter's untimely arrival but she didn't reckon with the radio telephone.

Someone called a friend in Pender Harbour who informed the local news. The story was picked up by a Vancouver radio station, passed on to the CBC national news, who wired it to the BBC who broadcast it to all of England. Before Lynne could tell them herself, they'd already heard that Baby was born in the boat!

So much for island isolation.

As the youngsters approached school age, the need for a school was always on the community lips. Harry Thomas volunteered space on his land, and arrangements were begun. There were sixty-four people in the Blind Bay-Billings Bay area at that time, and around 100 on the whole island.

The Forties in Cockburn Bay

Cherry left her young family in 1942 and Harry had three kids to look after with no close neighbors. Friends helped. Those from the city sent boxes of clothes and Dora Johnstone in Blind Bay, sewed for the three of them. Harry butchered one of the cows he brought from Welcome Pass on a float, and canned the whole animal in quart jars. Yo now says, "Seems we had that meat for years."

He stacked the storeroom in the center of the house with case lots from Woodwards, and home-preserves, and he also killed the odd deer. With the fresh fish and garden vegetables, he managed to keep his young ones fed. He scooped out a root cellar in the bank by the garden for keeping apples, potatoes, carrots, cabbage, and beets. Eggs were preserved in a crock of "water glass." But in spite of all the provisions, it was a tough time for the family.

The house was finally looking and feeling like home though, and everyone was fairly happy and in good health by the end of the year. Harry was a religious man and gave thanks to God for his home and children.

He was ingenious too, and rigged a windmill as well as a workshop with a water tank on the roof. In front of this tank facing the beach he had a four-bladed windmill attached to a pump at the bottom. In a southeast wind they could fill the tank using wind-power to pump the water from the well. It had one drawback, that of being too efficient in a storm. They often had a hard time stopping it then. One person would have to hold the brake while someone went up on top to tie the thing down.

He also had a "drag-saw." It was a single cylinder engine on an A-frame. The motor drove the saw back and forth like a hand saw. When the block was cutoff, the frame was moved over for the next cut.

Harry's resourcefulness illustrates the island ingenuity. If anything broke down, they fixed it themselves, and usually a back-up system took over while the work was being done. In later years the windmill was replaced by a gas-operated pump and a power saw took over the work of the drag-saw, but Harry's inventive talents were still being put to use to lighten the load in other ways.

If he ever had a problem he couldn't solve he would stay calm and quiet until the answer came to him. If it came in the night, he would get up and write it down by lamplight. Yo says, "He also had a way of running everyone's life which got him into some disagreements from time to time!"

Ann Pettigrew and her daughter Jacquie came to live with them in March of 1943. The goats and rabbits they brought along made them an almost self-sufficient homestead. They fixed up a bigger garden, put up hay for the goats, and built pens for the rabbits and geese. Harry sold the *Leyo* and built a bigger boat, the *Ha-Ha*. It was a busy time. Ann kept Harry's kids and Jacquie at their correspondence school in the mornings and they did chores in the afternoon. Seven-year-old Lee's job was to gather wood from the beach in a burlap sack and dump it in the woodbox behind the stove.

Ann stayed until 1947 when she took Jacquie back to West Vancouver to finish high school. The Roberts kids didn't get past grade eight. Their dad said they could always do it later, but Yolana wishes he had made them do it then. They took out books from the Victoria Public Library and finished their education informally, although Yo and Lee went to the UBC Extension Department for a youth training course later on.

They inherited an artistic bent from both their mother and father. Harry painted scenes and Cherry painted flowers. Yolana captured birds in water color, and Lee was always drafting plans for boats. Both Zoe and Yolana painted birds on the kitchen cupboards. The frogs and water lilies which can still be seen at Sunray were painted by Yo.

They had few friends in those early years. Their *Family Herald* subscription featured a pen pal page and they wrote to a number of pen pals across Canada. After Jacquie left, their cousins were old enough to visit in the summer.

Yo remembers her first visit to see these cousins in West Vancouver when she was fourteen. She went across to Pender Harbour by boat, took the *Gulf Mariner* to Vancouver, and the North Vancouver ferry to Lonsdale where the first bus was taken. A transfer to a second bus was needed to get her right to West Vancouver. Quite an excursion for a young islander.

Another time she remembers taking the open boat, *Ha-Ha*, to Roberts Creek to visit her cousins at the castle. "On the way we had trouble with the motor, got caught in a southeast gale and stopped behind Trail Islands. We didn't have a tent or blankets or anything much for spending a night. The tug, *H and L*, was tied up nearby with a boom of logs. Finally the skipper called us over and put us two girls in his cabin for the night. We couldn't understand why he locked us in. We had breakfast with the crew, and as the wind had gone down, we headed out for Roberts Creek."

When Lee was fourteen, he went to work on a tug for Len Hipp.

The two-week job was his first experience away from home. At fifteen he worked on the boom for Charlie Klein. Yo and Zoe did the housework, laundry, and cooking then, and charged him $50 per month for their services.

They used part of this spending money to go to the shows and dances at Pender Harbour and Madiera Park on nice weekends. They got to know some of the kids there, but went mostly with older fellows as there were very few boys their own age. If a storm came up they would spend the night at Davis' Garden Bay Hotel, returning home the next day.

When Yo was seventeen her dad built her a 10-foot boat with an air-cooled engine. She could then go for the mail and visit her neighbors by herself.

Cars were a different matter. Their first car experience was with a 1928 Buick that Lee brought home from Billings Bay on a raft of logs. He took it completely apart and got it running, doing most of his work from a book, as his dad knew very little about cars. They had more fun with that car. They had to cut all the old skids out of the road and fill the mud holes. If it wouldn't start, they would pull it up the hill with a rope and block, hop in, and coast down until the engine caught."They learned lots," says Yo.

Later, when Lee logged, he purchased several second-hand cars which allowed the three of them to go to Roberts Creek and Gibsons for their dances and visits. About this time, too, he finally built one of the boats he'd been planning for years.

Harry had a small sawmill that he bought in pieces and rigged himself. Lee cut the lumber on it to build this first boat, the *Black Wolf*. They worked hard for their amusement.

PART IV

The East Side of Nelson Island

Howie White Remembers Green Bay

My father, Frank White, first set foot on Nelson Island some time in 1949, as near as I can reckon. To this day I think he thoroughly regrets doing so, but none of us kids do. How could we? To him and Mom it was a tough luck show that robbed them of their prime years; to us it is the mold that formed us—to reject it would be to reject a basic part of what we now are.

Charlie Philp was to blame for Green Bay, as he was for so many of Dad's disappointments. Charlie was a rich guy who lived in Vancouver. He'd been a lowly car salesman at one time but then he got the Mack Truck dealership just as truck logging was sweeping the coast, and made a million. He enjoyed his surplus wealth by finding ambitious young loggers like Dad to go out and set up hard-scratch gyppo shows, then slowly torment them into bankruptcy. My dad had just gone through the process with one partner, Eddie Barnes, up in Cardero, before moving to the Fraser Canyon for a season. Now he was coming down and starting over again at Green Bay.

The camp itself was already set up when he arrived. It consisted of three small board-and-batten shacks on posts just above tide line and three somewhat more permanent shacks farther up from the beach. These were all located on the west side of the bay beside a waterfall that roared like a rushing freight train all winter and disappeared in the summer.

It was in 1950, on May 24 as I inexplicably recall, that Dad decided to move the rest of the family, consisting of my mother Kay, my older sister Marilyn, eight, myself, five, and my baby sister Cindy, three, into camp. We had just moved out of a failed camp at North Bend, after weathering the record-setting winter of 1948 in one of the province's most extreme climates (my father's luck wasn't good, but it was consistent), spent a few months of respite in the comfortable family seat at Abbotsford, then moved with all our effects aboard the fish packer *Moorpack* owned by the keeper of Pender Harbour's main store, Royal Murdock.

The house we kids slept in was practically at the foot of that waterfall and I'm sure that eternal roaring is still going on somewhere in the back of my mind; I know whenever I hear the rush of falling water now it does strange things to me. That house wasn't a part of the camp; it was finished on the outside with real siding and lined inside with birch veneer like a real house in the city, and had been built as a wilderness home by a family named Yates who still owned the twenty acres the camp occupied. All we kids knew of these mysterious Yateses was that they were Christian Scientists; the closets and attic of their abandoned house were packed with innumerable issues, not of the *Christian Science Monitor*, but a lesser true-believer publication on octavo-size pages with a vine border framing the covers. Millions of them. Frank Yates, the ageless Sechelt bus driver, is a scion of this family and is no doubt in possession of a very sensible explanation of his family's involvement with Green Bay, though I have never asked him for it.

I suppose Dad chose the Yates house for us because it appeared at first glance to be the most comfortable; it had two private bedrooms, a large living room, a kitchen with nice cabinets, an old wood range, and hot water, and an inside bathroom with a chemical toilet, all finished in handsome birch plywood, in contrast to the other bunkhouses, which were just bunkhouses, with the usual beaverboard and spiked-to-the-wall orange-crate appointments. But the Yates house was totally accursed. I still dream about it regularly; it provides my subconscious with a purgatory symbol that can't be improved upon. It was always dark, dank, and cold. It was built in a kind of muddy hole in one of the few locations with no view of the bay and was so overhung with droopy cedars the sun never shone. It was always wet; glossy magazines left in that house for more than a few days would turn to mush and clothes gathered mildew hanging in the closet. Dampness was endemic. A cool steam wafted over from the waterfall, filtering through trees burdened down with Spanish moss. Periodically the wetness would gather its energies and erupt into the open; during spring and fall rainstorms, an impromptu river might break down the back door and flood the whole house to a depth of six inches. I remember being delighted the first time I awoke to find my gumboots bobbing against the wall, then later when the waters subsided, discovering the plywood floor blistered into a series of springy hills that made good jumping on until Dad caught us. I remember him looking underneath the house and roaring, "They actually dug the goddamn thing down into a hole! How could anybody be so goddamn stupid as to build a goddamn house in a goddamn mudhole. They must have blasted to get it so bloody low!"

Everything had been done wrong in that house. Doors opened the wrong way, the steps made you trip every time, the water pipes couldn't be made to stop leaking in the summer or freezing in the winter, so they were simply never hooked up. As a result the bathroom was inoperative, the kitchen sink was only good for trapping spiders and the stove couldn't be lit because that would burn out the unused water coil. And yet here were all these good intentions; dish cabinets with glass doors, leaded windows, pretentious archways, laboriously built dry-stone terraces, all useless. It was like an arrested dream, that place. We very much envied the wife of the camp foreman, who occupied the boxy shack on the hill which had none of these pretensions but was warm, dry, functional, and commanded a clear view of the bay. The only good thing about the Yates house was the fact we kids had it all to ourselves, after Mom and Dad moved down the trail to the less gracious but more livable quarters in the back of the cookhouse. At first a teenage girl from Egmont was hired to watch that we didn't stay up all night and make us work at least a few hours a day at our correspondence lessons, but that lasted only until I chanced to observe to my dad one day that the men in the big bunkhouse must be short of blankets or something because one of them was coming over in the dark of night and sharing our babysitter's.

We kids often climbed in with each other when it was cold, so the man's behavior didn't seem all that unaccountable to me, except for the fact that they were so noisy, and I was surprised by the reaction my casual comment drew from my parents. They were thoroughly scandalized, but the situation must have been a tricky one. Dad had hired a crew of local boys from Pender Harbour and had already begun to discover some of the reasons more experienced heads had warned him not to do this. One young fisherman had persisted in showing up for work on the rigging crew wearing gumboots, and when the foreman fired him, the entire crew dropped their work without a word and walked down to camp.

When Dad realized what had happened he got one of the men aside and asked why he'd walked out. "Harry's my cousin," the young man said. "If you fire him I gotta leave too. Our family wouldn't like it if I stayed." One by one the others gave the same reason. To Dad's surprise, it turned out they were all related. Harry got his job back.

They didn't know just how our babysitter and/or her paramour fitted into the local maze of family relations, but there seemed no delicate way of finding out, so Dad came up with a strategy involving me. In the peculiar quavery hush I would come to know better as his talking-about-sex voice, he directed me the next time I heard the lovers carrying on, to barge in and put on a display of childish outrage. This, he calculated, would make the culprits feel so ashamed of themselves they would break it off, or at least become acceptably discreet. The actual words I was coached to say were, "What the hell do you think this is ... a whorehouse?" This astonished me because we kids weren't permitted to say even "damn" or "bugger," and I couldn't believe my father was actually coaching me to violate our cardinal rule. It put me in a quandary I struggled with all day. I was still awake fretting that night when the familiar noises began in the next room, but with my heart in my mouth, I leapt into duty. I stomped down the hall making as much noise as possible, as I had been coached, burst open the door and began my piece:

"What the ..." at the critical point my nerve failed. "What the HECK do you think this is, a hoorhouse?" I squealed at the shocked silence. "Hell" was the only part that stopped me. I had no idea what a whorehouse was, so that part didn't trouble me at all.

Dad's ploy worked like a dream. The noises were never heard

again; in fact the girl left of her own accord very shortly after for reasons she kept strictly to herself. The only result for me was that all the men in camp suddenly began treating me with extreme respect, and the particular man, who has grown old alongside me in Pender Harbour, treats me very warily to this day.

After the babysitter experience, we kids were left to our own rules, and it is instructive to recall how this worked out. Naturally for the first few weeks we stayed up all night and slept in each morning until Mom had the men away, the dishes washed, the lunches made, and trundled over to shake us out. Likewise, the amount of correspondence lessons completed was negligible, and of course the house was an impenetrable tangle of dirty clothes, cut-up Eaton's catalogues, stepped-on plasticine, peanut butter sandwich remains, and dirty milk glasses with clots of milk powder doing colorful things in the bottom. But within a reasonably short time we discovered on our own we could not go on this way, and our little system righted itself. We simply learned about ten years earlier than most kids about the basic necessities of looking after yourself on your own, and became a very responsible, self-sufficient, easy-to-look-after little group. My older sister Marilyn even got around to doing her correspondence, and kept her courses up so diligently that when we moved to Pender Harbour some six years later she was able to walk right into junior high school and start knocking over top marks immediately. I didn't fare quite as well. After four years I was still fumbling around in the early stages of grade one, although I had become the camp's regular dump winch operator. My mother finally became so disgusted, she completed my grade one course herself in two afternoons, doing the printing exercises with her left hand. I essentially omitted my first four years of schooling, but I can't say as I have ever missed them. All three of us ultimately graduated from high school and went to university, a relatively rare occurrence in Pender Harbour then, and my younger sister Cindy had the distinction of being invited to attend Simon Fraser University straight out of grade eleven, one of only a few so honored in the entire province. She graduated with an MA.

When we first moved to Green Bay, the camp was called Arbutus Logging and was run by Cam Prior, Harold Pearson, and Graham Whalley. But my father, through a combination of genuine capability (Bob Hallgren, then the general manager of the giant Rayonier Timber Company, once told me Dad was the most versatile all-round logger he ever knew) and inexhaustible gullibility soon assumed managership, then ownership, changing the name to Jervis Logging. True to his trusting nature, he took along one of the lesser qualified employees of the camp, Charlie Trebett, as partner. Charlie claimed to own the camp's yarder as well as knowing everything about running your own show. In the end he was a total disappointment. Not only did he know nothing, the yarder turned out to be on lease from a man named Samson, and then to top things off, he married my mother's younger sister Jean, who came up on a summer visit. The partnership ended in a real honest-to-goodness fistfight down by the light plant, wherein my dad, an old street brawler, landed a haymaker that sent Charlie head-over-heels right through the salal brush and onto the beach below. The barnacles left him looking like he tangled with a bobcat.

Ever since that time, Dad has been down on partners as a general thing. "Don't go into partners," he warns us younger entrepreneurs. "You just do it because you think you can get somebody else to be all the things you aren't, but it never works."

We kids loved Green Bay, or as we invariably called it, Greenzbay. There was nothing there for us—no schools, no playmates, no television, no radio, not even regular mail or newspapers, but for us it was paradise. We lived basically on our own in the Yates house, our parents were so preoccupied with business. Our entertainments, in spite of the lack of modern amenities, seemed endless. At night we would stay up as long as the light plant stayed on, enjoying movies which consisted of new car ads for '52 Plymouths and Chryslers from the Saturday Evening Post, projected on the wall with Marilyn's opaque projector. After lights out she would read to us by flashlight from risque bestsellers such as *Giant* and *Cannery Row*, which served us in place of *Mother Goose*.

By day we lived in a world of pretend. Each of us had one main pretend persona. Marilyn's was Marilyn-of-the-Stores, so named because we originally began by setting up pretend stores stocked with beachcombed bottles and cans. I was a strait-laced masculine hero named Sevward Billington, and poor little tagalong Cindy was a ne'er-do-well named Mrs. Bad Keeky. During most of our waking hours we lived in these made-up roles, snapping out only when confronted by grownups, and frequently branching off into innumerable lesser roles that altogether comprised a pretend world of such highly developed interrelatedness, the adults in camp were

"Logging camp kids" Howard, Marilyn, and Cynthia White catch dogfish instead of going to school. All went to university later.   H. White

The Whites at their Green Bay home in 1952. From the left are: Frank, Howard, Kathleen, and Cynthia.   H. White

Frank White's Green Bay camp was a typical independent, or "gyppo," logging operation (1950-55). H. White

The MV *Moorpak* calls in on the Whites in 1952. The supply vessel was owned by Pender Harbour merchant Royal Murdock. Howard White

continually astonished by the glimpses they caught of it.

In the course of our play we transformed the geography of Greenzbay into a fantasyland. Our parents were of the enlightened generation who followed the indulgent dicta of Dr. Spock and went him one better, allowing us the free run of the place as long as we kept our bulging kapok life jackets firmly buckled in place. We were provided with a rowboat my father had built for us using plans from *Popular Mechanics*, his hands-down favorite reading material. It was a blue painted, high sided, vee bottomed, blunt-nosed thing made out of half-inch plywood called a "pram," and we wore out one set of oar lock holders after another exploring the local landscape. Across the bay from camp was a sheer bluff which was nevertheless discovered to contain a cave which showed eerie signs of previous occupancy. Part way down the bay toward the north end was an equally evocative abandoned campsite and boat beaching grid where I found a five-inch barnacle grownups told me could only have come from the west coast. Legend was this site had been previously occupied by an old seagoing hermit who beached his sailboat there. Later another wanderer found it: the legendary Allen Farrell, who built his famous ketch *Native Girl* there some years after we left.

The north end of the bay ended in a mudflat surrounded by green slopes which had been terraced into gardens by some previous wave of settlement. Shortly after we came, two families of early-day hippies named Gregerson and Fraser beached a floathouse on these flats, enlivened by some completely unworkable vision of living off the land. Within six months they were gone, Dave Gregerson to become Pender Harbour's resident dipsomaniac electrician, Fraser I know not where, though I've often wondered.

Coming out of the bay from the north end, on the west side opposite the hermit's boat ways, was the foundation of a log cabin, mysteriously abandoned half finished, said to be the work of the mythical Yates family. Rounding a bend that led into the waterfall bay where our camp's log dump was, was a low mossy knob which owned a special place in our hearts because it was where the otter herd in its annual migratory visit set up a slide like a group of touring acrobats and enthralled us for an unforgettable afternoon. Directly in front of this mossy dome was "The Reef." The reef served two essential functions. One, it anchored the standing boom to which our camp's booming ground was tied. Two, it provided the camp with its chief summer entertainment—watching yachts smash into it, then blither about like chickens with their heads cut off. It's a particularly treacherous rock in that it is surrounded entirely by steep-to shores, and therefore unsuspected. In our day its insidiousness was increased by the existence of a six-foot boulder perched at its center, but in recent years some civic-minded towboater seems to have rolled this into the deeps. The reef was a favorite visiting spot at low tide, serving as a mock Treasure Island as well as a bounteous source of every subtidal life form from foot-long foot-shaped oysters and eating crab on down to clams, blennies, anemones, and fat juicy sea worms that made you feel sick just to look at them.

Going farther out the bay past the camp, on your right you had, first of all, Chair Bay. I forget why it was called that. Either we found a driftwood chair there or it looked to one of us at one time like a chair in its overall shape. The main feature it had, besides an enormous house-sized boulder with a stagnant green rain pool on top, was a flat shingly beach, the only decent one in the bay, which made it good for two things: wading at high tide when the rocks warmed the water, and collecting driftwood. Chair Bay supplied us with most of the rusty tins, glass bottles, and rimracked condoms that stocked the shelves of our make-believe general stores. The most prized items were the most exotic, such as aerosol cans of whipping cream with elaborate plastic trigger-tops, which would fetch at least 50 prime salal-leaf dollars, or items with unmarred labels, or anything plastic, which in the fifties was still a rare and magical substance. Opposite Chair Bay was Cover Point, a low, smooth nose of granite that faded out into the sea in a very gradual slope so that the water always seemed to be very gently lapping it. Cover Point was also a nice place to swim, its wave worn stone was so warm and smooth to the foot, but it was even more notable for its tidal pools populated with large hermit crabs. Hermit crabs, after otters, are perhaps west coast nature's most comical creatures, and we spent days howling at the antics of those unfortunates we captured and took home in jars. They proved ideal pets, surviving no end of clumsy attention and carrying on their bizarre underwater antics unbothered.

Cover Point was really the last named geographical area we regularly frequented. The little bay in its crook was called Maple Bay, for the huge overhanging maple which papered the water with bright leaves each fall, shore-to-shore, and the little angular bay adjacent, Mud Bay, because of the unpleasant muddy bottom which was pocked with icky sea worm holes but full of clams. At the very mouth of Green Bay on the left was Eagle Point, a forbidding place so named because of the gnarled snag there which, we felt sure, must be just the place for an eagle to roost, though we never saw one. On the right was the Crag, an old dead snag that had the profile of a pterodactyl and stood ominous guard over the Green Bay entrance until very recent times, when it finally crashed to the beach.

Unlike settlers up on the Blind Bay side of the island, down at Green Bay we felt virtually without neighbors. Technically speaking we had some, the Henrys. The Henrys were an old-world Finnish couple and I think the term my father used for them was "hard-bitten." They had the old cannery site in the little hole-in-the-wall just to the right as you came out of the bay. They called this little lagoon, which becomes landlocked at about half-tide, Hidden Basin, in memory of their first homesite up at Hidden Bay, which they had left some years earlier following persecution by the unreasonable people who lived up there, as they explained it. Elsewhere in this book you may find the other side of this story, which tends to place the unreasonableness on the Henrys' shoulders.

In any case, the Henrys managed to find a rather favored location for their second Nelson Island home. Unlike the big bay we occupied, it got sun, it had a bit of flat land where they could run their solitary brush-fed cow, and there were still a number of cannery cabins scattered along the beach bluffs which the Henrys promptly organized into a sort of low-budget summer resort, mainly for Finn millworkers from Fraser Mills. It was actually this piece of land which had been owned by the Green for whom the main bay was named. I never did learn much of this pioneer except that he took out a large tract some time before the first World War and he must have leased it to the cannery, because after the market for canned protein collapsed at the war's end, Green regained possession of the cannery site as well as the large two-storey 12-foot by 30-foot cannery building itself, which he turned into a shingle mill in partnership with a Vancouver millwright named George McConnell, Ian McKechnie, and another man named Sansen. This venture soon failed for lack of raw cedar to saw and ended in litigation between the partners, as—my father would point out—most partnerships do. Eventually the main cannery building burned, and when we were there the only sign of it was a scattering of barnacled, sea-worn bricks on the beach. Of the cannery operation itself I have never been able to find any written record. Jim Warnock of Pender Harbour tells me it was owned by a man named Windsor, who called it the Windsor Cannery and orignally set it up in Bargain Harbour before moving to Nelson Island to be nearer the big humpback run up Jervis Inlet. McKechnie says that when he went to work as a millhand there in 1923 there was still stationery headed Cliff-Lomond Packing Co. drifting about the premises. His theory is that there never was enough high-grade fish to support a cannery in the area and that the cannery was only set up to cash in on the wartime market, when you could can "anything that swam."

What this sketchy early history does indicate is a pattern of decisive failure and abandonment—a pattern that persisted through our experience, and ultimately through the Henrys' although in our time they seemed to have secured a pretty sound foothold. As Finns tend to be, the Henrys were inexhaustibly hard working, especially Mrs. Henry. Boats leaving camp at daybreak would always discover her out before them, jigging for cod off the bay mouth in one of the curiously designed sampan like boats they used. During the spring she toiled until dusk in the large garden they had built up on a rock knoll near their house, laboriously packing soil in pails and fertilizing it with star fish, dogfish, and seaweed until it blossomed into a heartbreaking jungle of fruits, berries, and vegetables, heartbreaking because, gawk and drool as we might, we can-fed urchins never got to sample a bit of it. Every scrap of food Mrs. Henry could lay her hands on went into jars to feed her summer guests. Again following the typical Finnish stereotype, everything about the Henry's place was sparkling clean, orderly and well kept. The house itself was quite striking, with large windows, crisp white painted shingle siding, a bright green tiled roof in the shape of a curved arch and odd projections at each of the four corners where the eaves continued clear down to the ground, the way we always assumed all the houses in Finland must be, though now I suspect it was just another of Captain Henry's quirks. In the midst of all that enclosing coniferous jungle, they maintained a neat lawn with trimmed shrubbery and charming flower plots that gave the place the aspect of a toy village in the Alps, or in Finland, I suppose. It was a kind of magic realm all of its own to us kids, just because its civilized charm was such a contrast to the bunkhouse and bulldozer universe we occupied, but on the few occasions we were admitted to the house with its fragile furnishings, porcelain trinkets, and unearthly cleanness, we felt suffocated.

The locals warned Dad that the two old Finns were "mesatchie" and troublemaking—a reputation resulting no doubt from their dispute in Hidden Bay—so, true to his perverse nature, he set out to win them over. This proved less than simple. Those first-generation Finns had a very hard face which they turned to the non-Finnish world, a peculiar expression which seemed so devoid of human feeling as to be completely intimidating, and this was the face we would be met with on any attempt to stop the Henrys for a chat on the Irvine's Landing dock, or to drop in on them for a casual visit. One's business would be crisply asked, and there being none of note, no quarter would be given. The seven-mile trip to Pender Harbour and back was a day's undertaking in those slow-moving days, particularly with the Henry's snail-like little sampans, but all overtures toward collaborating on shopping runs were dismissed without consideration. The initial attempt to deliver their accumulated winter mail was received with something akin to shock, and resulted in the postmistress being rudely dressed down and ordered not to allow it again.

They were also extremely jealous of the boundaries of their large tract of mostly useless bush and would be seen lurking behind trees whenever logging operations came near anywhere remotely in the vicinity. If we kids ventured out that way in our rowboat we would be shooed home, and once when some of the men fired a shotgun at some mallards they were stalking down the beach from the Henrys, the old lady popped out of a crevice in the rock and gave them such a ferocious tongue-lashing they retreated without attempting to retrieve the good sized drake they'd hit. They had been unable to determine whether Mrs. Henry was upset by the noise, didn't approve of killing, or just wanted to chase them off so she could put the duck in her jars.

There were two cracks in the Henrys' heavily armoured independence, however: their cow, and the internal combustion engine. Old Otto was a deep sea master mariner but his experience was all in sail and he had never really gotten the hang of keeping gas engines going. Since in the summer they depended on their boat to meet guests coming up on the Gulf Line steamers to Pender Harbour, this was a serious problem, and finally one morning Mrs. Henry appeared at our wharf in a dreadful state, pleading for help. She had the better English of the two and was normally quite comprehensible, but when she got worked up, you had to have a lot of Finnish to decipher what she was saying. This Dad couldn't do, but it was clear enough the problem was over at their place, so he towed the old girl home with our camp boat, a coffin-like ex-rumrunner entitled the *Suez*, and found the old captain almost dead of exhaustion from heaving on this one-cylinder Easthope in the sampan. He was just purple and gasping and his hands were raw to the point of being bloody. A quick check showed the gas line to be running straight rusty water, and after draining the tank and cleaning the carburetor, the engine ran like it was made to. The old boy was effusive in his thanks, and Mrs. Henry insisted Dad accept a King George dollar bill, neatly folded in thirds. She was so upset when he declined that he offered to take "something for the wife" from their garden, and came home with four carrots and a bit of lettuce.

The trouble with Henrys' cow was it was Canadian. They wanted a Finnish cow as frugal and orderly as they were, but this cow was haywire. For one thing it gave too much milk, and always at the wrong time, so she always had lots when there were no guests to feed and none when there were lots. This led to her next actual attempt to acknowledge our neighborly existence, which took the form of her approaching my mother with an offer to provide the camp with fresh milk. Mom of course happily agreed, even when it turned out the old lady wanted the same price per ounce as canned milk at Murdoch's store. Mom took it and even kept taking it after we discovered it was so queer tasting, a result of her cow's peculiar diet of seaweed and salal brush—that no one would drink it, so anxious was she to establish something approaching a normal human relationship with her only neighbor.

The other thing about Mrs. Henry's cow that helped bring us together was its propensity for wandering. There was no real road connecting our two places, they wouldn't let Dad make one, and Mrs. Henry desperately tried to keep it fenced and roped in, but that cow was over at our place every time you turned around. I don't know why. It just hung around. I think maybe it longed to hear its own language spoken. We kids naturally liked it and made a big fuss over it and snuck it pocketfuls of rolled oats, but Mom and Dad made a neighborly effort to send it home. Dad was afraid a logging truck would run over it and he'd have to pay Mrs. Henry its worth in T-bone steaks at Murdoch's. The trouble was, it was very hard to get home. It would get bogged down in swamps, jam its head between close spaced saplings, and get stuck trying to climb over fallen logs, bawling and thrashing as spike knots ripped into its udder. We could never figure out how it got around on its own, or why it was never killed by a cougar, or one of the area's numerous pit-lampers.

Its greatest caper was the time it ate the dynamite. Dad was a bit sensitive about the dynamite because by law it was supposed to be kept locked up in a special air-tight magazine built out of 6-inch by 6-inch timbers, while he had it stashed in a flimsy open lean-to just up the road from the shop. On top of this, you were supposed to destroy dynamite after a certain date because it becomes unstable and dangerous to handle, but he could never bring himself to just burn dynamite he'd paid good money for. Eventually ours got so old and cranky they were all afraid to go within a hundred feet of the magazine, let alone use the stuff. This was when Mrs. Henry's cow was discovered standing by the road chewing away on a stick of 20 percent stumping powder as contentedly as Fidel Castro munching a Havana cigar. Closer inspection revealed that the beast had been living for some days at the magazine, stomping boxes open and eating case after case of dynamite, evidently enjoying the piquant taste of saltpeter and nitroglycerine soaked sawdust.

"Holy jumped-up, bald-headed, bare-assed, black-balled Mexican Christ!" my father shouted, twisting his cap around on his head as the implications of the discovery sunk in. "Nobody touch that cow!"

"One hiccup and we're all goners," observed Jack Spence, the foreman. "Can you imagine what a time the cops would have trying to figure it out? Just a crater full of guts, hooves and hardhats."

They were afraid it would go home and blow up in Mrs. Henry's barn, or else the dynamite would get into the milk and poison half the crew of Fraser Mills. Finally they decided to drive it way to hell and gone up the logging road where it would take two weeks to get home, by which time it should have cleaned its system out. But nobody wanted to go close enough to tie a rope around its neck, so they hit on the idea of getting behind it with the logging truck and scaring it up the road with the air horn. With everyone else cowering down behind stumps, Tom Grey eased slowly up in the truck, but at the first blast the unsuspecting animal shot into the brush like a goosed kangaroo and was gone. We all spent the following week with one ear tuned for large blasts, actual or verbal, emanating from the Henrys' direction, but the case of the bomb that mooed closed without further incident. The next thing I remember about that cow was Dad killing it. I think the suspense got to Mrs. Henry, after so many years of sitting home fretting about losing all that potential bottled beef to a marauding cougar, and eventually she prevailed upon Dad, who she had somehow found out was a trained butcher, to do the thing in. Being of the opinion that it was never too soon to start disabusing his male heirs of any innate squeamishness about blood and gore, Dad took me along to "help." I remember there being a parental discussion on the matter, where it was concluded this would be good for me, so the event took on a ritual air. This was augmented by the careful laying out of tools, the erection of the hanging beam, and by Mrs. Henry's hysteria. Even before we arrived her face had the wrung-out, red-eyed look of a person suffering through a death in the close family. However this was equalled by another kind of excitement, at the veritable bonanza of bottled provisions which were about to land in her lap, and she couldn't pull herself away until the fatal moment was upon us, and then only with the odd request we summon her immediately the deed was done. Then she struggled off, wringing her hands, to hide in the house. Dad cocked his head in the direction of her retreat to make sure I learned my lesson.

"What's wrong with Mrs. Henry, Dad?" I said. "Well son, she's like most people," he intoned. "They can't bear the sight of blood, but they like to eat meat. That's why there has to be men like you and me around to look after them."

Then he told me to put down a handful of hay under the hanging beam and when the cow walked over to it and lowered its head to munch he quietly suggested I hand him the ballpeen hammer we'd brought along in our bucket. I fetched it and he delivered the cow an easy thud on the back of its head, collapsing it in a heap exactly on the spot he wanted to hang it from for skinning and splitting.

"Gee, is Mrs. Henry's cow dead now, Dad?" I said. It didn't seem like much of a spectacle, for all the buildup there'd been.

"That's all there is to it, son. Farmers, you'll see 'em get the animal rearing all around beating on its nose with a claw hammer, but this is the way you do it."

Coming from the Fraser Valley, Dad always used farmers as the example of people who did everything haywire, although after he'd been up the coast for a few years he began to cite fishermen instead of farmers. I grew up thinking of both the way prairie wasps think of Ukrainians. It wasn't until I was fully grown I heard fishermen refer to gyppo loggers in the same spirit.

I looked at Mrs. Henry's cow lying there whole, unmarred, as unchanged as if it were asleep, except for the odd finality of its stillness, and found death didn't impress me at all. Then Dad reached down and drew our butcher knife across the cow's silken brown throat and my heart stopped as an ocean of blood burst out over the dry fir needles.

"Take a stick and draw a groove in the ground so it will drain over there and we don't walk in it," Dad said. But I was transfixed. At this point Mrs. Henry came puffing up the trail. "Is it done? Is it done?" she kept calling, not wanting to get too close in case it wasn't. Then she followed my pale stare to the blood.

"Ohhh! I wanted you to call me." She produced an enamel milk pitcher and stared from it to the brilliant puddle now dispersing amongst black fir tree roots and spongy moss.

"I ... I wanted to keep it," she stammered. "We always keep it, in the old country ..." And then she knelt with the pitcher to her cow's clotted jugular, but the flow had stopped. This was too much for me.

"What's she doing, Daddy?" I shrieked, jumping up and down. "You told me she couldn't stand blood and now she's going to drink it!"

I survived their pained explanation and the full spectacle of slaughter as it unfolded before my now thoroughly impressed eyes. Mine, but not Mrs. Henry's. Her squeamishness forgotten, she fastened herself to my father's elbow, snatching every scrap and drip for her jars. The stupendous eruption of guts did not faze her; she hungrily seized upon the tripe, lights, brains, heart, hustling them off to the kitchen and returning quickly for more.

"What's that?" she would demand in the angry-seeming way that was more her normal tone, with that singular Finnish blanche beginning to seize her features, as Dad went to throw another piece on the compost pile.

"Bung," he said.

"What?"
"Bung."
"What's it good for?"
"Well, Scotchmen use it for haggis ...."
"Give it here!"
Dad gave it.
"What's that?"
"Bladder."
"What's it good for?"
"Well, when we were kids we used to blow it up and play football with it ...."

For his efforts Dad was allowed to take home a roast of his choice, so he cut out the sirloin—she didn't know one cut from another anyway—and amid much festive feeling and dynamite belch and exploding oven jokes, the camp crew sat down to eat it that Sunday, but true to form, Mrs. Henry's cow was completely inedible.

Captain Otto Henry was a good deal older than his wife and once you learned how to decipher his mangled English, actually proved the more sociable of the two. Once or twice when Mrs. Henry was off on one of her occasional trips to Vancouver, Dad and some of the guys went over with a bottle and even discovered the old guy to be a bit of a rounder. He could laugh, tell stories, and his history was fascinating. Finland had built up a merchant navy early in the century by buying richer countries' mothballed sailing fleets and crewing them with destitute farm boys who worked under seventeenth-century conditions. Captain Henry had begun as a cabin boy on one of these ships, and told horrific tales of the hardships the Finn sailors suffered from hard work, bad conditions, and harsh discipline.

One of young Otto's tasks was to take care of the raisins—raisins were the one luxury on the ship's menu—and while he had the raisin locker open to squish weevils and count out portions, he was under orders, under pain of the lash to keep continuously whistling.

Despite the hardship of life in his native land, Captain Henry never ceased to be homesick for it and scornful of his adopted one. His dream was not only to once again see the old sod, or old tundra as it were, but to build himself a fine little ship that would take him back to all the wondrous places he'd seen in his youth and provide him a long retirement of leisurely drifting on the tide. The whole time we were on Nelson Island, Captain Henry worked on this perfect vessel as assiduously as his wife did her jars. It took shape in a shed a few hundred feet down the beach from the house, but so painstakingly was he piecing this last command together, double-planking it with yellow cedar over oak ribs and teak fittings, that the progress from year to year was barely perceptible. It was a very strange looking ship, for a dream boat, about thirty-six feet and rather tubby, with a long foredeck and a high house admidships with tiny round windows. Of course, it was designed to sail, I'm not sure he even planned to bore the keel.

The end of the story goes without saying. Not too long after we left in 1954, victims of the Social Credit government's policy of closing the woods to small free enterprise and delivering it over to the big monopolies, Captain Henry, who must have been eighty, died with his little ship still on dry land. I went up to look at it and noted that he had gotten as far as painting a name on the bows— *Esto Utopia*. I once thought *Esto Utopia* to be a marvelous piece of arcana evoking a special Finnish valhalla but my friend Raimo Savolainen tells me it was just the English word "utopia" paired with an acronym made of the Henry's two anglicised names, Esther and Otto. A few years later Mrs. Henry sold it to a fisherman who cut off the outlandish house, bobbed the stout mast, painted out the *Utopia* and converted it into a very prosaic gillnetter called simply the *Esto*. I never saw it tied up to the *Whisky Slough* fish barge without stopping to marvel at its romantic history, but its new owner only complained of its screwball design and the rot in its timbers.

By the late fifties, Green Bay had thus won its sunless, rockbound solitude back to itself once again, and buried another generation of settlers' dreams. My parents never forgave it and remember the period only with bitterness. As for us kids, as I say, it has remained a place of dreams, and my dreams of it are the pleasantest I have. Every time I dream about it, I resolve to go back for a visit, and at at least once a year Marilyn and I do. But it gives us a funny feeling. The falls are still there, and Dad's old log dump, but all trace of the camp is gone. Even the one permanent structure, the Yates house, has been so thoroughly consumed by salal and elderberry we can never agree exactly where it was. The great looming bluffs across the bay are gone, replaced by an anonymous unimposing low hump, and nothing seems mythic at all. I swear someone has moved the reef a hundred feet closer to the shore where the otters used to romp, and somehow changed the way it looks. There are traces of the intervening decades—the burned-out hulk of a west coast troller, Clarence Cook's old *Morien II*, below the falls, and around in Mud Bay a tug in similar condition, I think the *Viking Prince*. Over in Hidden Bay, Henry's successor, an even bigger Finn dreamer named Ken Viitanen, who spent several years there trying to grow exotic hothouse orchids for worldwide distribution has vanished without a trace, although his son-in-law, Walter Ibey still booms salvage logs in the main bay. The Henry's house is gone too, having burned in disgrace during the hippy era, which brought the most recent wave of dreamers to Green Bay. Thirteen of them went together and bought the old Yates property, but already the little shacks they dotted through the woods have been left for the ravens.

The Yates and Follets in Green Bay

Howie White's mythical Yates were a very real part of Green Bay for a few years, and their house that Howie's dad had cursed was just as damp and cold for them as it had been for the Whites. While the Whites had blamed the builders, the Yates and Follets blamed the cement board finish which was all they could purchase just after the war.

Lorene Yates and her daughter Lola had holidayed at Captain Henry's resort and had fallen in love with the area after their first row around the bay. When their husbands, Harry Yates and Ron Follet, came for the weekend they talked excitedly of building a summer resort themselves.

They approached Captain Henry who agreed to think about selling them the land around the waterfall. When the deal was made, 198 acres for $2,500 they set to work to build their ill-fated home. The two-bedroom cabin was built over the creek and close to the waterfall which supplied the power for their electricity. They moved into it in October of 1945. The cement board they placed their shoes on at night would seep water into the soles and soak them by morning. Between the green lumber and the creek spray, the glue on the bed refused to hold, and Follets were always landing on the floor. The next day would be spent in propping the bed over the Coleman stove to dry the new glue. Condensation ran down the glass canning jars on the open shelves and gathered in a pool on the floor which eight-month-old Chris loved to play in each morning. The keys were stuck on the old oak piano they had brought with them on the fish packer, and the drawers were swollen on the new bedroom suite.

All of Harry's savings and Ron's retirement cheque from the army went into the property, leaving them with very little to live on. They remember getting up at 2:00 a.m. to dig clams to sell. Ron even tried trapping, but his trapline only produced two mink, one that sold for $18 and one that sold for $20. This little bit and Chris' $5 a month family allowance was all they lived on for awhile. When loggers moved in above them, they received some money from them for keeping their logs in the bay.

It wasn't enough to build a resort though, and the men went logging to earn the money needed. They had logged their own timber first and Ron had towed it to the LM & N Logging Company in the Sechelt Inlet. It wasn't until he was through the Skookumchuck that he learned of the treacherous rapids and the wait needed for slack tide. He was a bit ill when he thought of what might have happened.

While the men logged with LM & N (and before that DeLong's Logging), the women tended the garden and kept the 8-foot deer fence in repair. They gathered oysters and clams, and Lola shot ducks, with the fishy taste that only she could eat. They canned venison and garden produce.

They used oil in their stove, which astounded Ott Henry. He couldn't understand them not chopping wood. As *Mrs*. Henry chopped all their wood, and did everything else as far as they could see, they ignored the comments. He was only known to them to go out and bring the guests in from the steamer.

Mrs. Henry caught the salmon for dinner and tended the huge vegetable garden. She was a wonderful cook and served salad in an unusual but welcome fashion. A large platter of shredded vegetables was set on the table and each person picked what they wanted. It was served with good wholesome food.

Henry's resort boasted a new sauna the year the Yates arrived, and guests were treated to the Finnish custom. They were also taken across to Lake Kokomoon the peninsula for a hike.

Their only other neighbors were Jim and Lou Read and son at the head of Green Bay. Green owned the property across from them but never lived there while the Yates were there.

The Yates and Follets traveled around in their boat, the *Emu*, which was a rebuilt lifeboat from a steamer. It had a galley and cabin with bunks, and even had a head in it, its main selling feature.

They had lived in Green Bay for four years, enjoying the life and still nurturing the idea of a summer resort, when a tragic logging accident in Jervis Inlet took Ron's life. Lorene says it "squashed their plans" and they had to abandon their dream. One man couldn't continue all the heavy work alone. Lola stayed in the Jervis logging camp until she began to get upset about the men coming in off the steamer and asking where they could find the young widow. Kindly loggers moved her down to the peninsula.

Lola sold her half of the land to the Dubois for $5,000, and Harry and Lorene moved to California. When they sold some years later, they recovered double that price for their portion.

The Reads on Caldwell Island

Caldwell, a small island in Agamemnon Channel was home to the Read family for over twenty-five years. These exceptionally tall people, the men were well over six feet, were familiar to the Nelson Island area when they arrived on their island in 1951. They had lived in Green Bay for at least seven years before that. Jim and Lou's only son, George, renamed the island "Alcatraz" as a joke and erected a sign with this name on it.

They named the bays as well, funny little names, although the work that went into making the terraces and planting shrubs and gardens was no joke. They cleared trails and put up bridges on their showpiece.

George grew up on the island, always on the water, running the boat or walking logs, but unbelievably, he never learned to swim. He did his correspondence courses, all twelve years of them, in the boat while tied alongside the float which held their small donkey engine. His mother ran the donkey, yarding out the logs while Jim logged. The logging and a bit of beachcombing kept them going.

When he was through his schooling he worked for a man from

Pender who boomed logs near their island. All went well until one day George set out to pick up his folks who had been to Vancouver. He had an open 14-foot outboard that was taking in a bit of spray in the choppy water. He slowed his engine and got up to get a tarp out of the bow, something he'd done a thousand times. Apparently he lost his balance and went overboard. The young man who had always lived on the Agamemnon Channel, daring fate by never learning to swim, lost his life to the turbulent waters.

His parents sold the island shortly afterwards and moved to Vancouver in 1976. So much more should be written of their many years on Alcatraz and in Green Bay, but both Jim and Lou have passed away now as well, taking their stories of island life with them.

Westmere in the Forties

The life of resort owners appealed to Lawrence and Kay Wray after spending a vacation with the Hardings at the View Point Lodge in Blind Bay. When Westmere came up for sale in 1944, they decided to move their five children, two girls and three boys, to the east side of Nelson Island, to try their luck. With gas rationing still in effect, vacationers sought out the coastal resorts.

Lawrie had owned a shoestore in Jubilee, and was no relation to John and Walter Wray already on Nelson, so they knew no one on their side of the island. There were no "Do-it-Yourself" books then, and they never even had a radio phone over the years. All bookings were made by mail. They learned as they went, occasionally taking advice from a passing fisherman on how to anchor your boat so it wouldn't leave on the tide, or some other important island knowledge.

There were more people on the coast than when the Wests built the original hotel, and Lawrie soon added an addition to the "half-of-hotel." Nonfunctioning old post office equipment was found in the office of the resort, well as buckets of odds and ends hanging from the rafters.

The lodge never did more than pay for itself, and the Wrays dug clams and picked oysters to supplement their income. Kay raised chickens and sold eggs as well as young roosters in the spring. Betty Wray, who was seven when they moved to the island, remembers

Just a morning's catch at Westmere. Lake fish are in the foreground and salmon are on the rack. Wilf Crowe is in the center, and Mr. Buckley is on the right. L. Wray

Hotel after Lawrence Wray added his addition to the half-of-hotel. L. Wray

"Mother would end up with this vast production line in the kitchen, chickens that were half-plucked, chickens that were half-cleaned, half cut up, it was a big job." Kay's kitchen also produced fresh bread and baking that was long remembered by guests.

When word spread of the good lake fishing and fair salmon catches, guests came continuously from spring to fall. They had nine bedrooms, some of which were used by family. They had no bridal suite, but one "brutal suite," a primitive cabin used only by younger members of the family. As well as caring for the lodge, Lawrie built several of the fourteen summer homes on West Lake and checked them all winter. He serviced them by boat, picking up their grocery orders and propane in his 26-foot launch, the *Elkay*.

"We were a close family," recalls Betty, "especially my younger brother and I, but were considered a bit of an oddity with our wall of books, and our piano, and record player. We played a lot of music. We always had sing-songs. We'd try to set Dad up as a solo. Mom would play a song that he knew well and when he got into it, we'd all fade out. He'd sung first tenor with various choirs." The guests enjoyed the singing, and they enjoyed the guests, often speaking of them through the long winter months, some with a chuckle, like the stout fellow who dived into the water and lost his bathing trunks. View Point Lodge had a guest who went into the water without a suit, too, but she wasn't completely naked, she always wore a hat. Betty left when she was seventeen, but found her once-a-year trips to the city for dental appointments and the exhibition, didn't prepare her for her "burst into the world." She felt she had none of the normal abilities to deal with people her own age. Her younger brother, Alec, stayed on after his parents left in 1972. He and Fred Buchamer owned Westmere together for several years before selling to Forrest Angus. The resort had served the area for more than half a century.

The Milligans in Vanguard Bay

About the same time that Jervis Logging began its operations in Green Bay, another small logging outfit was setting up its tents on the shores of Vanguard. Lew Milligan's eight-man outfit was preparing to log the area for the next three years.

Little did Joan, Lew's wife, know when she arrived by Cee Bee to this makeshift camp in the summer of 1949, that more than thirty-three years later she would still be calling Nelson Island her home.

Lew had leased two acres of land with foreshore rights and set up a donkey engine on the beach earlier in the spring. He had purchased the camp from Gustafsons who owned Deserted Bay Logging, and had barged the equipment in from Sliammon. Among the equipment was a fifty-year-old poker table that is still in use as a summer table.

L & J Timber, as they called their company, logged the home site first, pulling every tree out by the roots. Large gaping holes filled the site. The road was the next project, then with the help of Lew's uncle, Bill Milligan, Bill's son John, and six other men, they logged the area around Vanguard Bay.

Chris Neilson was their cook in the early days, although Joan's friend, Polly Barker, nee Powell, came the first summer and pitched in, thinking it would be a lark.

The carpenter only had the house half finished when they moved in with Doug, four, and Kathy, two-and-a-half. Little Sue stayed behind in Vancouver to be spoiled by her grandmother for the first while. There was no trim around the windows and doors and during the 1949-50 winter they were really cold. They wore the same clothes inside as out.

Around the middle of January, they got the northeaster. The wind began to blow in the morning and by evening it was howling into the bay. The huge waves heaved booms onto the float, smashed the freight shed, and pushed their boat, the *Vanguard*, onto the beach and piled boomsticks on top of her. The whole float, freight shed, and boat were jumbled together like pieces of driftwood. Everything iced up the moment the water hit it. There was deep snow everywhere, and ice across the bay.

There was no one else in camp at the time and Lewis ran over and tried to get the boat started to get her off the beach. But there was nothing he could do. A walking icicle, he returned home.

There they were with just a rowboat and no phone, during the worst winter in fifty years, as Judd Johnstone told them later. "I don't really think we were terribly upset, except to see the boat go," Joan remembers. "It was just one of those things that happened in the wilderness."

A weather-whitened hulk of a boat wrecked on the beach is a reminder of that ill-fated day.

They burned oil in an airtight heater in those days, not having time to chop wood steadily enough to heat the too-well-ventilated house. Lew would take the 45-gallon drums and put them in the small open boat and go off to Egmont, twelve miles there and back. It would take all day and Joan often wondered if she would see him again each time he left. But like the mail he always arrived, eventually.

Mail arrivals were weird and wonderful over the years. The Milligans have had five different addresses to date, but have never moved. Cherry Sandvold acted as postmistress when they first arrived and would row around from the steamer with their mail, and news of the island. After the steamers stopped coming, Davidson Marine Freight delivered until they folded. Then for a while it was left at Pender Harbour where once for a three month spell, it piled up and fell over before finally being located for Lew. The Gulf Lines, the *Wing* and *Mariner*, did postal duty after that, and now the mail is picked up at the Saltery Bay mailboxes.

The *Jervis Express* of Tidewater Navigation, and later as Union-Tidewater (1956), also serviced the Milligans. To catch the boat they would have to go to Egmont. One time they had made it to the "crossroads" of Agamemnon Channel and Jervis Inlet when the steering cable broke. As they couldn't maneuver close to the Jervis Express, it had to maneuver to them. Their good friend Polly (ex-cook) who had been visiting, was unceremoniously heaved up on deck.

Life has never been boring on the island. Hard-working Lew has met challenges that would stop lesser men in their tracks. The engineers from B.C. Electric, forerunner of B.C. Hydro, said it was impossible to put some of the roads in around the area, but Lew went right ahead and did them anyway. This was in 1955-56, when the first lines were going across to Nelson from the peninsula. He and his men did the road and rock work and took all the equipment up for them. A helicopter took the spars up for the towers.

The first aircraft warning balls that were put on the line would spin each time a boat went underneath which meant that the wires all had to be cut and the lines fitted with a new design of ball. Finally it was completed to satisfaction.

Fire added unwanted excitement in 1951. A lightning strike on the south side of Vanguard started a forest fire which came around the road by West Lake. Lew was up Jervis when this big one broke out. He spotted the smoke and knew at once it was near his property.

Pushing his boat for what it was worth, he arrived to help in record time. Loggers and forestry and anyone who could handle a shovel were pressed into service. It was dirty work remembers Tom Peddie of Powell River who fought the fire and wind. When the wind eventually died down, allowing them to surround the flames, it had left a blackened area halfway to Captain Island.

Two fires closer to home panicked the Milligans for a time, but they were under control before the bush could catch fire. One of them was in the light plant, the other a 3,000 gallon diesel tank on the edge of the trees.

Ironically, the Black Ball ferry sailed on past without hesitating during the light plant and tank fires, when help could have been used, but when the Milligans were lighting fireworks for American guests one fourth of July, the ferry came all the way in to view the display. Lew assured them by radiophone they weren't flares, but they came anyway.

Between storms and fires, the Milligans routine ranged from mundane to magnificent. There were occasional visits from the public health nurse on *White Arrow No. 1*, and weekly visits from Oscar Orpana, the old bachelor who lived in the Walter Wray homestead, and those by various other islanders. At first Orpana just came for Christmas dinner, then it was Sundays, then Saturday and Sunday, and finally he came Friday and stayed until Monday. Joan cooked for everybody. Even Mr. Johnson from Gibsons, who ran the school taxi, stopped for breakfast on his route.

Summer saw the most company and cooking. Long languid days of visiting and sunbathing and outdoor barbecuing turned the Milligan float into a glorious marina. After the International Power Boat Race each year, the boats would come from Vancouver, Victoria, or Nanaimo. At one not-so-glorious time, fifty-five people arrived at once, mostly teenagers, and it poured rain. The usually sparkling surf against the bright blue of the summer sky and the many hues of green were replaced with Nelson's alternate colours—seven shades of gray.

With the arrival of fall each year, plans had to be made for school. When Doug first started, he went down to St. George's in Vancouver. The next year he went across to St. Vincent's Bay with his cousins, where there was a nice logging camp with a beautiful garden and water wheel. Brenda Milligan, Doug's aunt, would usually take them across in their fish boat. For several years after

Blair and Susy Milligan watch Canon Greene play "Little Jimmy." J. Milligan

The first Milligan Logging Camp in 1949. J. Milligan

that, all the Milligans went to the Ballet Bay school. Blair, who was born to the Lew Milligans on Halloween in 1951 in Vancouver, spent his first school years on Nelson. With Sue, he finished his elementary schooling at Henderson School in Powell River, then went on to Brooks and Max Cameron as the others had done.

Although Lew has long since finished logging on Nelson, and Vanguard Bay is no longer a sorting ground for his company, at seventy-one he is still based on Nelson Island. He has formed a partnership with Blair, his youngest son, in Powell Lake Contracting, which bought out Nelson Island Contracting, the successor to L & J Timber. The eight or nine people he employed in 1949 have grown to thirty-five today.

He has not been without problems. A crooked log broker almost broke him at one time. Sue remembers that her dad took out his frustrations on his hard hat, and he went through many over the years. (But another time one of these same hard hats had been used to bring Joan a ladyslipper.) He's been one of the few, possibly the only one, to recover from a loss on the island and make a success of his business.

The original one-room house has expanded to a modern comfortable home with a greenhouse and guest home. Gardens, manicured lawns, and tubs of geraniums belie the fact that garden soil was nonexistent in the early days and had to be made from compost—compost that in the later years has been put through a food processor first, to speed the rotting. There had not been a deciduous tree around in the beginning.

The Milligans have become as permanent a feature on Nelson Island as the temporary dam that Lew built for their water supply a third of a century ago. It too is still in the same place and working most effectively.

PART V

Community Notes

The Place Names and Origins

Would-be historians love to know the origins of place names, but often the hoped-for stories that accompany the name aren't there. If there was a bay or point unnamed after the surveying ship had passed, it was simply named for the original owners as Green Bay was named for W. E. Green. In later years, it became customary for the Hydrographic Surveys to commemorate soldiers from the Fatal Casualties List when a name was needed for a geographical feature.

The natives on the other hand had a more literal way of naming their areas or waterways. The rhythmic sounding names are a combination of short meanings describing the locale. KOHK-SOH-WHE-AHM, the name for the Harmony Islands, contains the symbol AHM which indicates a startling of the inner self. The full name means "surprisingly broken up."

I am indebted to Lester Peterson for the following Indian information on the area.

CHART NAME or AREA	INDIAN NAME	THE MEANING or LEGEND
Blind Bay	AUTH-OH-LEECH	"outer harbor"
Clam bed on Hardy	AY'-UHL-KHAIN	This was where one of the first human beings sent down by the Divine Spirit brought with her the art of cooking clams
Agamemnon Channel	LEAL'-KO-MAIN	"little channel" *The symbol KO indicates that the water is looking up, watching.
Jervis Inlet	LEG(K)-OH'-MAIN	"big channel"
Cape Cockburn	SKWALT	According to Sechelt lore, a renegade band somewhere up the coast where native peoples had come into contact with liquor and guns, raided this spot and killed many villagers.
Freil Falls (in Hotham Sound)	TAY'-EH-KHAIN	KHAIN denotes height, both literally and figuratively as in rank.
Hotham Sound	SMAIT	"his was not an easy place to come upon marine foods"
Saltery Bay	SKUHLP	
St. Vincent Bay	TAHK-WHOH'-TSAIN	"from land to water"
Neville Rock	KWAH-KAH-NAYSS'-AHM	"an amazing number of sea lions" (near Scotch Fir Point)

When Captain George Richards surveyed the area in the *Plumper*, he renamed the whole area for Lord Nelson's glory. As well as Nelson Island, Hardy Island, Telescope Passage, and Blind Bay which were mentioned before, other areas smacking of naval history include:

Captain Island	named for *HMS Captain*, the seventy-four gun flagship of Rear Admiral Sir Horatio Nelson at the battle of St. Vincent in 1797.
Vanguard Bay	named for *HMS Vanguard*, seventy-four gun flagship of Nelson's at the Battle of the Nile.
Agamemnon Channel	named for *HMS Agamemnon*, the sixty-four gun first line battleship Nelson was appointed command in 1793.
Bruce Lake	named for Rear Admiral Henry William Bruce, commander-in-chief of *HMS Mon-*

Nile Point	*arch*, 1754-57, and midshipman on *Euralus*. named for the successful win of Nelson's at the Battle of the Nile.
Caldwell Island	commemorates Captain Benjamin Caldwell, RN, first commander of *HMS Agamemnon*.
Fearney Point	commemorates Lord Nelson's bargeman and follower, William Fearney, who received the swords of the Spanish navel officers as they surrendered on the quarter-deck at the battle of St. Vincent in 1797.
Cape Cockburn	named for Admiral Sir George Cockburn, who as Captain Cockburn of the Minerve frigate, bearing the broad pennant of Commodore Nelson, joined the fleet of Sir John Jervis the evening before the battle of St. Vincent when Nelson transferred his pennant to the *HMS Captain*.
Jervis Inlet	commemorates Rear Admiral Sir John Jervis who, after his great victory over the Spaniards in St. Vincent's Bay in 1797, was made Earl St. Vincent (named by Captain Vancouver). Jerry Jervis who came to Hidden Bay in 1938 was a great-great-great niece.
Billings Bay	is named for William Thomas Billings, a naval officer and assistant surgeon who served on the surveying vessel, *Herald*.

In 1887 or thereabouts, the local people named two locales in the Indian fashion—Quarry Bay and Granite Island. Granite Island was renamed Kelly Island for one of the owners of the company who worked the granite. With the exception of the chart and tourists, the name didn't stick. It had been known too long as Granite Island. Another area aptly described is Strawberry Island named by the Harry Roberts family.

Areas named for people other than those associated with naval history include:

West Lake	the namesake of the West family who settled in the very early 1900s.
Alexander Point	is presumed to be named after Alexander Grant who was crown granted Lot 1486 in 1892 on Hardy Island.
MacKenzie Lake	commemorates Laughlin N. (Jack) MacKenzie who was crown granted Lot 2195 in 1913.
Maynard Head	is named for the Lorne Maynard family.
Ballet Bay	Midge Thomas, Harry's wife, named it in honor of their daughter Audree, who became a professional ballerina.

Zoe Lake, Lee Lake, Yolana Lake	are named for Harry Robert's offspring.
Chack Chack Lake	commemorates Harry himself, whose bald head reminded an Indian Chief of a bald eagle, chack chack in Chinook language.
Fox Island	is thought to be after R. L. Fox of Seattle, who contracted Nelson Island granite for the Port Orchard dry dock in 1894.

Hidden Bay had the most interesting story attached to it. Bertrand Sinclair, the author of several novels set in early B.C., spent some time in Hidden Bay with the Hammond family. Before that time the lagoon was either referred to as Billings Bay, the same as the outside bay, or Billingsgate, tagged by some of the loggers and fishermen of the area. While writing of Chinese smugglers, Sinclair used this Billingsgate area as the setting for his novel. He called both the area and the manuscript, Hidden Bay.

May Hammond wrote to the B.C. government telling them the story and asking that the name be legally changed to Hidden Bay. Her request was granted. Although Ora, Sinclair's wife, says that Bill received a prepublication cheque for *Hidden Bay* in 1915, to her knowledge no book was published under that title. In 1919, *Hidden Places* appeared in print with the slightly broader setting of Toba Inlet. The government had a scheme at that time to settle returned veterans to the land at the head of Toba at the end of W.W.I, and perhaps that idea influenced Bill's choice of location. In later years a cartographer dubbed the lagoon Hidden Basin, but to early islanders it is still Hidden Bay.

The Floats and Post Office

In the Blind Bay-Billings Bay area, the final plans were being made for a school in the fall, and another project was being discussed, a government float and post office. Everyone agreed on the need, but the location was cause for heated debate. Although it seemed a simple matter of geography, the Blind Bay people objected to the proposed Billings Bay site because they felt the water was usually rough there. Lorne Maynard, who was to be the postmaster, naturally wanted it to be close to him; and the people of Hidden Bay, Ballet Bay, and Billings Bay who were close to Lorne, agreed. Even the Union Steamship Company got into the act as they were not anxious to go into Blind Bay because of the reefs.

In the end, two floats were built in the summer of 1950. The one in Billings Bay held a freight shed which contained slots for everyone's mail. The other float was built behind Clio Island. The steamer made two stops for freight, but the mail all went to the Billings Bay float. Those who still objected, got a mailbag and took their mail to Pender Harbour.

A quarter of a mile through the woods was the Maynard home, where stamps and postal notes could be purchased and mail registered. A difference of opinion was voiced over the naming of this post office as well. Some thought it should be Nelson Island and not Billings Bay, but fear of confusion with Nelson, B.C., and Nelson Forks eliminated this obvious choice. Still there was confusion; Carole Maynard remembers one letter that was marked N. I. with a short upswing on the the "N" which went to the Virgin Islands before reaching them.

Often the steamer would be delayed into the night and Lorne would be up to get the mail in the early hours of the morning. One morning after such a night, Lorne and Carole had sorted the parcels and put them in the allotted spots by nine, but still had the first-class mail to go through.

The wife of a hot-tempered islander who'd been described as "someone sitting on a powder keg," came by and picked up their package and left again. Later, her irate husband appeared, demanded his mail, and knocked Lorne cold. Thus were the duties and experiences of the island postmaster.

So much had been said during the arguments over the location of the post office and float, a rift was driven in the community that took several years to close. On the surface everyone carried on as usual, getting together for school functions and celebrating birthdays. There was even space cleared, and talk of building a community hall and playground on Hardy Island, for which Mrs. Macomber had given them permission.

In the meantime, community functions were held in the quarry dining hall in Blind Bay. The women got together regularly in each other's homes where they did handiwork, beautiful embroidery, and carvings for their sales. Christmas drew them altogether as it had united the island for half a century.

The Ballet Bay School

When Mrs. Jessie Sherry, Ballet Bay's first official school teacher, stepped off the Gulf boat in October, 1950, the Billings Bay float was new. As it still needed its ramp approach built, the teacher balanced her way to shore on the planks.

Nine pupils attended that fall. The girls still outnumbered the boys as they did in the earlier schools, but only by one this time. They all came by boat, paid for by the Sechelt-Gibsons School District #46.

Lorne Maynard applied for the contract to taxi the students, and bought a new boat the *Arab II*, a 24-foot motor cruiser in June, 1950, especially for this purpose. As the owner had wanted to keep the boat for the holidays, Lorne agreed to pick it up in the fall. It was launched from the mouth of Roberts Creek as they all stood around. The boat was lowered into the water, its fine lines settling deeper and deeper, until they realized it was sinking. Too late they discovered the previous owners had removed the plugs and forgotten to replace them.

The new school boat was truant the first month of school while the submerged motor was overhauled in Vancouver. An interesting aside to this story was that the mechanic in Vancouver told Lorne, to his dismay, that the motor would have to be professionally attended to at least once a year, that Lorne couldn't do it himself. This was quite a blow to the independent islander who always handled his own repairs. When the boat was ready, he tried it out and found the timing to be all off. Disgusted, he took it all apart and did his own work, as he continued to do every year thereafter.

He ran the boat for three or four years, then Art Harding took a turn at taxiing, as did Mr. Johnson from Gibsons. Mr. Johnson would pick up the Milligans from Vanguard and come around while the others went only as far as the Krentz' where Lew Milligan or his sister-in-law, Brenda, would have dropped them.

The school boat offered a dimension to school that mainlanders missed. Some were not sorry to miss it, mind you, but they cannot deny the adventure it often had to offer. One blustery winter day, Mr. Johnson tried to return the Milligans to their warm fireside when the sheer force of the northeaster blowing out of Jervis Inlet struck him. It blew straight into Van-

Art Harding taking kids to school. The taller boys are John and Rick Milligan, cousins of Kathy, Doug, and Sue. J. Milligan

Mail Day at the new float in Billings Bay, with the *Gulf Wing* **attracting the islanders.**
M. McIntyre

Susan, Doug, and Kathy with life jackets, ready for school in Ballet Bay.
J. Milligan

All the island enjoyed Sports Day, June 1959, the last year of school. J. Milligan

guard Bay, pounding the waves against the vulnerable craft. He looked at Milligan's float covered in spray and decided to head across to the far side of the bay where a small island offered protection to the logging outfit nestled in behind. The camp cook took in the chilled youngsters and warmed them with hot chocolate and cookies. She had given them supper and had them all bedded down when a worried Lew Milligan arrived with food and sleeping bags awhile later.

Joan was worried about young Susie being scared, but she needn't have been. All she talked about when she finally got home to Mom, was the pretty yellow nightgown the cook wore.

Of course, there were beautiful fall and spring mornings when the air was clear and the water reflected the soaring gulls. Cruising to school was sheer pleasure then. A mainlander knew nothing of this delight. Sitting in school on those days cramped the independent spirit though. Their eyes would stray to the window where an eagle was dive-bombing a duckling and the gulls were running interference. For the first three years, the Ballet Bay school consisted of the Hardings, John and Royal Maynard, and the Johnstone grandchildren—Dorothy and Richard Krentz, Gary Vaughn, and Franny Deberri. Fran remembers, "It was a little rough there, different, us kids weren't little angels."

Agnes Harding filled in until Mrs. Sherry arrived. Mrs. Sherry taught the first three years; Mrs. Armour from Gibsons came next; then Mrs. Harper; and finally Miss Waterman. Fran Deberri also remembers a Mrs. Peters and a Mrs. Armstrong. Cherry Sandvold kept the one-room hut in order.

The school inspector who came to visit showed a special interest in the new school; in fact the whole area, and particularly Hardy Island. Mr. Frederickson later told Carole Maynard that he had been that first teacher to the Hardy Island school that collapsed on opening day in 1915.

School populations waxed and waned as people moved in and out of the bay. When John Milligan came with his family, and others from Lew Milligan's Logging camp were coming over, the number of students totaled nineteen. This was during the 1954-55 school year. That year the teacher was teaching every grade to grade eight, except three and seven. Those busy teachers produced wonderful concerts that would rival any high school production. Talented mothers used island ingenuity to make intricate costumes that twenty-four years later could still be described in detail. Sue Milligan still remembers Linda Fedosov's wonderful lamb costume made from the stuffing of an old mattress.

Mrs. Harper from Pender Harbour taught at Ballet Bay for two or three years, so the kids that "weren't little angels" couldn't have been too devilish. During the 1956-57 and 1957-58 years there were pupils in each of the eight grades, presenting quite a challenge to anyone in the profession. When the school closed in June, 1959, ten pupils said good-bye to Miss Waterman. The hut was removed by the school board to the Gibsons area.

Most of the families had left the bay then, some with older students moved closer to the Gibsons high school, others moved across to Saltery Bay. Some of the students have managed well with just their Ballet Bay schooling. Lew and Joan Milligan "battled" with the Powell River School board to allow their four to attend Powell River schools in 1959. They argued that it was much safer and quicker to take them to Saltery Bay where they could catch Mr. Lang's school bus, than to take them to Pender Harbour. Their point was well received and Doug, Kathy, Sue, and Blair spent their remaining school years in the Powell River School District.

Since then, there have never been enough year-round students to have a school. The students all take correspondence courses from Victoria. There is a $50 a month stipend that the government makes available to anyone who teaches four children correspondence, and from time to time two families have doubled up to enable one mother to take advantage of it. But for the most part, they have worked independently in their own bays just waiting for another Hammond-size family to move in with its built-in school enrollment.

The Fifties

The actual island living carried on much the same in the fifties as it had earlier. A telephone had been added to the island, at Art Hardings, and Lyn would row about the bay with phone messages. Most thought life was still too challenging to ever make one feel deprived. Only the teenagers felt they were missing something.

Allen Farrell, Sharie and son, Keray, moved into Blind Bay in 1953. He was no stranger to the island having visited as Mel Daniels in the forties. They arrived in a fifteen-foot inboard rowboat, *Klee Wyck*, at their ten acres of property bought for $500, almost all their savings.

Allen fished and built the *Ocean Bird* during the five years they lived in the area, and often painted pictures as a hobby. "We sure had it good compared to the problems of today. Every week the steamer brought absolutely anything we wrote away to town for. Groceries, boat material, clothes, even some guy's wife." It also brought a procession of housekeepers to Frank Ficek, all of whom left on the next steamer.

"Old Mitch," who had come a few years before Allen, supplied him with lumber for his boatbuilding. Geoff Partington remembers Mitch, Raymond Mitchell Shuck, as a "perky little guy, nothing ever put him off. He was an ex-cattle rancher from Alberta who arrived here in a nice fish boat towing a houseboat. The *Sheila Fay* was the boat; George Larson bought it later. They pulled the houseboat up on the beach. He was just going to relax and enjoy his last years, game for anything. Little fellow with a big smile who went commercial fishing with Bob Johnstone." He lived on a point nearest to Telescope Pass on Nelson, on the coast that he remembered from 1903 when he worked on the *Dauntless*, one of the last coal tugs.

After homesteading from 1907-46, he came west to retire. He had a sawmill put together in Vancouver and had it hauled up by George and Alice Larson with their boat, the *Wonderbird*. The sawmill almost didn't make it, as a storm came up and they had to head for shelter near Gibsons.

When the compensation board began making regulations about having a first-aid person on hand, he gave up the business. He retired again in 1964 and went back to Alberta. His sawmill was later sold to John Picken in 1972.

He enjoyed knowing the Johnstones and Old Tom and was friendly with the Hardings and Partingtons. He entertained his friends with his violin and often played *Silverheels* for Dora Johnstone who would thank him with another drink of rye.

A few years after Mitch arrived, Marjorie McEwen, who later married Harry Roberts, visited the area. She hoped to write a novel set on an island and came to Nelson for local flavor. She hadn't long

The Hidden Bay view of Billings Bay. M. McIntyre

Frank Johnstone and Frank Ficek at Ficek's place, now owned by John Picken.
T. Deberri

to wait as she arrived at the onset of a southeast gale, and felt Art Cherry's boat heave in the heavy ground swell. Floating debris was everywhere and swarms of bird life flew off of it. It was "like driving through a snowstorm of seagulls," she noted in an account of her arrival. They made good time, arriving at the entrance to Hidden Bay an hour before slack. On hearing of a trail through the woods to Sandy Millard's, she had Art leave her on the beach and sent him back to Pender Harbour before the weather got worse.

The December trail was soon covered in water and the ground sank beneath her feet. Salal was everywhere beneath the trees. In less than an hour she was lost. She panicked momentarily, then got on to a rotting log and made her way from there to the shore through the brush. On coming out she found herself on the opposite side of the peninsular piece of land. It was only a matter of hours before Sandy and Grace Millard came along and rescued her, but it was enough to give her a taste of island isolation. In this case, a bad taste.

Even so, she returned to live at Sunray, first as housekeeper, then as Harry's wife. As Harry's health was not as good as hers, her writing efforts went into his book, *The Trail of Chack Chack*, 1968, and her novel was never completed. Ironically she died several years before her ailing husband. She came to know the island well and was familiar with the saying, "God willing, and weather permitting," particularly fitting at the cape.

People often wanted to live on Nelson Island after visiting for awhile, and would go to Lorne Maynard to get him to locate a piece of land. Frances Wilson and the matron of St. Mary's were two of these visitors. They had nursed Lorne in the hospital and wanted to see this island he boasted about. They were quite taken by Blind Bay at once, and soon were building on their own land across from Kelly Island:

Once more islanders watched and speculated while two women built a cabin in the bay. They were doing all right too, until they came to put on the peak. Stumped as to how to go about it, they were still puzzling it out when the *Lake Biwa* came by, and a tall handsome man stepped out of his boat and into Frances' life. Not only did Frank Johnstone put the peak on their house, he kept coming back until he could put a ring on her finger.

The wedding was held in the Johnstone home in Blind Bay, October 30, 1954, with Reverend Stringer of Powell River officiating, and Lorne Maynard giving the bride away. Dora and her

The wedding of Frank and Frances Johnstone, October 30, 1954. Back row: Lorne Maynard, Tom Brazil, Rev. Stringer, Judd Johnstone, Slim Deberri, Allen Farrell, Bob and Chris Johnstone. Fourth row: Frances and Frank Johnstone, Evelyn Roberts, sister of Doris. Third row: Grace Millard, Cherry Sandvold, unidentified person, Sherrie Farrell, and Dora Johnstone. Second row: Doris Johnstone, Carole Maynard, Fran Deberri, Dorothy Krentz, and Alice Johnstone. Front row: the Johnstone grandchildren.   T. Deberri

"The Birthday Party." Back row: Evelyn Roberts, Cherry Sandvold, Ann Pettigrew, Dora Johnstone, and Thelma Deberri. Front row: Madam (Lotte) Wehner and Grace Millard. T. Deberri

daughters outdid themselves for one of the last parties ever held in the big house. Family and community friends lined the living room to wish the couple well.

Year-round living wasn't quite as satisfying as summer camping on Nelson for Frances. They lived in a float house between Clio Island and the adjoining islet, with no fresh water. She carried pails of water from Thelma Deberri's house around the bay and used each three times over before it was dumped. Also the logs under the float house were almost completely eaten away during the first three months they were there, and the house began sinking. When it was refitted with new foundation logs, they moved it behind the islet.

During the next year, Thomas Forrest was born. He was named for his two grandfathers, but Tom Hughes and Tom Brazil both thought Judd's grandson was named for him and were as proud of their "namesake" as Judd was. He was still pretty small when the north wind began to blow. The sky was a brilliant blue and the air was clear and cold. So cold that Frances held the baby just inches over the kitchen stove and never felt any warmth on her hands. At night the wind whistled through the uninsulated walls as they knelt on the bed with the baby between them and a tent of blankets over them. They talked all night trying to keep each other awake. When the pink dawn showed through the window, they packed everything and went up to Frank's parents to wait out the wind. Then, when it was safe to do so, they towed their home into a protected bay near Judd.

Judd's sons, Frank, Bob, and Chris were all well known as good fishermen during their time on Nelson, although Bob logged, Chris beachcombed, and Frank did both generally, before going fishing full-time. Frank often found the best spot, told the others, then found himself with the smallest catch, remembers his niece Fran.

Bob was the subject of a fish story that traveled the bay in the early fifties. They were in Richard Krentz' boat with the seine piled up in the mast, when they made too quick a turn in the overweighted boat. It flipped over, trapped George Larson in the cabin, and threatened to drop Bob to the bottom of the brink. But Bob was quick—he climbed over the gunnel, up on to the bottom of the boat, and hardly got wet. "It's true," writes Allen Farrell.

Television came to the island in what Fran Deberri thinks was 1958. The Deberri family were the first to get it, then the Milligans.

Ballet Bay was named for Audree, who was "Anna Istomina" in a Russian Ballet.
H Thomas

Public Health Nurse arrives by water taxi from Sechelt Health Unit.
J. Milligan

Sue remembers her dad attaching the antenna to the top of a 60-foot fir behind the house. Every time the antenna had to be adjusted, Lew would go up with his belt and spurs while the kids were down below shouting, "That's better ... better ... worse ... back ... better." Later he rigged a system with board and lines to move the antenna from the ground. "Better" was still pretty snowy, but it added something new to island evenings.

There had been much talk in the early fifties on how the proposed new road to Vancouver would affect the islanders. Freight service by Gulf Lines was threatened by the reduction in passenger service. Airplanes were on the increase and bus service to Vancouver was planned.

When Mike Costello, newcomer to Blind Bay, made the inaugural run on the Black Ball Ferry, Quillayute, in 1954, changes in the island life were already evident. With the fishing declined and the handlogging finished, the men were looking for different areas to work. In the next few years the children would all be high school age, and too few young ones would be left to keep the school open. With the steamers gone and freight service starting to break down, life on the mainland looked pretty attractive.

Frank Jenkinson owned land at Saltery Bay which was selling for $500 per half-acre, and houses could be bought reasonably from B.C. Forest Products at Brittain River. The temptation to buy land with road access, and be able to put the kids on a school bus to Powell River, and still be close to Nelson Island and all the fishing, clams and oysters, was too much for some. Judd and Dora and Frank and Frances Johnstone were the first to buy from Frank, and Evelyn and Grace's families were soon to follow. When Bob and Chris Johnstone also moved their families to Saltery, Judd's family, all but Thelma and Alice, were back to the spot where Judd had spent a year in his youth. It was a Japanese fish saltery then and an Indian and Japanese fishing rendezvous.

Six of Judd's grandchildren that had been born to the Nelson Island settlement were now mainlanders. The thriving community which had attracted John Picken when he purchased property in Blind Bay in the fifties, was no longer there when he brought Frances and their young sons to the island in the mid-sixties. Summer people had purchased most of the vacated homes in the area. Only the occasional newcomers, idealists like Pickens, or workers on the new ferry, like Costellos and the French family, tackled year-round living.

Jottings of the John Antle

The *John Antle*, and earlier, the *Columbia*, of the Columbia Coast Mission, brought not only the work of God and the teachings of the Anglican Church, but a good friend to all, Canon Alan Greene. When the blast of his whistle was heard off Arland's Point, Ann Pettigrew says, "We all dropped what we were doing, grabbed whatever coat was handy to cover up our sins, and rowed out to meet the boat."

They would have only ten minutes to make the service that Canon Greene gave once a month. He visited all the remote logging camps, forestry areas, and Indian villages on the southern B.C. coast, while Heber, his brother gave services from the hospital ship, the *Columbia*, in the northern waters. On "Little Jimmy," his portable organ, Canon Alan Greene played the hymns appropriate to the occasion. Jesus Bids Us Shine with a Clear Pure Light was a favorite for the children of the lighthouses.

He baptized and married the islanders, then when it came time to "swallow the anchor," he buried them as well. He was a visitor to the sick, librarian to the isolated, projectionist to the camps, Santa Clause to the children, and friend to all. "He was someone you could love immediately," recalls Ann.

The men of the logging camps enjoyed visiting with Cannon Greene, joking about the times he'd put the *Columbia* or the *John Antle* up on a reef, but they were always a little embarrassed about the church services. He could never have pushed the church on the people or he would never have been accepted. They politely listened to what he had to say, and went back to their former ways on his departure.

He was often called upon to settle disputes in remote areas. One east side Nelson Islander was getting quite old and a victim of the isolation breeding paranoia. He'd been noticing his old cedar trees had large squarish holes and was sure that a particular neighbor had been chiseling these holes just to bedevil him. He complained to Alan Greene who laughed. Assuring him it was no neighbor, he walked around his property with him until he found the culprit, a large woodpecker who was busy tapping out yet another "square" hole. Not all neighborly disputes were settled so easily.

Another of Canon Greene's less favorable duties was to go into

Annis Bay and bring out Anna. Anna was a Finnish woman who had built a cabin in the bay all on her own. With just her dog for company, she lived there for years never bothering anyone. Occasionally she stopped at Westmere, and is remembered coming in with all her goods piled up on her boat, with her pooch perched on top.

Unfortunately, the isolation caught up with her as well, and she became "bushed." When she began shooting at people, Alan Greene was notified to go in and investigate. The then-hostile hermit was taken aboard the mission boat and brought out for help.

Alan Greene kept a log aboard the *John Antle*, into which he wrote some of the coastal happenings. His writings and those of the other missionaries in the Columbia Coast Mission were published in *The Log*, the official publication which was subscribed to for a dollar in the fifties. Alan Greene was editor of the welcome periodical.

The January to June, 1959 issue, was particularly interesting to the islanders when under the headline *Nautically Speaking*, Canon Greene gave an account of the marriage of Master Mariner Geoffrey Partington to Jacqueline Pettigrew. As a master mariner himself he enjoyed officiating at the marriage aboard the *John Antle*, and writing of it afterwards.

> The small alter in the ships's pilothouse was flanked by chart tables, a ship's clock, and a radio telephone, and out through the pilothouse windows we could watch passing ships. Mercifully there was no sea running, or it might have been a trying ordeal for all concerned as fourteen of us crowded into the pilothouse. Just to remind us that we were aboard a ship, the John Antle rocked gently to the wash of passing vessels. The marriage register lay on top of the charts on the chart table, and the parallel rulers used in chart work lay alongside the register as a symbol of the course these two were "taking off," as in the sacredness of the marriage service, the Church stressed that only as they were one in their vows and intentions, could they steer a true course, as laid down in Holy Scripture, the wonderful old manual that gives us "The rules of the road." Then as we photographed

Geoffrey and Jacquelyn Partington in front of alter. J. Partington

The *John Antle* at the Westmere float. J. Partington

Miss Edith Jacquelyn Pettigrew

and

Mr. Geoffrey Walter Partington

wish to announce their marriage

on Board

The Mission Ship "John Antle"

Tuesday, June the ninth

nineteen hundred and fifty-nine

at Nelson Island, British Columbia

Reverend Canon Alan Greene officiating

"The Wedding Party." Back row: grandmother of bride, Ann Pettigrew (mother), Yolana Roberts, Canon Alan Greene, and Geoffrey Partington. Front row: Robin Partington, Jacquelyn Partington, and Charles Fathergill (uncle of the bride).   J. Partington

them it just happened that behind them was the ship's steering wheel, on whose center spoke they both chanced to lay their hand, suggesting again that the great voyage they had undertaken needed agreement as to the course, please God, they would try to follow.

This all happened at Nelson Island in Agamemnon Channel, names that again suggested a very nautical background. Their hosts were Mr. and Mrs. Lawrie Wray of Westmere Lodge, at whose wharf my ship lay that afternoon, June 9. I wish a city society editor had been there. She would have been stumped in her effort to give the wedding a nautical flavor. I know she could have done real justice to the wedding gowns of the bride and the bridesmaid, but I feel she might have slipped a bit in her ship terminology. Instead of coming up the aisle "supported by her father," the bride as did all the others, came down alone on a wobbly ramp at whose head was the ominous sign One at a time, please. No dancing on the ramp. She was followed by her bridesmaids, and they were both encased in cellophane to shield them from the torrents of rain that really let go, as the wedding party came from the Wray home to the ship. The bride's great uncle, Mr. Charles Fothergill, gave her away. Someone whispered to me that he was seventy-nine. He did his part nobly, and later made a very happy speech in proposing the bride's health. I liked the way he included the husband in his toast. Captain Partington, true to the tradition on the "silent service," said nary a word in reply. And nobody noticed it!

Everybody who came to the Wray's came by boat. And they all went back by boat. And I started the fine young couple off on their honeymoon on my little ship, taking them around Nelson Island to Blind Bay, where Jacqueline had decided their honeymoon should be spent in the peace and quiet of Tom's Island.

As they landed their gear and Jacqueline shared in getting the cargo ashore, Geoffrey spoke of her as a very good deckhand. Alan Greene wished them, "Good sailing. Kindly seas. And safe anchorages." then waited until he could see the smoke from their chimney before he left.

The Parties

Holidays and special events, weddings and birthdays were celebrated with a dance. G. Y. Smith at Vanguard held these parties in the early teens of the century, but later in the thirties and forties they were most often held at the Johnstone home or the Harding's View Point Lodge. Guests would come from miles around to attend these functions which would last until dawn. Only the occasional person didn't come—Heikennin (Captain Henry) never did, thinking they were "great foolishness."

Music was supplied by anyone and everyone who could strum a banjo, play a fiddle or blow on a harmonica. Talent wasn't really a necessary requirement. The islanders enjoyed their efforts and danced as if it were Guy Lombardo himself supplying the accompaniment. It was all good clean fun. Most often the drinking was kept outside. Sometimes the party was "dry," meaning coffee drunk from jam jars if the crowd was large. This usually only happened if the still owners were away fishing. Everyone was glad to have a respite from the never-ending work. The women were just happy to see the other women, to hear something more than engine-talk.

They would bring the sandwiches and cakes and the men would bring the liquid refreshments. One "still on the hill" produced a powerful brew with quite a punch to it. One very proper woman got "spiflicated" on some of the stuff at one do and when she went to go home, the sight of the ramp at low tide left her feeling a little heady. She refused to go down the steep incline, and stayed the night. As this party was at one of the bachelor's homes, she was mortified when she realized what she'd innocently done, and spent the morning rowing about explaining the predicament to her neighbors.

In later years the Liquor Control Board rye took the place of the moonshine and results were more predictable. Most of the time they all left when the dance was over, sometimes rafting their boats together, and partying the whole way home.

Boatbuilding

To live on an island without ferry service, you must have a boat. Even a house isn't necessary if the boat is livable. It seems only natural then, that boatbuilders would be attracted to an island, or that islanders would become boatbuilders.

The Harding brothers became boatbuilders after coming to Nelson, hand-sawing the planks that built their boat the *Agnes H*. The boards were steamed with care in a hand-built box, to form the ribs and planking of the sturdy boat.

Allen Farrell was well known around the coast for his many hand-built sailboats before he came to live on Nelson in 1953. Two of his boats were built and launched on Nelson: *Ocean Bird* in Blind Bay and *Native Girl* in Green Bay. They were built without power tools, with some of the lumber of *Ocean Bird* coming from Old Mitch's sawmill.

Native Girl, a thirty-nine-foot ketch, was launched in 1965 and sailed to Hawaii in 1968, returning in 1969. After changing her rig to brigantine, they sailed down the coast as far as Puerto Valarta in 1978, over to Hawaii, and back to Lasqueti Island in 1979. There he began building a forty-foot Chinese junk which he has just recently launched.

Harry Robert's boats outnumbered Allen's boats, but stayed closer to home with them. Perhaps the most famous boat on these shores was his Chinese junk, *Chack-Chack III*. Most famous because it never had to have its bottom scraped of barnacles and never had to fight the cape storms—never even was launched.

Unfortunately, it succumbed to dry rot before it ever touched the water. It has been called repeatedly "a carpenter's dream." Each drawer was lovingly crafted by a master craftsman. It contained a variety of inventive touches that gave Marjorie and himself a great deal of pleasure during the three years they called it home. Harry's family was afraid that he was too frail at seventy to handle the thirty-two-foot schooner with just his wife as crew, and talked him into leaving the boat in its cradle. Skipper Chack-Chack built four fair-sized rooms and a full scale bath into the boat that was fashioned from a huge red cedar, found on the beach. He carved a figure head in the form of a bald eagle.

Harry built three schooners, two twenty-foot speedboats, several thirty-foot work boats, a few ten-foot sailboats, and many rowboats throughout his life. At ninety he was still planning to build another one, a twenty to twenty-four-foot *Lady Sabot*, a weekender for a couple or two. This was almost seventy-five years after he'd built his first flat-bottomed boat. Over the years he was remembered for *Chack-Chack I* (originally the *Odamit*), *Leyo, Ha Ha, Chack-Chack II* and *Chack-Chack III*.

They were all made from lumber cut in his own sawmill, from salvaged logs or hand-felled timber. Often they were put together without the necessary clamps to hold the planks in place (the reason for the *Odamit's* name), but they were all skillfully done.

Other boatbuilders of lesser fame and ambition have called Nelson their home. Jack Hammond was the first we know of; Ott Heikennin (Captain Henry) was another, although Hidden Bay neighbors questioned this ability of his. Green Bay neighbors seemed more impressed with Captain Henry's boat skills. He had been a skipper of a four-masted schooner in his early years and was building a boat called the *Esto Utopia*, with the perfect piece for every part. He never finished it. Chris Sandvold also built beautiful boats in Blind Bay; Lee Roberts at an early age built the *Black Wolf*; Doug Milligan at a young sixteen built the *White Wing II* in the guest house at Vanguard Bay; and John Picken, the latest boat builder, has built a sixteen-foot cabin sloop, *Cygnet*, among others.

Boats Familiar to the Waters Around Nelson Island Throughout its History

THE STEAMERS
Mermaid   This paddle steamer serviced the earliest quarry workers who traveled across to the peninsula to meet it.

Comox	The first steel ship to be put together in B.C. and the first new ship bought by the Union Steamship Co. in 1891. It docked at Irvine's Landing where islanders went to meet it until 1919.
Selma/Chasina	Although built as a luxury yacht for the wild Duke of Anglesea in the Glasgow shipyards, the *Selma* was the first steamer to service the west side of Nelson on its route to the coastal logging camps. It was owned by Captain Polkinghorne and Sam Mortimer of the All-Red Line and began service in 1910. She made three day-trips weekly from Vancouver to Powell River.
Santa Maria/Chilco	The *Santa Maria* was a sister ship of the *Selma* built as a clipper-bow steam yacht for John A. Rolls and later owned by Lord Hartswell before being steamed to the Pacific in 1914 for sale to the All-Red Line. She also made three day-trips weekly, passing the *Selma* across from the peninsula. The All-Red Line was sold to the Union Steamship Co. in 1917 and the two ships were renamed the *Chasina* and *Chilco*. They continued on the run until replaced by the Union's *Lady* boats.
Lady Cynthia & Lady Cecilia	These two Union ships were converted World War I minesweepers. They served the Nelson-Hardy Island area until 1951.
Capilano	The *Capilano* was remembered by Enid Hammond as having served the islands at some time before its sinking off Savary Island in 1915.
Cassiar	The *Cassiar* was another Union Ship seen in Nelson waters before 1923. The *Cardena* was also mentioned by former islanders, but it was considered too grand for regular day runs to the coastal camps.
Gulf Mariner	The Gulf Line boats were faster than Union ships and gave them stiff competition in the late forties and early fifties. The *Gulf Stream* hit Dinner Rock off Lund and sank in 1947.
Jervis Express	The Tidewater Navigation ship serviced the east side of the island in the early fifties.

THE COLUMBIA COAST MISSION

Columbia	Canon Alan Greene brought this early Anglican Church boat into the Nelson area before 1940.
John Antle	The *Columbia* was replaced on the southern run by this boat, also piloted by Canon Greene.

Harry Roberts and John Picken in 1973. J. Partington

Native Girl, **Farrell's thirty-nine foot ketch.** A. Farrell

Ocean Bird and *Grey Gull*, **Allen Farrell's boats.** A. Farrell

Curious onlookers lined the rail of the *Selma* when Nelson Islanders came to Hardy Island for their mail. Powell River Museum

Gua Yee	A lay ship of the CCM, this one was owned by Ernie and Nell Christmas who settled on Nelson in the fifties.

FERRIES
Quillayute	This Black Ball ferry was the first one on the Saltery Bay-Earls Cove run when the new road to Vancouver opened in August 1954. Mike Costello was captain.

STORE BOATS
The Pappy	The earliest of the remembered storeboats. Edwards (Whitehead) and Garfield went around to the logging camps with jewelery, gifts, and bulk foods.
Adventus	George and Lorna Bradshaw's first store boat, the *Adventus* was burned and replaced by a lovely old classic, the *Spartan*.
D'sonoqua	A romantic delivery boat of the early '70s.

SMALLER CRAFT
Agnes H	*Aggie* was built in the late thirties by the Harding brothers and is still tied to the pier of Bill Harding's home.
Arab I and II	These were boats of Lorne Maynards. The *Arab II* was the school taxi for the Ballet Bay school.
Belmont	Excitement was created when this ship was salvaged by Walter Patrick and Frank Stager in Vanguard Bay, 1950.
Beryl G	The ill-fated rumrunner of W. J. Gillis.
Black Shark	Judd Johnstone lived aboard this boat of his in the early thirties.
Black Wolf	This was Lee Robert's first hand-built boat.
Blithe Spirit	Jim Spilsbury's *Five B.R.* was replaced by this boat.
Brant	The *Brant* belonged to Richard Krentz.
Chack Chack I, II, and III	These were three of Harry Robert's many boats. The *Chack Chack I* was called the *O Damit*.
Cygnet	John Picken built this sailboat on Nelson.
Delta Dawn	Sis Harris still fishes in her cod-boat.
Derald H	The *Delta Dawn* replaced this boat of Sis and Henry Harris.
Dirty Gerty	This unusual boom boat of Louttit's amused many a tourist.
Elkay	Westmere guests were transported to and from the steamer by Lawrie and Kay Wray's launch.
Emu	The Yates and Follets enjoyed this converted life-boat.
Esto Utopia	The dream ship of Captain Henry.
Fidler	Frances Picken's sturdy boat is a later addition to Nelson's shores.

Five B. R.	Jim Spilsbury serviced the depression radios from this craft.
Fraser Lad	Frank Johnstone was owner of this one twice.
Gary	Johnny and Evelyn Vaughn named their boat for their son.
Ha Ha	This is another of Harry Robert's boats.
Happy Tramp	Tom's Island still sports this boat of Jacqueline Partington's.
Harbour Warrior	Chris Johnstone owned this familiar one before selling it to Frank and Irene Johnson.
Henry Bay	Sue Milligan owns this flooded cod boat bought from Ed Warnock of Pender Harbour.
Hoo Hoo	Bertrand Sinclair often visited Hidden Bay on this one and entertained fishermen at sea by telling some of his stories on the radio-phone.
Istomina	The Thomases lived aboard this vessel for their first years on Nelson.
Kauki Lani	This Hawaiian-sounding boat was the fifth boat of Frank and Frances Johnstone.
Kenbern	Bob Johnstone bought the *Kenbern* from his sister, Thelma Deberri.
Klee Wyck	Allen and Sharie Farrel came to Nelson Island aboard this boat in 1952.
Lady May	The pleasure craft that brought the Hammonds to Hidden Bay in 1907.
Lady Peggy	The McNutts of Green Bay arrived on Nelson via this lady.
Lake Biwa	Frank Johnstone came to the rescue of Frances when he pulled in to shore in this early craft of his.
Larry H	This was the last of Frank Johnstone's six.
Leyo	This was one of Harry Robert's early boats.
Morien II	This Green Bay wreck was once Clarence Cook's.
Native Girl	Farrell's 39-foot ketch launched in Green Bay.
Ocean Bird	Farrell's 30-foot cutter built in Blind Bay.
Ocean Girl	Farrell's clipper-bowed brigatine built at nearby Seven Isles.
Principia	This yacht of LeRoy Macomber's spent summers on Hardy Island.
Ruf-n-Redy	Art Bishop's boat was originally the *Fircom*.
Sailfish	Zoe Roberts occasionally sails her craft into Nelson Island waters today.
Sandy Cape	This is Nelson Island's most recent wreck, now found on the shores of Vanguard Bay.
Sarita	Slim Deberri owned this fish boat.
Scooter	Sue Milligan now owns this little one built by her brother, Doug.
Sea Wave	Lorne and Carole Maynard had this small boat during their earliest days on Nelson.

Sheila Fay	Raymond Shuck was the original owner who later sold to George Larson.
Skeena Chief	This fish boat of John West's was later owned by Doug Wray of Westmere.
Small Fry	This reliable little clinker of Harry Thomas' met many an island emergency.
Suez	Frank White's family remembers this boat.
Tamerlane	One of the "navy boys," Mike Costello, skippered this craft.
Therma I	Lorne Maynard owned this charter boat which took the government boiler inspector around.
Triton	This unlucky craft of Fred Easthope's was often seen off the shoals of Nelson.
Vanguard	Lew and Joan Milligan owned this boat.
Veracity	Ernie and Nell Christmas' sailboat which moored in Hidden Basin.
Viking Prince	A tug wrecked on the shore of Green Bay.
White Arrow No. 1	The Jervis Inlet water taxi helped many an island child when it brought the Public Health nurse.
White Wing I and II	Familiar to Vanguard Bay were these boats of Milligans.
Wonderbird	George and Alice Larson highlined from this beauty.

Storms

Islanders were always at the mercy of the weather. Vanguard Bay residents suffered from the northeast winds which whip off the glaciers and whistle down Jervis Inlet. They dangerously iced up the boats heaving in the winter seas. On the west side, the Roberts at Cape Cockburn got the full force of the southeast winds that would shake the very ground they were on in its ferocity. The noise would change as the tide came in or went out. The high tide pounded the driftwood and logs together, sometimes upending them and crashing them down again. The winds forced the sea spray and torrential rains up over the trees on the rock bluffs.

The Blind Bay-Billings Bay residents escaped the full fury of the storms but were still subject to their severity. They feared for their floats coming loose from their moorings and they feared for their boats. Ballet Bay was the only safe year-round anchorage. One particularly turbulent storm ripped out both Bill and Bert Harding's floats. Bill dashed about in the dark, untying lines and starting the engine of his boat, *Agnes H*, desperately trying to keep her from the rocks. Finally, he headed her into the lashing blackness to Ballet Bay.

Bert and his son David were in town that night when Daphne checked their float and found it coming loose. With sinking heart she realized it was up to her to save their boat. She jumped onto the float, pulling threateningly at the last mooring, and pleaded with the engine to turn over right away. Then with the motor barely audible above the roar of the wind, she untied the cold wet ropes and pushed herself away from the float. Wind and waves battled her valiant efforts to find safe moorage, but after what seemed like hours she anchored by Bill. The float pulled completely away in the night.

As if to make up for the havoc they wreak, the storms dropped peacemakers along the beaches. An assortment of deck chairs, cushions, life rings, oars, bottles, cans, drums, glass floats, and old boats were washed ashore. Good logs for firewood, pieces of cedar suitable for shakes, and even lumber, were gleaned from the high tide line. Hal Hammond's find produced the teacherage; Harry Robert's beachcombing, the big shed he used for a goat barn/workshop; the men in Green Bay covered the cannery with number one clear fir drop siding, shipwrecked from a scow.

Whatever the spoils, they couldn't make up for the loss of moorage, boats, and worse, the loss of life. Yolana remembers walking along the trail leaning into the wind, and keeping a watch out for boats that got into trouble as they went. They spaced themselves apart as their father had taught them, keeping an eye open for falling limbs and trees.

One of the first shipwrecks she recalls was between their house and the cape where the rocks are so steep the beach stands on end. The engine had stopped out by the island and the boat was drifting. The anchor wouldn't hold in the howling gale. Harry watched to see if the boat would stop, then got his rowboat down to the beach. He fought the waves to get out to the boat and somehow was able to rescue the man. Later in the house, cold and wet, he sat around the fireplace with the Roberts. From the window he could see his boat slowly fill with water and sink.

He was lucky. Another night they saw a light drifting towards the cape. The wind was just coming up for a southeast storm. Suddenly the light went out before it got to the cape. They grabbed their rain coats, took down the big gas lantern and flashlights and went over the goat trail to the cape. With the rain and nightfall, they couldn't see much. They searched the shoreline and as far out in the waves as they could see. At last they saw the top of a wheelhouse of a gill net boat submerged in the water. A quick look assured them nothing else was there before they ran back to tell their dad about it.

Radio news the next day stated that the storm had claimed the life of a Pender Harbour man. Local news spread fast as well. If the telephone was not put out by the storm, islanders phoned around to check on how each one had made out, and offered to help those who needed it.

On the east side of the island, Lawrie Wray at Westmere, had to cope with keeping his launch off the rocks with each storm. Someone had to hold the boat out, while another clambered over the side, started the engine, and took it out of the bay. His daughter Betty recalls one stormy night when Lawrie was over seventy years old, and his wife Kay was past clambering, he spent one whole night up to his armpits in icy water holding the boat off the treacherous rocks.

Somehow they all managed to outlive the storms and pick up the pieces to carry on.

The Telephone

Nothing links the island as effectively and as quickly as the telephone. If it's working.

Since the first line was put in through the trees around 1916 or '17, enabling John Wray and Tom Brazil to hold their nightly conversations, the telephone has been alternately blessed and cursed. The overland line, which was always being put out by falling trees in the early days, was installed by a man named Phelan with the help of George West and John Wray. John was the telephone lineman who many times tramped through the miles of woods to find the downed line between his home and the Macombers on Hardy Island.

Even the superior marine cable had its problems. The only official record of this line to be found is in a notice to mariners dated February, 1938. Jacquie Partington recalls hearing or reading of this, or a later cable in the fifties, being used previously on the Nanaimo or Point Grey line, but no records have been found to substantiate this.

This expensive area to service was purchased by the B.C. Telephone Company from the Northwest Telephone Co. L. D. and Toll Station facilities on January 1, 1955. It was after this that the Blind Bay residents received their party lines.

Islanders and visitors alike have broken the line repeatedly and it has been out for up to a month at a time. Once it was put out while someone was building a stone wall, another time it was burnt in a bon fire. It's been torn out by a tractor, cut with a chain saw while getting wood, dragged over and over again by anchors, snipped by a toddler developing his small muscles, chewed by puppies, and eaten by a goat. There was even a time when 100 feet of line was quietly cut when an islander needed a bit of wire.

The most puzzling of all occurrences was a time when the phone only worked when the tide was out. Islanders had for years scheduled themselves by the tides, but this was the first time the telephone had been affected by the ebb and flow of the ocean. It was some time before the cause was found. A break in the wire at high water line was causing it to short when the tide came up. When the tide was low and the line had dried out, it would work again.

Party lines are necessary. To call one of the seven persons on your line, 18 is dialed, the receiver is replaced, and the caller counts to ten before lifting it again. Discreet clicks of party-line eavesdroppers are often heard above the noise of the phone which at times sounds like a steam engine coming into a station. More than once too, an islander has been startled by the phone ringing in his own kitchen rather than in that of the person being called.

Most of the time the phone works well and is cheaper and easier to use than the radio telephone that was used before the party lines went through in the mid-fifties. No line is through yet to the sparsely populated Vanguard Bay where the Milligans live. They are still using the radio telephone. At long distance rates, it's a business-only convenience.

When the first land telephones came in, the search and rescue men would often come into Maynards to use theirs as the radio phone allowed reporters to eavesdrop easily.

Large CABLE signs mark the homes with telephones and warn boaters not to drop anchor. When the Loutitts visited Green Bay in the sixties, there was still an old phone in a box nailed to a tree, a reminder of the first overland line. Much progress has been made in more than six decades and islanders appreciate the service.

The Outhouse, The Backhouse, The Privy

Whatever the owner called it, the outhouse was an important addition to almost every islander's domain. To those coming from the city, using it (particularly in winter), represented a hardship second only to coping with medical emergencies.

Many stories have been told of the various outhouses. The girls in Hidden Bay built several before resorting to nature. The most noted of these privies was one built of odd-length boards around four trees standing more or less in a square. The whole thing swayed and creaked in the wind and threatened sudden revealment of the user.

Grandpa Maynard always told of the whole building he was sitting in shaking violently one Sunday morning. He yelled to his young grandsons to cut it out, and came out to find the two and five-year-old boys quite innocent of any shenanigans. He always had an interesting answer though when people asked where he was during the earthquake of 1946.

The Hydrographic Survey office has never noted Outhouse Point on a navigational chart but it was well known in the fifties. A sketch by Allen Farrell shows one of several similar views on the island. It must have saved digging a lot of holes in that impenetrable rock.

Even today the outhouse plays an important role in island living, often just as a back-up system to the indoor plumbing, but sometimes as the main convenience. One islander, John Picken, is noted for designing unique outbuildings for summer residents. "French Telephone Booth" or "Gothic" architecture are his specialties. John was just finishing the shake roof of a Gothic original for a neighbor, John Mitchell, when the Mitchell family and guests arrived at their dock. One of the guests hurried up the path to the privy and stopped short, called to Mrs. Mitchell, "Oh Billee, it's priceless!"

Little Suzy, who had been handing her dad the shakes, looked crestfallen. With wide eyes she whispered to her dad, "Does that mean we don't get paid?"

The paid-for structures include varnished seats, interesting windows, and a touch of carpeting, noticeable improvements over the many island forerunners. These present-day anachronisms, despite the refinements, are a very real link with early island history.

Island Kids

The survival rate for kids on the island was excellent. In most cases a strong patriarch was in command and they learned what was expected of them, as well as their limits, very early in life.

Almost every family can tell a story of a youngster's close call, but the kids all lived to try it again. A lot of adventures are naturally linked to boats, like the time a young Picken wandered down on the dock and climbed into the speed boat. Just like Dad, he turned the key, started the motor and ran the boat—at a year-and-a-half, no less. Fortunately for all, the boat was in reverse, someone was quick, and the solid rock in front of him remained as intact as he did.

They soon learn to handle a boat with ease, or almost with ease. The Roberts three and Jacqueline Pettigrew rowed around the island when Zoe was only seven and Jacqueline was just fourteen. There was a great deal of discussion on how that boat was to be navigated. Two of them rowed, or tried to row at once, which led to some heated words and a wake as erratic as the Nelson shoreline. Jacquie and Yolana could row quite well together but Lee and Jacquie had a problem "because you couldn't speed Lee up no matter what," Yo remembers.

With a few potatoes and Tinker the dog, they rowed from Cape Cockburn to Vanguard Bay, more than fourteen miles around the island. They stopped then to boil a few potatoes in sea water and to stay the night. They pulled into a little cove in the late afternoon and Yolana and Jacquie boiled some more potatoes.

Curling in their blankets, they slept until the gray light woke them. With a breakfast of a few more of the hearty spuds, they started off for home. After rowing for an hour the sky began to darken. Expecting a storm brewing, they rowed harder. Soon it became quite dark, as dark as night. They pulled harder on the oars. Then they realized what had happened. It was night. They had slept for a few hours in the late afternoon and early evening and had started out again before dusk.

When morning did finally arrive, the water on the horizon was black, and the wind blew the firs along the shore. It was sometime later that they pulled the heavy clinker well up into a bay on the north side of Cape Cockburn. The water was pretty wild around the point and the kids had enough sense to take the last part of their journey overland. As they approached the house, they could hear the worried voices of Harry and Ann wondering about what they were going to do about their long over-due kids. But, despite the adventure, they survived, of course, like they all did.

A healthy respect for work was engendered in them. They were sons and daughters of pioneers and as such were expected to help provide the family rations whether they pioneered in 1900 or 1960. At the tender age of eleven, Hal Hammond shot his first deer, the first of many in the years to come. They fished too, their play overlapping this pleasant work. The rigid boundaries between what was girl's work and boy's work were pretty flacid on an island, and in later years nonexistent. Although the girls were more apt to be in the kitchen with Mama in May Hammond's day, in 1983, Simon Picken's pizzas are rivaled by no one.

The kids were hardy, too. Sue Milligan remembers wanting to go timber cruising with her dad, from Hidden Basin overland to Vanguard Bay. The two men from the Forestry took one look at the small twelve-year-old, and said no at first, then relented, saying, "But we're not carrying you back."

They started out at seven in the morning, hiked through the bush, and climbed right to the top where one of the Forestry men had to sit and rest. Lew stayed with him and Sue went on ahead, and beat them all back.

They all learn to run a boat an an early age, putting their competent mothers into the passenger seat. They become adept at repairing motors or sinks or whatever. A keen appreciation too, is developed for their surroundings. Imaginations are freer to explore and develop as Howie White relates in his memories of Green Bay.

Island kids viewed life from a different perspective. When the Milligans drove to Vancouver on the new road, Sue was heard to ask her father, "Where are we going to tie up Dad?"

Tying up the car was one thing. Viewing the city lights and stores at Christmas was quite another. The hotel rooms, watching Howdy Doody on television, the windows, and the toylands were wonderful. But the glamour of it often gave the young people the idea that they were missing too much by being on the island. Most of them tried what they thought was a better life after leaving Nelson, but many of them have returned to a similar life in a different setting, valuing their sense of independence.

Island Pets

All the island children have had their share of cats, dogs, and rabbits, and even the occasional goat, but some have been able to tame the more unusual. The Hammonds had a majestic eagle with an injured wing. He became so used to them that he would let the little girls come close and pet his silky feathers.

Zoe Robert's crow was not as grand as the Hammond eagle but just as tame, and would light on her hand or shoulder.

Kathy Milligan had a white pet duck, Oswald, who had something wrong with him. The oil on his feathers made his swimming difficult, and he would sink if he got too low in the water.

Susy, her sister, had a particular rabbit that she was especially proud of and entered him in the Powell River Fall Fair. Her "buck" turned out to be a doe and caused quite a commotion in the cages. She couldn't understand why he hadn't won a blue ribbon. She felt *he* was healthier and more beautiful than all the others.

The Milligans also had a pet seal they called Flippy, who was unusual even for a seal. He lived in their bathtub, without water, and thought Satan, their dog, was his mother. Not only that, but they also had to teach him how to swim.

As seals in captivity are prone to enteritis, Joan went to a lot of trouble and expense to keep her orphan alive. Five times a day she had to feed, or shove down his throat, cod-liver oil with milk and a spoonful of the $11 worth of antibiotics. (This was quite a sum for an animal in the late fifties.) He survived through the first crucial weeks and began to thrive. By the time he was three weeks old he ate three pounds of herring a day. This kept Susy, and Lew's crew busy. The crew spent all their lunch hours catching small fish for him. Flippy got lots of attention, starting at five o'clock when he yelled, "Ma!"

He became a favorite of everyone and they had him for several months before he was tragically killed by one of the dogs, not his "mother."

Hubert and Bunny Louttit who came in the sixties, had two baby flying squirrels for a year. The lovable, curious pair had free run of the house and entertained many a visitor with their escapades. They left each night through an opening under the kitchen door or through the kitchen drain hole, and returned at dawn to sleep the day away. As they do not interbreed, they left for good when they were ready to mate. "It was a rare experience having them around," Bunny remembers, "and one that we wouldn't have missed for the world."

Ann Pettigrew always has several squirrels for company around her cabin on Tom's Island. She often carries a pocketful of nuts for the cheeky creatures who also come and go freely.

Oscar the Otter was the latest pet. He was actually an import to Hidden Basin from northern Manitoba. A relative of the Thomases, summer people in the basin, is a girl bush pilot who had arranged to pick up a trapper at a lake in Manitoba on a set date. When she arrived to get him he was followed by a baby otter. He explained that he had trapped his mother and finding her young one, had looked after him. Now that he was ready to leave though, he was going to leave it to fend for itself.

The bush pilot insisted that he take it, that she wouldn't take the plane up without him. "OK" he agreed, "but you take him." Which she did—first to her apartment, and then for the sake of the apartment—to Nelson Island.

He traveled around the area, adopting the Hopes for a while. Oscar was no fool, Brad and June Hope were just beginning their fish farm then. As well as eating fish, he acquired a taste for cheese and would go boldly into their house and flip out their drawers looking for some. He became quite a nuisance as he hissed and snapped if they disciplined him. They finally discouraged his company and he went "on tour."

He arrived at the Picken's one day and threw himself down on the dock to have his tummy rubbed. Duly done, he flipped himself into

Zoe Roberts and pet crow. M. McIntyre

Clara Hammond and sister with tamed eagle.
M. Hammond

"Flippy," Milligan's seal. J. Milligan

the water and swam playfully with the Picken kids, rolling against them in the summer sunshine. But the smell of salmon frying soon put a stop to the play. He scrambled aboard a visitor's boat and literally had one flipper in the pan before they could get to him. He was quick and slippery. Nipping a boy in his way, he stole a loaf of bread and whipped off the dock and into the cove.

The Mitchells next door, were packing up to leave for the winter, and were picnicking with friends from Japan when Oscar joined the picnic and became the star of reels of Japanese home movies.

The film-starring, bread-thieving cheese freak was destined to move again. When his antics became too much for the islanders, he was given to Sealand in Victoria. Here the nautical performer again made a nuisance of himself, and was again moved on. The last anyone heard he was a mascot at a Vancouver Island college on the ocean. The college is right beside a salmon weigh-in station that had to erect a sign that stated "BEWARE OF OTTER" when he arrived. As he had a habit of making off with the salmon before they hit the scale, Oscar the Otter from northern Manitoba, may have yet seen another move.

Nelson Island Uniqueness

Nelson Island had some unique features that larger islands often couldn't claim. Long before skylights or hot tubs were fashionable, two island residences sported them. Harry Robert's home, built in the late thirties, had a beautiful skylight in the kitchen, and Captain Wehner's place housed a hot tub in the forties. He was often reported sitting in his hot tub with his captain's hat and his binoculars, looking out to sea.

And not every area had its own Father Christmas, as Ernie Christmas was know to his friends. He and his wife Nell had been lay missionaries up coast on the *M. C. Gua-Yee*, and had visited the Maynards for several years before retiring to Hidden Bay in the fifties. Nor did many places have a Bavarian opera singer, as Madam Wehner had been before coming to Blind Bay.

An orchid business was another unusual distinction. The Viitanens of Green Bay grew orchids in large plastic greenhouses. They produced an array of delicate blooms grown on moss and fir bark,

Inside the Sunray kitchen with its unique skylight. M. McIntyre

Chack-Chack III in ruins. Powell River Museum

A coypu (nutria) similar to those Art Harding raised. B. Weems

Yolana, Lee, Zoe, and Jacquelyn in loft at Sunray. J. Partington

for export to Edmonton and New York. They left when the government began to tax them heavily on their undeveloped land and it became unprofitable.

For awhile, too, Art Harding raised nutria, also called the coypu, a South American rodent almost two feet in length. The softness of the fur resembles that of our Canadian beaver.

Sunray itself and *Chack Chack III* were as distinctive as their builder, Harry Roberts, whose name is now synonymous with Nelson Island. The bald head of Harry, which the chief of the Sechelt Indian Band once likened to the bald eagle "chack chack," could be seen on the island for forty-seven years. This fact in itself is unique as most islanders moved on after just a decade or so.

Nelson Island Stores and Delivery Service

Keeping the larder supplied, the equipment running, and the family outfitted, has always been a challenge for the islanders. Even the early quarry workers found a need for more than the steamer service. In 1898, the B.C. Directory states that the first general store on the island belonged to R. Dan Trevor. As the voter's roll of that year lists only seven men, there hardly seems that there would be enough nonvoters and families to keep the poor man in business. And indeed there probably wasn't, as it is the only time he appears in the Directory.

May Hammond was next to try her luck with island business. Enid remembers, "Mother opened a very small `general store' in the parlor of the big house. There were very few customers, but it enabled her to buy everything for the family at wholesale price. Fishing boats and other craft helped too, the folks on there always spending a few dollars. She talked Hal into putting a sign outside the bay, facing bravely out into the gulf to snare passing boats. He climbed a big mast-straight hemlock and bolted a large board to it saying: STORE - HALFWAY UP LAGOON."

Tom Brazil was a frequent visitor to the store both here and its other location, Hardy Island. Business was brisker on Hardy with the addition of the quarry workers, but never was it a thriving concern. The early stores were just a supplement to the steamer's delivery service which brought the newspaper that advertised what Woodward's had to offer. "No order too large or too small," the ad in the *World* proclaimed. Many a pair of $3 logging boots were delivered to the island in those days.

Staples were ordered a month at a time usually, or a winter's supply of case lots was ordered in the fall. Woodward's was the main supplier in the early days and later Eaton's offered the same service. They each had a "personal shopper" who would fill orders from a description in a letter, a wonderful assistance to the isolated. But most everything could be found in the catalogue, which next to the tide book, was the most important reading material in the house. A story is told of one woman who was so excited about receiving her Eaton's catalogue that she couldn't sleep all night.

More exciting to most was Boat Day itself. While east side islanders went to Irvine's Landing for the day, westsiders met the boat near a group of islets around Kelly Island. It was the one day of the week that everyone got together to visit. For those who had rapids to deal with, the day began by consulting the tide chart, and waiting for slack tide. As the boat schedule depended on the state of the weather and how long it took to unload their various amounts of freight at the numerous logging spots, no one was sure just when the boat would arrive.

During the late thirties, and until the government float was built in 1950, everyone met the boat in midstream. They sheltered just off Kelly Island in the lee side of the islets. Fish boats and rowboats of every description tied together or fished in the area. A feeling of genial comradeship filled the islanders as the coffeepots bubbled, and they discussed the local fishing and doings of the week, in various accents. In wet weather they sat inside one of the larger boats, tobacco smoke and steam from their clothing enveloping them like a fog. In good weather they deepened their already rich tans sitting out on deck.

The whistle of the mail boat, anywhere from noon to nightfall, would stir them into action. Ropes were untied, anchors were pulled, oars were put into locks, engines were fired, and the small flotilla made its way to the gaping freight doors of the *Lady Cynthia* or *Lady Cecilia*.

The steamer would slow down and turn to make a lee for the smaller craft. Curious passengers would crowd the rail to watch as the deck hands passed the packages and crates to their owners. If the waves were unusually bad, only the larger boats would go out, and even then, oars and hooks were often broken in holding the fish boats off the steamer, and freight was lost overboard. Quick net handling often retrieved the soggy parcel, but like as not it was lost to the brine.

They would all return to the smaller islands where Tom Brazil, or later Harry Thomas, would bind the mail together and toss it to their owners. Some of these rugged men only came for the company, rowing out week after week without receiving so much as a postcard.

Gonzalves and Dames at Irvine's Landing and later Lloyd's and Murdock's stores at Pender Harbour supplied islanders as well. The better part of the day was spent rowing or chugging back and forth to these outlets.

Before the road went through to Saltery Bay that gave easier access to Powell River businesses, George and Lorna Bradshaw ran a store boat, the *Adventus*. They were the agents for Jones Tent and Awning, among other companies, and even brought a hairdresser around occasionally. Until they moved to Cockburn Bay where they were joined by Mrs. McKenzie and Don, Lorna's mother and brother, the Bradshaws lived aboard the *Adventus*. Even their honeymoon had been spent aboard ship while they traveled north selling along the way. The boat burned in the late sixties and was replaced by their second store boat, the *Spartan*, a lovely old boat with a history.

Bradshaw's was a utilitarian service that couldn't match the romance offered by the *D'sonoqua*, the floating service that appeared in the early seventies. *D'sonoqua's* name was based on an Indian legend about an evil spirit who captured native children if they were out after dark. It was a barkantine sailboat with a ferrocement hull. With auxiliary power they served the coast as far as Church House. The skipper had a crew of half-to-completely naked girls who served honey and health foods to prospective buyers. He was a good ship hand but enjoyed socializing and wasn't too prompt on delivery dates or quoting fixed prices, and lost a lot of business because of it. They brought groceries and construction materials mainly, but would also deliver furniture on occasion.

The Bradshaw store boat spanned decades. The *D'sonoqua* only gave the area service for about a year-and-a-half, but left lasting memories that appear with a smile on the faces of former customers.

Islanders don't row for their groceries anymore, and haven't had steamer service for more than thirty years. Even the store boats are history. Freight service is a problem, and going for groceries and repair equipment means maintaining and insuring a car at Saltery Bay as well as a boat, and a lengthy drive to Powell River. Pender Harbour facilities are still patronized by boat alone but as it is a small center, they don't offer the variety that Powell River can. There is a nostalgia for days of the *Lady Cynthia* and *Lady Cecilia* with its gaping freight doors and convenient service.

Christmas on Nelson

Christmas was particularly dependent on the steamers. Although the pick of fresh-scented trees was at their doorstep, the steamer brought the trimmings for the festive season, the nuts and fruit, the cakes and Christmas pudding from home-folks, the cheerfully wrapped gifts, the newsy letters, and the colorful Christmas cards. The grocery box from Woodwards was promisingly bigger before Christmas and sometimes protesting turkey crates were tossed down from the imposing steamer to the waiting boats rolling in the winter-gray waters.

Exciting were the Christmases when aunts, uncles, and cousins were also unloaded through the freight doors to swell the Christmas table and add to the general gaiety. The Hammonds almost always had visiting relatives who enjoyed the cordiality of the holiday runs on the steamers. The coal oil lamps on the *Chilco* and the *Chasina* lit up their brass clocks, wearing festive holly wreaths in their white-linen dining salon. A fresh-coated steward served the locally-famous Union Steamship pound cake and seasonally garnished pudding. The captain and officers were more friendly than usual and made a point of showing the wheelhouse to the visiting children. A party atmosphere could be felt by everyone.

Christmas day at the Hammonds was a happy, busy event as all the bachelors in the neighborhood joined the family for a dinner of roast goose. In the center of their living room stood a huge fir with flickering candles clipped to its thick branches. The bright candles were magical in the soft glow of the lamplight and cast pretty reflections on the glass ornaments. Strings of red cranberries and puffed popcorn looped the bright greenery. After dinner the Hammond children and their cousins would join hands and dance around the tree merrily singing the yuletide favorites. A blazing fire warmed the room, and the spirit of loving and giving warmed those within.

And so Christmas was spent in Hidden Bay, snug in their home, insulated from the winter frost or occasional snow—or more likely, the lashing rain that so often accompanies coastal Christmases. But one Christmas stood out from the others in Clara's memory as the year she lost her belief in Santa Claus. Santa in his red wool suit and white cotton beard, was reaching for a present from the tree when his arm brushed too close to a candle and his suit was aflame. At once, May had him wrapped in a rug, and when the fire was properly smothered, she unrolled poor Santa to reveal Cliff! The youngest Hammonds stared at their brother in surprise, learning the secret of the jolly old man the hard way.

Sis Harris' Christmas memory is of a Veda doll hanging on the tree in the early 1918 morning. Her mother had bought the small glass doll, and carefully dressed it with homesewn clothes. Sis' brother had taken a pithy wood which he used for making whistles, and had run a hot wire through it, then threaded it with waxed string to make a tiny swing. They fastened it on the tree and sat the glass doll on it to surprise nine-year-old Sis.

Thelma Deberri (nee Johnstone) remembers one year that the steamer didn't cooperate in bringing the Johnstone's their Christmas parcels until very late. For some reason, either the weather or the unusually heavy freight unloadings, the boat steamed right on past the regular island stop both going up and coming down the run. It wasn't until it went up and back again, that they finally unloaded their holiday ware. All that time the Johnstone Christmas turkey had paced its crate, gobbling half-heartedly, getting thinner and more seasick with every roll of the steamer.

In later years, another generation of Johnstones, Fran Lambert, then Deberri, remembers having to go to Pender Harbour for the turkey, now plucked and cleaned and packed in ice. The steamers had finished their runs and the small boats made annual Christmas trips to Lloyd's store for their bird, no matter what the weather.

Not too many had cranberry sauce to eat with their turkey though. In Green Bay, cranberries from around Goose Lake bubbled and steamed on the kitchen stove while the Yates and Follets spent Christmas Eve yanking and pulling on the dresser drawer that held their Christmas presents sent from Ron's mom five days earlier. No matter what they did the damp swollen drawer refused to give up its booty unil long after the holidays.

But the turkey or goose wasn't always the dinner fare for the big day, many had a roast of venison, and the Harding boys remember a depression Christmas dinner of stuffed cod wrapped in bacon, cooked by Paul and Bert, and enjoyed by all.

In fact, what went on the table often set Island Christmases apart from mainland ones, for it wasn't unusual to have dishes of steamed clams and oysters with melted butter, tasty crab legs, tender muscles, baked red snapper, and smoked salmon, to be tasted by all who visited. And they all visited, in fish boats and clinkers, by oar and sail, whatever would float and take them through the icy spray. By the early forties there were a number of families in the Blind Bay-Billings Bay area, and parties were held in the homes, but by the fifties, the community had grown too large and a camp dining hall in the Blind Bay quarry was used to hold a community dinner before Christmas. Marjorie McKewen, a newcomer to the area in the early fifties vividly recorded a community dinner in her writings.

The Community Dinner

by Marjorie McKewen Roberts

Dinner was to be at 1:00 p.m. on Saturday, December 15, 1950. Word was passed around by word of mouth perhaps at the tea two weeks previously. The charge was $1.50 per person but that included the children of the family free.

Bill Westbrook, who used to be a professional candy maker, living now at the far end of Hidden Bay, was given $15 for ingredients and made boxes of dipped chocolates, pretty colored stuffed dates, large quantities of coconut ice, fudge and a candy cake. The latter was raffled.

The ladies brought homecooking, linen, and novelties. On the

Last Christmas concert at Ballet Bay School in 1958. Left to right: Lyn Harding, Kathy Milligan, Mary Harding, and sister. J. Milligan

Rick Fedesov; Kathy Milligan; Mary Harding as Santa; the next two belong to Art and Lyn Harding; unknown; Susan Milligan; and lamb, Linda Fedesov. J. Milligan

way up, Sandy Millard took us to see a bay in which he would like to someday build. In spite of it we arrived there just before one, horribly cold.

The hall was just a little above tide level at the base of the mountain. It had been a camp dining hall. It was very dark, cold, and damp from a recent scrubbing. The windows were small and far apart. When one thought of the voluntary work which had been done there, the cleaning and decorating, and the spirit with which these people came, many from long distances away in open "kickers" on a raw cold day, and made the best of what they had, one felt shamed into doing her utmost to make it enjoyable for all.

There were two huge maples with curving moss-grown trunks in front of the building with branches spreading out over the hall and over the water. We were helped ashore by Bill Westbrook, who was meeting people with his skiff. The steep ramp felt positively greased and it was something of a feat climbing it with handbag, club bag, and another parcel.

The hall remained very cold, even after vigorous stokings of the huge old cook stove, but with the later addition of fifty-five people it began to warm up. People began to arrive by boatloads. Some in fish boats, many in kickers. These were anchored out a little distance from the rocky shore and skiffs pulled up to the water's edge. The men waiting outside to help with landings would form a chain and pass the babies and children up over the rocks. The children, all bundled up in parkas or snowsuits, peeped out from their fur-trimmed hoods with fresh excited faces. The babies looked a little wonderingly at each new face, as they went from one pair of arms to another.

Mrs. Johnstone and her four daughters began heating the turkeys and cooked vegetables, and others joined in. By two o'clock the rough board table and a collection of other antique kitchen tables were covered with brown papers—whoever was supposed to bring the building's table cloth had forgotten it—and set with a big platter of carved turkey, sauce pans and bowls of peas, potatoes, sweet potatoes, carrots, turnips, cranberry sauce, apple sauce, crisp celery, jars of olives, and pickles all arranged buffet style. Paper plates were supplied and we took our own cutlery and cups.

We all tucked in and did full justice to the dinner, even to the pies and coffee and cookies, which were delicious. There were some interesting faces among the group, dear old Mrs. Jeffries, (mother of Mr. Jeffries who took me out seining for herring, and Vera Grafton who acts as guide to wealthy Americans on cruises up the coast, also mother of Mrs. Johnstone). The young men, mostly loggers and fishermen, were big well-built fellows with a sort of wholesomeness about them. They talked to the children and handled them so nicely. They were some of the prettiest youngsters I've ever seen. There was such a spirit of happiness among the people, and color and race didn't seem to matter.

Old Tom Hughes was there, and dear Lottie (Wehner) looking so sweet in a lacy sweater set and black skirt, and black and white shortie coat.

After the dinner it was surprising how soon the tables were cleaned off, and the candies, home cooking and novelties spread out. There seemed to be a general rush of buying, and then in no time people were leaving. I found the Maynards gone before I could give her the candies for the boys.

We came home in blowing, drizzly-cold rain, now in among the islands, now far out from shore in a rapidly darkening world. The phosphorescence behind the boat was like silver Christmas balls dancing in the water.

Sandy gave her the gun through the Skookumchuck (local name for rapids at the entrance to Hidden Basin) so I guess the tide was running out as we had no difficulty. We were home, very cold, at six p.m.

After the school opened, each teacher put on a production for the annual Christmas Concert. Elaborate costumes were made by the mothers, a Christmas tree was decorated, and presents, Japanese oranges, and candy canes were brought by parents. The whole bay was invited, children or no children. Guest of honor, Canon Alan Greene, came as Santa Claus every year. Sue Milligan recalls him "coming in and telling us how many seals he'd eaten, big pillow on his stomach, red suit, the perfect Santa Clause."

In 1958, the last Christmas that the school was opened, the CBC came and filmed the Christmas party for posterity. It was the passing of an era, the last of the Ballet Bay school concerts.

Logging After 1920 on
Nelson and Hardy Islands

The "Christmas trees" of Nelson fed many a family over the years. Most of the men logged, whether they did it for a living or just supplemented their other incomes. Handloggers were seen less often after 1920, but they still were around.

The B.C. Directory lists a few names that others have forgotten. In 1920, the Shamrock Lumber Company was given as the employer of John Shannon, a logger, and Anna Swanson, who was most probably the cook. Frank Swanson is listed separately as a teamster, but no indication is made whether he was in charge of the horses, or whether this was the first introduction to truck logging on the island.

Ten years later, D. Amscold was given as the manager or owner of Shamrock Logging Co. He was possibly from the Amscold family who lived on Nelson when the Laughlins were there after World War I.

The McNutt Brothers logged Green Bay from 1934 to 1942, about the same time the Jorgensons were in the Hidden Bay area. The Delongs: Lim, Robert, and S. S., were logging around Nelson from 1935 or so, into the forties.

There was a surge of logging in Cockburn Bay at that time. Pete Klein and Rae Phillips logged in the head of Cockburn Bay on the north side of the creek early in the decade. Soon to follow them were Ralph Williams and Paul Green who lived in the old Roberts cottage. They were still there around 1947 when Art Marshall came from Cortez Island, bringing a cat driver with a family of two or three children.

The logging boomed after the war and attracted Charlie Klein from Pender Harbour in 1948. He was the man who could lift a full gas drum, amazing the young fellows like Lee Roberts, who at thirteen, went to work for him on the boom. Bill Cook and his son Clarence also worked for Charlie, as did Frank Campbell from Pender Harbour. Art Marshall took on the Hall boys, Clarence, Irvin, and Ernie until they had logged out Cockburn Bay. Art finally went up to Jervis Inlet and Charlie Klein went to Gibsons. It's been said that Art eventually made his fortune, not from logging but from buying boarding houses.

Fred Helliar logging on Nelson Island. H. Helliar

Paul, Bill, and Bert Harding cutting trees with power saws, 1953. A. Harding

Frank White logged in Green Bay from 1949 to '55 while Oliver Lauson logged elsewhere on the island. The early fifties saw several logging outfits come and go—Ollie Sladey's day camp in Green Bay and other areas of Nelson; Milligan's L & J Timber in Vanguard Bay; Bill Hodge's day camp around '50 to '54; and Oliver Dubois' camp after the White's left.

Powell River Company and Mahood's Logging both worked on the strip for the B.C. Electric line in 1955-56 which went across the top of Nelson in the Vanguard region. One of the men from Mahood's camp told of infringing on Walter Wray's "territory" and of watching him and his sister put out porridge for the deer each day.

After Mrs. Macomber sold Hardy Island to Gibson and Howay in 1951, it too was logged. It has changed hands several times since that time, always to owners who had it logged. Gibson bought out Howay; Howay sold to Northern Development Ltd. (known locally as Scott Paper Products) for $75,000 in 1953; and they sold to T & S Logging Co. Ltd. in 1979 for $3,800,000. The final transfer was made to Hardy Island Developments Ltd. for a total of $600,000. A "reservation of timber" on the transfer allowed T & S Logging to take the timber until December 31, 1983.

It's been reported that owners of Hardy Island Developments, Digby Porter and Ian Mahood, wanted to exchange the southwest end of Hardy for another tract of timber, preserving this area for parkland, but the government wouldn't approve the plan. Loggers have tried to log away from the main Indian middens.

Logging operations have desecrated the once beautiful island. Single spindly trees lean weakly, apparitions of the solid giants which once lined the hand-swept trails. Great areas have been stripped and flattened, a sight that would make the selective handloggers rise out of their graves waving their double-bladed axes. Even Macomber's luxury home, in a sad state of decay, was torn down in recent years.

It is rumored that $17 million worth of timber has been removed from the island that sold for almost $4 million in 1979, seventy-three years after MacKinnon bought it in a tax sale for $217.

The Failing of Frank Ficek

Keeping chickens on a raccoon-and-mink-infested island has always been an aggravation to the islanders. It was a problem which often got blown out of all proportion, with grown men lying in wait with fire in their eyes and revenge in their heart. The following ballad, with apologies to Robert Service, relates an incident which happened to Frank Ficek in his pursuit of the island enemy.

>Now Blind Bay's crew used to like to chew
>   the fat at barber Frank's
>They'd take the chair, and he'd cut their hair,
>   then they'd brag about their pranks.
>Just one or two of Frank's own brew
>   would tangle the legs of most,
>And they'd take a row in any blow
>   to be with this genial host.
>
>A bold raccoon in the empty lagoon,
>   was eating a tasty clam,
>And he seemed to say as they passed his way,
>   "Oh what a coon, I am!
>I'll be back for more, beyond the shore,
>   as soon as I get the chance."
>And they swore a wink, from that mask of ink,
>   went into his parting glance.
>
>They climbed the bank and greeted Frank,
>   who'd been eyeing the greedy coon,
>"It's my belief, I'll get that thief,
>   and it won't be any too soon.
>He can have my clams, but not my hens,
>   it's there I draw the line,
>If he shows his face around my place,
>   his head he'll leave behind!"
>
>The night wore down and the brew went 'round
>   all the boys who were there in throng,
>Then they heard the hen in the chicken pen
>   croaking her dying song,
>"He's having a feast, that rotten beast,
>   it's the last he'll ever eat
>For I've got a scheme that will end his dream
>   of a chicken-a-night for a treat."
>
>The battery-pack from his homespun sack
>   he held up to the men,

"See this radar lamp that I got from camp,
    it'll help me clear the pen."
('Twas a different shape then, like an old jam can,
    with a round rim stand beneath),
And with a scoop, he grabbed the loop,
    And grimly set his teeth.

Beneath the chin of the stubborn Finn
    they tied the lantern tight,
Like an old pit-lamp from a miner's camp
    it would light up the darkest night.
He looked at once like a naughty dunce and
    the men all whooped with mirth,
Then he grabbed his gun and silenced their fun,
    and told them to give him girth.

By the light of the moon, he could see the coon,
    whose eyes were shining bright,
"By God, one blast and he'll see the last,
    of this chicken-thieving night."
He vowed to the men, as he aimed at the pen,
    and prepared to stalk his foe,
He took one stride, he'd have that hide
    before the guys could go.

But his leg flew out, and a strangled shout
    had the boys in a wide-eyed trance,
They heard the shot but Frank was caught
    his feet just seemed to dance.
The shot of the gun had the 'coon on the run,
    for the gunfire seared the stars,
But he paused in his flight to look back through the night,
    and laugh at this comical farce.

They checked Frank's head, to see what led
    To this very unusual sight,
Saw the loop of the light that had caught on a spike
    and pulled their host up tight.
For it seemed instead, it was almost his head
    that was lost in this island clash
Of coons and hens in chicken pens,
    and an islander high on mash.

    Judd Johnstone and Old Mitch had one solution to the problem. In the age before protest groups, they began trapping the coons in the area, preparing and storing the skins until they got enough for a full length coat and a jacket. Rowena Underwood, Mitch's daughter, says the jacket is still being worn by her daughter in Alberta. They've hardly seen a coon on the island since.

Part VI

After the Exodus

Possibly this history of the early days of Nelson Island and area should end here with the breakup of the community in 1956. The era of the steamships had ended; the opening of the road to Vancouver left Nelson less isolated and more open to change; the quarries were seldom working and logging was almost finished.

But some of the old-timers carried on despite the changes—Harry Roberts, the Thomases, Maynards, Bill Hardings, Larsons, Deberris, and a few others. And on the Agamemnon side, the Lawrence Wrays and the Reads were untouched by the exodus of Blind Bay residents. Then too, a few of the newcomers, particularly the Milligans, deserve their mention since they span a third of the recorded history. Most of the island activity from that time on though, is touched on lightly.

Harry Robert's family had all grown by the mid-fifties, instilled with a confidence that only island life and Harry's teachings could give them. The same year, Lee and Yolana went to a Youth Training course at UBC for two months. They met kids from all over B.C. but found without their high school education that they couldn't get into other courses.

The next year saw Yo married to Clarence Cook from Gibsons, where they lived for a few months. With Barb, Clarence's daughter from his first marriage, they moved from there up the PGE to Devine, near Pemberton. After another move to Gibsons, where Clarence logged, they came back to Cape Cockburn where he worked for Oliver Dubois until 1960. It was then that he bought the troller, *Morien II*, and went fishing for a living.

Lee had married Betty Merrick the same year as Yo and Clarence tied the knot. After living with Harry one winter, they settled in Roberts Creek for a year while Lee ran the garage there. They made more moves after that, North Vancouver, Craycroft Island, and Campbell River. Tod, Tammy, Jenifer, and Kim were born along the way.

Three years after Yolana and Lee, Harry himself married again. His wedding to Marjorie McKewen took place in 1957.

Florence and Harold (Freddie) Frederickson came permanently to Hidden Basin the year before this event took place. They were another couple who had visited the area for years before making the move. Florence was the postmistress after the Maynards left in 1965 until the Trudeau government took over in 1968. Tyee Airways flew the mail in to her and it was picked up there, or at the boxes in the shed at the government wharf.

Bunny and Hubert Loutitt arrived on the island in the sixties. Hubert did selective logging for Fredericksons, and other private owners as well as logging some crown timber. They lived in an old VLA home on a fifty-foot by fifty-foot cedar float for fifteen years, pulled from camp to camp by a tug. They were pretty comfortable, propane stove, Coleman heater, and coal oil fridge. They didn't have to chop wood, although Bunny carried fresh water from a hose attached to the float. The pipes of the house had been frozen at one time and never fixed. Their indoor toilet was flushed with salt water.

"There were always neighbors around in the early days, in the bays where we tied," remembers Bunny. "There were beachcombers, telephone line crews, and surveyors, and they all hung out in our camp if they were in the area. The stories and the drinks flowed freely some nights. There were false teeth puked overboard and fished out again at low tide; there were experiences that had nothing to do with history but were nevertheless interesting."

Everyone enjoyed the baby flying squirrels and Loutitt's small pooch who chased the ducks. The ducks would stay just out of reach of her on the float, then dive, and she usually did too, scrambling back on the logs herself most of the time. When they were in Cockburn Bay, the pooch would chase the deer that fed freely in Robert's Orchard, and cheekily raided the garden. He was more of a nuisance than a threat to them.

They viewed nature at its finest, the loons, deer, grouse, coons, ducks, and hummingbirds; more than a hundred fed from the gallon wine jug, often refilled with sugar water.

Truckloads of supplies and parts were taken with them and more were added by Woodward's delivery service which was still going strong. Freight was brought in to the Billings float by barge then. Groceries were banded with aluminum, and it was a full day's chore lugging them home in a boat, up a wharf ramp, often at low tide, and storing them away.

"We traveled by fish boat and our own boat, and for years flew with *Tyee Airways* out of Sechelt. Al Campbell and the crew were fantastic, and many a tale I could spin about our times with them over the early flights.

"Many winters the bays we were in froze over, and we had a boom boat we called *Dirty Gerty*, don't ask me why, I never did know the story behind that name. We would break ice for boats, or use it for transportation to get the postmistress in or out with mail. It was two old plane pontoons salvaged from Texada Island, filled with styrofoam with a frame around it. It went like crazy and could turn on a dime. We used it to ram logs etc. There was no place to sit on it, but there was a bar across to hang on to, and a railing, and a rod with a steering wheel on it, and an outboard on the back. It turned many a tourist's head, no one could figure out what the hell it was."

They also had the use of an army jeep the last three years, to haul firewood and tour their side of the island. They were caretaking then, having quit the gypo logging. They had a cat and a skidder and just one man helping, a small outfit contracting for a larger one.

"Hunting season was always a pain in the butt, people beached their boats and walked all over the island, private property or not. It wasn't safe to walk the dog at times. I can understand city people not being able to fathom 800 acres being private land, and not knowing where it began or ended ... but their behavior was beyond understanding. We have seen a deer running in front of the skidder on a logging road and some guy in hot pursuit firing away like mad, 'til my husband stopped the skidder and chewed him out. They even hunted with motorcycles at times, mind you they got nothing, but the local people never saw a critter of any kind for weeks after they left."

Accidents or illness in fall or winter were the worst hardships they encountered; then being scared silly while being bounced around in air pockets as the plane took advantage of a "calm" in the storm to bring them out.

Loutitts lived in the old Bradshaw house for three years. There were some old bottles of hooch found from the rum-running days but whether anyone drank it, they have no idea. Arrowheads from an earlier period of history were often found, and stories were told of pirates being shipwrecked, and burying their gold on Robert's beach. The legend of the Indian princess being entombed beneath the rock at the head of Hidden Basin was often repeated. As no one could touch the princess and live, the two braves who dug her grave had to take their lives and be buried with her.

Bunny says they never lived life the hard way, but she canned and baked bread on a wood stove in Bradshaws. In the winter they heated with the fireplace and read by coal oil lamps, much preferring the peace and quiet to the noise and conversation. "Believe me it is a true test for a marriage, if you can stand your own company and each others ... if you have any faults or any good points, island living will bring them out."

Like others, she remarked on the children who acted and spoke like adults and the old folks who were as spry and active as youngsters. The island was a great equalizer.

"People who live on the water are a special breed," she says, "and you just don't land on the beach one day and move into their circle. You have to prove yourself and earn your place in their society. They are honest, helpful, and don't like getting used, so if your intentions aren't honorable, you won't be welcomed back again."

Margaret McIntyre's book, *Place of Quiet Waters*, describing her stay on Nelson was published in 1965, rocking the island boat for awhile. Some thought that she and Jerry Jervis had "used" their neighbors, but Miss McIntyre says that "no slighting remark was ever intended to be taken unkindly." She remembers that the "simple fishermen and loggers of the thirties were the kindest, most helpful, and finest men she had ever known."

In the same year as the book came out, Dora Johnstone, Judd's wife and friend to all over the years, succumbed to a heart attack. This helpful, dignified woman had been a mainstay to Nelson for the almost twenty-five years she had lived in Blind Bay. Everyone felt the loss keenly, but no one more than Judd, who gave up the will to live afterwards. He followed her four years later. People missed Judd's sense of fun, he was always laughing and telling stories. Allen Farrell remembers that Judd always said everything was good—food, people, boats, everything. "He never criticized anyone," he added. Few could ask for a better epitaph.

Very few families scratched their living on Nelson during the seventies and early eighties, but if a newspaper had existed, it would have recorded a number of incidents which touched their daily lives—cougar sightings, floats broken loose, chlorine barges last seen off Cockburn, another death at the quarry, killer whales in Hidden Basin, aquaculture beginnings, Aristotle Onassis visiting, Harry Robert's death, and of course, other lesser happenings including island gatherings and new arrivals.

An interesting event that crackled the telephone wires from bay to bay was the shooting of a local resident. A story is told of the Coast Guard receiving the call while in the midst of an argument over which of the fellows were going to do the dishes. "It's your turn, I did them last night," could be heard along the dock at Saltery Bay.

The distressed voice on the line pleaded with them to investigate the shooting on Nelson Island. Apparently a jealous lover had shot a man in the leg for visiting his girl, and was still waving his gun.

A man with a gun? They looked at each other, all in their very visible orange survival suits, and at their very vulnerable rubber dinghy, their only means of transportation to shore. Suddenly the dishes didn't seem like such a bad idea, and the argument was on again. "You go, I know it's my turn, you two did them last night."

The victim fortunately hadn't been hurt too badly, and the culprit was apprehended and jailed.

Another shooting caused less excitement, but still added fare to the dinner table, both literally and figuratively in John Marian's case. The Marian's had rented some Green Bay property in 1976 from which to base John's beachcombing operations. For quite some time in the early eighties, a cougar had been spotted coming in close to the old cannery/shingle mill site, threatening the family pets. When it came close enough that John felt his daughters might also be in danger, he killed the marauder.

Stringing B. C. Electric's power cable across Jervis Inlet. Black Ball Ferry *Quillayute* **passes beneath.** J. Milligan

Tyee Air, a more modern form of transportation. B. Loutitt

Harry Roberts and Marjorie, 1956. Y. Mortensen

A Johnstone family picture. Back row: Alice, John Vaughn, Evelyn, Judd's brother Steve, and Grace. Front row: Thelma, Dick Krentz, Dora, and Judd. T. Deberri

The animal proved to be old with dulled claws, not quick enough to compete in the wild. Again, a Green Bay canner was pressed into service as Australia Marian filled her jars with cougar meat, possibly with less zeal than Mrs. Henry would have done it, but just as effectively. And very probably the Marian girls will say, when they talk about this in later years, "Seems we ate that canned cougar forever."

The Marians differ from most of the families living on the island today, as they are not into aquaculture. With the demand for rock diminished, and the new growth of trees not yet ready for harvesting, islanders have had to investigate new means of surviving. Mariculture offers not only the chance to be in on a developing field suitable to their environment, but also reduces the taxes on their attractive waterfront properties. These promising new ventures may turn the tide on what has generally been an unlucky island for business.

The pattern of failure didn't fade even when the economy brightened in later years. Ocean-Lake Estates, a budding resort on West Lake, was developed in the late fifties and early sixties—a wharf was built, roads were put in, as well as a caretaker's cottage, laundromat, store, showers, and a dock on the lake. For a time, the American company was attracting attention on the lower mainland, but it fell through. A local story is told of one of the owners getting drunk and putting gasoline in a diesel engine, blowing himself up.

Less dramatic, but just as unsuccessful was a development in Cockburn Bay and the top of Cape Cockburn in the early seventies. Vern Paulus, principal stockholder of Dunhill Developments, envisioned a strata title subdivision of approximately 320 acres divided into thirty-five lots of various sizes. Residents would own some property outright, as well as sharing common ground such as the wharf and park. Owners were to get one vote on all issues pertaining to the strata corporation. At a general meeting a strata title council would be elected to provide for maintenance, preservation, and architectural control.

Paulus hired Hubert Loutitt to log the area and put in a road. Then with the help of Rick Fedosov, he also dug a lake to service the lots. It was quite a production, but didn't appeal to would-be summer residents. The property just sat there until B.C. Hydro bought it to put the Cheekeye-Dunsmuir line through.

Although Tom Brazil was just a memory in the seventies, a story of his was revived when a visitor to Blind Bay came down a trail from the outhouse swearing she'd seen a monkey. Tom had made a driftwood monkey which he kept attached to his fireplace with a huge boomchain. If anyone asked why the chain, he would say with a straight face, "If the damn thing gets out in the bush, I have a devil of a time catching it."

This visitor gave up trying to catch the monkey she saw and tried to enlist help. Someone picked up her empty glass and commented dryly that she'd probably had enough to drink, but she ignored him and insisted she'd seen this monkey swinging in the trees.

Well, Blind Bay residents were apt to agree that Nelson's pretty much of a tropical paradise on hot summer days, but no one could swallow the monkey story. That is, until they'd heard from neighbors that during their absence for a few days, Aristotle Onassis' yacht was anchored in the bay, lit up like a Vancouver street on a flat barge. Through the binoculars a woman had been seen on deck with a monkey draped around her. It was assumed that they'd come ashore and the monkey had escaped. It was never seen again. They should have borrowed Tom's boomchain.

Bigger animals in another season were cause for alarm when killer whales came into Hidden Basin one New Year's Eve. Trapped by the rapids, they cavorted in the water near Hope's fish farm, ringing in the New Year with strange-sounding noises. The Hopes feared for their young fish, afraid the whales would scare them. They called the Vancouver aquarium for advice, and then assured the fish would be all right, enjoyed the antics of the visitors until they left on the outgoing tide.

More potentially dangerous than the whales are the chlorine barges that were last seen off Cape Cockburn. They were on the way to the MacMillan Bloedel Pulp and Paper Mill in Powell River when they broke loose in a storm. Experts say the poisonous gases will be so diluted if they ever escape, that no harm will be done. But it's hard to believe that the sea life will be unaffected, and the islanders wait expectantly for proof.

In April of 1979, Harry Roberts, boatbuilder, artist, and philosopher, passed away in his ninety-fifth year. He had been a resident of Nelson Island for forty-seven years, longer than anyone else in recorded history. His funeral, and family reunion that followed, were held in Roberts Creek where he first pioneered in 1900. His grandnephew, Paul Merrick, carved a bald eagle on his casket for

"Chack Chack," and one of his granddaughters remarked, "It seems like the end of an era, we've known him forever."

Sunray lives on after him, having not yet given way to the constant dampness of the rain-forest climate.

Danger and Death

Over the years there have been many men who wintered on Nelson or spent two or three years and left. Some went out to sea and never came back. Some met their fate in logging camps. The woods could be cruel, much more cruel than the ocean. A broken cable could make hamburger out of a muscular body. Most of them are forgotten, but now and then someone will say, "Do you remember `Auld Reekie,' the old Scot, or `No Talk'?" No Talk, the Czechoslovakian whose real name is forgotten, was a good electrician. Then there was Lapollainen, the fiddle-playing fisherman who never bathed. He believed water was bad for you, inside and out. The old Russian was another. They added color for awhile, then moved on.

The men were offhanded about the dangers they confronted daily. This same unwashed fisherman told a story about falling overboard in open water further north. It was said he was all alone with his boat going full tilt. He couldn't swim fast enough to catch the boat, but he managed to grab an anchor rope trailing behind. He held on to this until the boat ran out of gas. By this time, it was said, he was somewhere off the tip of Alaska. He was lucky, he lived. No Talk died tragically in a fire. One islander talked about how the old-timers never got sick. I guess they just died, she added.

But some of them did get sick, and before they died they were cared for by the sympathetic women of the area. Cherry Sandvold looked after Old Tom Brazil before he was taken to a nursing home, and Florence Frederickson spent four years caring for the extremely arthritic Harry Roberts. When his knees gave way in early 1975, he was carried overland through the trail from Cape Cockburn to Hidden Basin.

Thelma Deberri looked in on Madam Wehner faithfully when her husband was away. Lotte was crippled with arthritis, had high blood pressure, a bad heart, and had suffered two strokes. Her fear of boats, unheard of on an island, kept her imprisoned in her home, but Thelma Deberri kept her in touch with the community. Ann Pettigrew and Agnes Harding helped Tom Hughes before he died.

Most had lived to be a ripe old age, but it seems to be a human trait to add inches to a fish, miles to a road, and years to an old man. All the old men were reputed to be in their nineties, but only Harry Roberts and possibly Fred Easthope, actually were. Tom Brazil was close at eighty-eight, but Judd was only seventy-eight when he died.

Sue Milligan Returns

Of the four Milligans that grew up on Nelson, only Sue has returned to the area to live. She and Bob Harris have bought Copper Island at the entrance to Telescope Passage. Like the Roberts kids, she tried what she thought was a better life; she worked in a bank, and then spent ten years as a legal secretary to J.S.P. Johnson and Rod Johnston in Powell River, only to return to island living.

When she first came back, Lew gave Bob a job right away but refused to hire Sue to do a "man's work." When she threatened to take a job that the opposition had offered her, he consented to let her count boomsticks and run the crew boat at Vanguard. The men she carried were leary of the boss' daughter at first and were always waiting for her "to hit something or screw-up a docking." Gradually they realized she could handle a boat pretty well.

Only one stretch of weather made her doubt her ability, fog for ten days straight. She had four to ten men sitting behind her and no radar on board. The fear of getting between a tug and its tow was a constant plague, and she admits that it got to her.

The return to island living, Milligan style, with lots of vehicles, road clearing, and elaborate water system, has been a reflection of Sue's early life. Even the fishing career she's chosen dates back to her first love, catching fish for her cat, then catching perch to catch ling cod. "Cod fishing is the only kind of fishing I ever wanted to do," she states. Today she owns the thirty-seven-foot *Henry Bay,* a flooded cod boat that carries 10,000 pounds of water. She fishes from April to November.

Sue Milligan with seventy-five pounds of halibut. S. Milligan

Old 1950 air force ambulance present problems in moving to island. Sue Milligan is accused of being a woman driver. S. Milligan

Geoffrey, Jacquelyn, and Peter Partington loading reluctant goats onto boat. J. Partington

Their small island boasts 300 feet of road, a large shed to house a tractor and all the mechanical junk and paraphernalia collected (a habit learned from her father), a light plant, a cabin, and an outhouse. A thirty-year old army jeep and a more modern van were brought to the island by using equipment borrowed from Lew, and help from Blair and friends.

She likes to be in control, and employs various back-up systems to ensure that she is, right down to her grandmother's flat irons—one for the fire and one for the board. Extra tanks of propane and stores of dry wood carry them through rough days, although the reliable *Henry Bay* is equal to any weather the inlet has to offer.

One of the most interesting projects Sue and Bob have ventured in during their four years on Copper Island, was laying their new waterline on Thanksgiving of 1982. Lew had told them of a little spring up on Nelson, with a clay bottom and bedrock, which he had piped down to camp to water-cool the brakes on the trucks. Even in the heat of summer it never dried up. The project involved laying an almost continuous piece of one-inch plastic gas hose underneath Telescope Passage, which would defeat most people before they started, but illustrates the resourcefulness of the islanders.

Sue recounts that "We got these big cable reels that the cable comes on. We took the *Beaver*, which is a self-propelled steel barge with a double drum winch on it. My younger brother, Blair, helped me with this down at Annis Bay. We mounted two cables, reel cables, on the front of the *Beaver*, and then we had 125 PSL gas hose (and it's all on a big coil). Blair made a spool stand for it and he picked it up on a crane that they use to lift boats in Annis Bay. That turned the cable and fed it down to the reel on the *Beaver*. Then he took a five-eighths cable that he had there, and rolled it onto another drum. Then we went over to the property next to Frank and Irene Johnson's, where Alice and George Larson used to live. We brought the hose down and connected it there. We had a side winder tie alongside the *Beaver* 'cause the *Beaver* could move forward and back on her own power but couldn't maneuver sideways. We had a couple of us reeling off the cable, and we tied the cable and the black plastic line together with heavy duty electrician's ties and halibut ground lines and cement weights that we had.

"Then we had a diver, Kenny Stevens, who went along the line making sure there were no kinks in it and not hung up over a cliff or anything, and putting more rocks on it where it needed them. Once we got it started, it went really quickly."

The bottom of Telescope is dead flat sand and the water is fifty feet deep at the deepest spot. They erected cable signs on each side to warn boaters not to anchor. Altogether the hose is 5,000 feet long: 1,000 feet from the dam to the beach, 2,500 feet under water, and 1,500 feet to the cabin.

If this Milligan work holds true to form, this line will still be in use when he next history of Nelson is written. If not, Sue has her back-up system ready, the rain barrels are out.

The Sunray Roberts Today

by Yolana Roberts Mortensen

I have attempted to tell what I can remember about growing up at Sunray. It may seem like a unique way of life now, but at the time we didn't think it was out of the ordinary. I think we did miss out on some things, particularly schooling. But we made up for it in other ways, by being very self-confident and practical in almost everything that we have done since. We are all living the same sort of life now, even in a much different time.

Zoe is living on her sailboat, the *Sail Fish*, where she is fishing abalone at Porcher Island, out of Prince Rupert. She married Al Lloyd at Pender Harbour and made her home there for over ten years. There are five grandchildren there.

Lee is tow-boating around Quadra Island with his own tow boat and chief deck hand, Joan. He also had been married and has four children and is now a grandfather.

I am living on a farm in the Bulkley Valley near Smithers. I married a second time, to a man who has five children. They are almost all grown up now. I spent ten years looking after most of them. Now we have a farm and all that goes with it.

Each of us had tried to fit into what we thought might have been the better way, of the regular job and the city life, just to find that we didn't really fit there at all. We found that we needed more independence and freedom. I think we may have all found what we have been looking for. I'm sure that our dad would have been proud of each one of us. None of us are after the dollar and I think we are all satisfied with what we are doing and what we have done. Dad always said that we were here to give our children a better life so they could pass it on to their children. Let's hope that some of them can do just that.

It has been fifty years since I was born. Sunray has been a good part of all the lives that started there, or ended there for that matter. It has been sold several times. B.C. Hydro has it now. They cleared a wide swath across the hills for their transmission line right-of-way. The house is falling apart and the woods are growing up around the grounds. Seems a shame that such a beautiful place so close to Vancouver and the gulf couldn't have been put to better use than this.

The beautiful beach will always be there, and the memories of the place will always be with us.

West Lake Today

For long eons, the call of the loon has been heard over West Lake, breaking the stillness of the night. The natives listened to its yodeling cry; the Senklers heard it in the early 1900s and today their grandson, Jack Manley, still a visitor to the lake, warms to the sound.

The big house with the shady verandah where the Senklers watched the loons returning to their nests, is no longer there. It had been built in 1918, a magnificent palisade style log house—by a man named Smith (possibly G. Y. Smith of Vanguard Bay). It sat on Manzanita Island, earlier named Vicars Island by the surveyor, but most commonly called Senkler's Island by guests today. The beautiful 48-acre island was purchased as a summer spot for tenting around 1909 for $10 an acre.

After the lodge was constructed, four tent floors were built around it as well as a sizable workshop and a boat house for the various canoes, rowboats, and motor boat that became part of the camp scene. The Senklers were the only summer people on the lake until the late forties when Don McDougall arrived. The lovely palisade home was gone then. It had burned in the summer of 1940 when Jack's grandmother put the ashes for the outhouse into a cardboard box, and an ember flared. "Almost everything went up in smoke except the workshop, the boat house, and one tent," Jack remembers. "The sad thing was that so many irreplaceable mementos of bygone years were lost."

"The island was sold in 1968 to the Oswald family and I am the last member of the Senkler family remaining on the lake. My wife and I have a tiny leasehold property on the south shore and from there I look across the lake to the island and to nearly sixty years of happy memories."

The other summer places on the lake appeared slowly over the years. In the 1950s there were between six and ten cabins; today there are over twenty. The J. Alan Traynors visited the McDougalls in the early fifties and liked it so much they bought their own retreat several years later.

Dr. Traynor recounts that, "We gradually grew as summer people and the West Lake Community Association was formed around 1972 with an annual meeting and several executive meetings during the year. The majority live in Vancouver but some are on Vancouver Island and several families (at least three) are from California. We have guidelines for the use of West Lake and they are well adhered to. Motors are under ten hp and there is no racing or water skiing."

As the lake is a loon nesting spot with nests built very close to the water, any large wave could wipe out their offspring for the year. They often have just a single young one and are in danger of becoming extinct without protection.

Art Bishop and his wife Millie lived on the east side of Nelson, coming in 1973. They lived near the lake and Art patrolled during the winter months and checked the cabins, replacing Lawrie Wray as custodian and helper. His boat *Ruf-n-Redy*, one of the last Turner-built boats of the forties, was once the *Fircom*, a taxi for a church camp for kids.

The summer people hold an annual regatta, which began as a birthday party organized by Millie for Art, around the end of July. At that time, many of the lake residents didn't know each other, and the Bishops got them all together for the day. The event became a regatta about five years ago.

Pansy West was back for the regatta last year. She still owns part of the land which was left to her by her father, but has sold most of it to B.C. Forest Products.

Ann Pettigrew, who once cooked for Lawrence Wray at Westmere, is sometimes still part of the summer scene on the lake. Her uncle, Charles Fathergill, willed her Fathergill Island, another small haven on West Lake. Ann has the distinction of owning both a lake island and an ocean island in the Nelson Island area. Her Blind Bay cottage is home for her from late summer to November.

Dr. Traynor shares the view of other lake dwellers when he says, "Our great joy is the ecology, the quietness, and the loons, and these attributes continue up to the present day. May they continue on for our grandchildren."

Conclusion

Roots didn't push too deeply into the solid granite. Only the Johnstone family saw a second generation raised on Nelson, but it was a generation that wasn't content to be isolated. Some of the Wray grandchildren, children of Emily's and Walter's marriages, made their home at Fearney Point for awhile, but the families left when the children were school age.

The quarries are all silent now, no powder blasts to startle the fish.

A carefully built rock reservoir is still in good condition on Kelly Island where nearby an old boiler and other equipment are rusting away. A vertical wall of granite shades a man-made valley where early twentieth century houses succumb to the coastal weather. Draft dodgers from the Vietnam War lived there for awhile in the seventies, surviving on puffed wheat.

Vanguard Bay, where illegal Chinese immigrants were once smuggled in the early part of the century, is just a booming ground now. Another wreck, the *Sandy Cape* has been added to the beach in recent years. Sis Harris can still be seen cod fishing around the Vanguard area, and sixty-four years after her first clam-digging picnic there, Sis is still getting clams from Blind Bay.

The area's pearl in the oyster, Hardy Island, that private sanctuary of hand-swept paths and soft-eyed deer, is only a memory. Macomber's home and outdoor barbeque is gone, but the swimming pool remains. A chestnut tree on the northern shore still drops its golden leaves where the deer once walked to the sea to lick the salty rocks. Scrap granite from the quarry operations litters the western beaches, and large booms of logs that were once the island's cool forest, take shelter from the northerly winds on the lee side of the island.

A second growth of timber is rapidly growing to replace the logged-out areas of Nelson. Sophisticated helicopter logging outfits will probably be seen someday on the mountain tops which once felt the rough hooves of logging oxen and horses.

Abandoned fruit trees, gnarled and scabby with age, still send tired branches upward to compete with the rapidly producing firs and cedars that threaten their existence. A huge holly tree marks the site of the John Wray family, Nelson's first pioneers, and stately English oaks near the remains of an ivy-covered shake house are reminders of Walter Wray and his sisters.

One of the Hammond daughters, Enid Wright, tells of visiting the Fredericksons of Hidden Bay, where the English walnut tree their family planted still casts its shade on the front lawn. While there, she drank a glass of bubbly champagne made from the Hammond's apples. Wehner's beautiful property is now a preserve for Ducks Unlimited. Haven Island is still in the Charman family and Fran (Deberri) Lambert's family still have property in Blind Bay. Most of the old homes have been bought by summer people who are happy to enjoy the solitude of the relatively nonindustrious area.

A number of residents of Nelson found their final resting ground at Pender Harbour or Powell River, but for years a special permit allowed the early people to be buried on their property. One of the last of these was Tom Hughes who rests in a shaded spot within the scent of honeysuckle on the island he left to Ann Pettigrew. A tombstone of Nelson granite marks the grave.

In 1979, Robert Harding died suddenly of a brain aneurysm and his ashes were taken to Blind Bay to be scattered near those of John Maynard, a boyhood friend who at seventeen, had met his untimely end in a road accident.

The inhabitants had come in waves, with each quarry contract or logging settlement. The largest wave crested in the late forties and early fifties when around one hundred British Columbians called themselves Nelson Islanders. By contrast, the winter population of Nelson and surrounding islands was just over fifty residents in

The *Agnes H.* "Aggie" still is tied at pier on Nelson Island. Here it is shown in the forties.   A. Harding

The four Wray sisters in the 1980s. Back: Sarah Edmond and Harriet Helliar (born in Quarry Bay in 1895). Front: Emily Dillabough and Ruth Lewis.   S. Edmond

Harry Roberts in front of Sunray window around 1970. Y. Mortensen

Old deserted cabin at Granite Island. K. Southern

1982. New ripples are being formed in mariculture around the island, and may develop into the wave of the future. Hope's fish farm in Hidden Basin (Tidalrush Farms) is well established now, and smaller fish and/or oyster farms are being tried by Linda and Tom May in Cockburn Bay; Cliff and Sue Foreman in Hidden Basin; Ray Lipp in Blind Bay; Jean and Dave Shearer in Hidden Basin; and John and Frances Picken in Blind Bay. With the fish farms in Sechelt, and three processing plants in Hotham Sound, the area is coming on strong.

With the promise of increased interest in aquaculture, will come the need for another freight service to transport the millions of tons of fish feed to the area, and the millions of tons of salmon and oysters from it. A freight service akin to the beloved Union Steamships would again make island living more viable.

Diving, though not an industry, may bring a rush of enthusiasts to the crystal clear winter waters of the mouth of Jervis Inlet. From the air, several submerged hulks can be seen. National Geographic referred to the area as a "fantasia of strange and colorful sealife."

A gravel company is opening again soon on Cape Cockburn, treading on the ancient Indian Village of Skwalt, and threatening the rugged beauty of Harry Robert's former shores. It will employ the local boys for awhile, but until then, Billy and Tony Harding, Bill's sons, and the last of the Hardings on Nelson, can be seen occasionally beachcombing the shores. The old *Agnes H* is still tied to the pier at the family home.

Most of the old-timers are gone now, the Wrays, Tom Brazil, Judd and Dora Johnstone, Harry and Marjorie Roberts, Fred Easthope, Lorne Maynard, Bill Harding, Tom Hughes, and Slim Deberri; but some are still with us, displaced in cities like the displaced Nelson rock. But like the stable rock base of the buildings, the island life gave them a firm foundation for the rest of their life. They're thankful now they have no firewood to cut for winter, no floats to tend, no ramps to lug supplies up at low tide, no water pipes from the stream to freeze, and no snow to shovel or boats to bail. They are also thankful for the wonderful memories of summer sunsets reflected on still water, the early morning fishing, or weekly visits on Boat Day—of raising their families in a simple time when honest hard work and cash and carry were the bywords.

Epilogue

It's been three years since this story was finished. As far as I can determine by the available government records, 1987 will be Nelson Island's Centennial year. One hundred years will have passed since the first quarry workers split the high quality granite at the Quarry Bay site, and settled the surrounding shores.

For the first time in its recorded history, a fourth generation is living on the island, two-year-old Wills Harding. His great-grandmother, Ann Pettigrew, came to housekeep for Harry Roberts in 1943, with her daughter Jacqueline, now Will's grandmother, who married one of the "navy boys," Geoffrey Partington (remember the wedding aboard the *John Antle*?) and gave birth to Marjorie Ann, his mother. Although Marjorie Ann grew up in the Victoria area, she spent summer holidays on Tom's Island, where she met Billy Harding, the son of Bill, Sr., who, with his brothers, logged the hefty giants during the early years of the depression to build the View Point Lodge.

Bill and Marjorie Ann have a small salmon farm and have successfully raised smelts which will become root stock. Their nets off Tom's Island don't alter Ann's view, which has remained the same for thirty years. Not too far from them is Tony, Bill's brother, and his Pender Harbour wife, Cindy. They have two second generation island youngsters, Mark Anthony and Starr. After trying commercial fishing, and helping Bill, Tony is now setting up his own sawmill.

Tidal Rush Farms has grown in the past three years to become a showpiece for B.C. aquaculture. Both Tidal Rush, and Hardy Island Sea Farms, the newest salmon venture in the area, under the general managership of Mike Mulholland, were unaffected by the algae bloom that swept through the lower coastal farms in the early summer of 1986, wiping out two-thirds of the stock in many areas. Quick action at the Hardy site saved their pens of young fry. They pumped the deeper water to the surface, and created currents with the dozer boat which would keep the bloom from getting in close.

It was rumored that the Nelson Island Sand and Gravel Co. didn't fare as well when they delivered a poor grade of gravel to the construction site of Expo '86. When they lost their contract, they went the way of so many former island businesses.

As the island is almost ready for re-logging, Nelson will once again come into focus. Young and old alike foresee a battle brewing between the logging outfits and the aquaculture. But just as important to the history of Nelson Island, are the families the logging will attract, the new wave of islanders.

I began this story with a mention of the Pickens, and would like to end it that way as well. This year is the twentieth anniversary of their involvement with Nelson Island, and marks the high school graduation year of their daughter, Suzy. An island gathering helped her celebrate her many years of correspondence schooling, with a hot tub party, as true to island ingenuity, John has designed the oyster-larvae tank to serve as a hot tub when not incubating future restaurant fare.

All three Pickens have now completed their high school years mostly through correspondence courses, alternating their textbooks each day with a turn at helping John in the sawmill. They learned early that to live on the island meant hard work. When Ping was being built, it took all five of them to push the 29-foot frames through the planer, a slow inch-by-inch grinding. But they learned too, that hard work reaps its rewards, and celebrated heartily when Ping was launched at Stan's graduation party. The boat was to become Stan's living quarters through his first year of college in Nanaimo, when he took his course in aquaculture.

Stan is now assisting Jim Wilson at the Hardy Island Seafarms, which is almost in his old backyard, and Simon has graduated from selling muffins to the yachts in Ballet Bay, to becoming a full-fledged chef at Malaspina College.

Like so many of the former islanders, Frances and John have now become summer residents, enjoying the comforts of winter living in Burnaby. Our families still get together occasionally, but now someone is always missing. Our oldest son, David, is working for a spell on Hardy Island for Andy Wheatley, manager of the forestry division of Hardy Island Sea Farms, and I often eye property on Nelson, which would one day give us a permanent link to its granite shores.

Bibliography

The British Columbia Archives:
British Columbia Directories, 1898 to 1940
British Columbia Sessional Papers, B.C. Schools Reports 1915-20, 1950-59
British Columbia Voter's Lists, 1898-1923, 1920, 1924, 1952, 1956, 1975
Public Archives, Canada:
Archivist, Trade and Communications Records, letter, re: telephone, June 10, 1983, Sept. 20, 1983
Minister of Environment, B.C.
J. McIntyre, Geographical Names Clerk, letter, May 9, 1983
Ministry of Mines:
Calcareous Deposits of Southwestern British Columbia, 1957
Calcareous Deposits of Georgia Strait Area, 1947
Report of the Building and Ornamental Stones of Canada, 1917
Yearly Reports from the Minister of Mines, 1899 to 1983
McIntyre, Margaret, *Place of Quiet Waters*, Longmans Canada Ltd., Don Mills, Ontario, 1965
Patterson, T. W. *British Columbia Shipwrecks*, Stagecoach Publishing Co. Ltd., Langley, B.C., 1976
Sinclair, Bertrand W., *Poor Man's Rock*, Little, Brown and Co. Boston Walbran, Captain John T., *British Columbia Coast Names*, J. J. Douglas Ltd., Vancouver, 1971
Holbrook, Stewart H., *Tall Timber*, Macmillan Co., New York, 1946
Jackson, W. H., *The Handlogger*, Alaska N.W. Publishing, Anchorage, 1974 Marshall, James Stirata, and Marshall, Carrie, *Vancouver's Voyage*, Mitchell Press Ltd., Vancouver, 1955 and 1967
Newal, Gordon and Williamson, Joe, *Pacific Coastal Liners*, Superior Publishing Company, Seattle, 1959
Peterson, Lester R., *The Gibsons Landing Story*, Peter Martin Books, Canada, 1962
Rushton, Gerald A., *Echoes of the Whistle*, Douglas & McIntyre Ltd., Vancouver, 1980
Rushton, Gerald A., *Whistle up the Inlet:* The Union Steamship Story, J. J. Douglas Ltd., Vancouver, 1974
Sinclair, Bertrand W., *The Hidden Places*, Ryerson Press,

Toronto, 1922 White, Howard, ed., *Raincoast Chronicles*, Harbour Publishing, Madiera Park, B.C., 1976

The British Columbia Archives

The Daily Colonist, June 4, 1972; Feb. 2, 1975

"Hijacking of the Beryl G" *The Shoulder Strap*, winter 1940

The Vancouver Sun, Sept. 20, 1973

The Powell River Historical Archives:

The Powell River News, Oct. 1, 1959; Dec. 24, 1970; April 13, 1949

The Town Crier, May 21, 1945

"Around Nelson Island in Western Jervis Inlet" by Ree, from *Sailing Life*, August, 1982

"The Hunters Who Never Starved," by Robert Pinkerton, from *True Magazine*, 1948

"An Ancient Village," by A. J. Charman, *The Coast News*, Oct. 30, 1935 "Nautically Speaking," by Allen Greene, from *The Log*, June, 1959

"Nelson Island Granite," *The Colonist*, June 2, 1894

"Tragedy off Trial Island," *Victorian*, March 28, 1973

"British Columbia's Cold Emerald Sea," by Larry Kohl, *National Geographic*, Vol. 157, No. 4 (April 1980)

Index

Adams, Frederick, 13, 14
Adventus, 179
Agamemnon Channel, 24, 54, 65-67, 97, 125, 126, 130, 191
Agnes, H., 157, 211
Alaska, 64, 66, 69
"Alcatraz" (Caldwell) Is., 125
Alexander Point, 37, 136
All Red Line, 37
Amscold, D., 186
Amscold family, 55
Andersons, 32
Anderson, Captain, 12-14
Angus, Forrest, 128
Anna of Annis Bay, 152
Annis Bay, 152, 203
aquaculture, 198, 211, 213
Arab II, 139
Arbutus Logging, 108
Armour, Mrs., 142
Armstrong, Mrs., 142
Armstrong, Robert, 15
Arnold, Harold, 74, 89

B.C. Directory, 177, 186
B.C. Electric, 130, 188, 196
B.C. Forest Products, 150, 207
B.C. Hydro, 130, 198, 205
B.C. Police, 61
B.C. Slate Co., 19
baby, first born on N.I., 21
Baggs Bay, 27
Baggs family, 27, 54
Baker's Sawmill, 97
Ballet Bay, 90, 136, 149, 164, 165
Bargain Harbour, 115
Barker, Polly, 129, 130
Barnes, Eddie, 104
beachcombing, 195
Beatons, 32
Beryl G., 61
Billings Bay, 88, 100, 103, 136-140, 145, 164, 182, 193
Billy the Kid, 63
Bishop, Art & Millie, 163, 206
Bjorklund, Hugo & Bea, 73, 94
Black Ball Ferry, 131, 196
Blind Bay, 10, 37, 54, 56, 69, 70, 73, 83, 97-101, 126, 135, 137, 138, 144, 146, 150, 155, 158, 164, 182, 199, 207, 208, 211

Blithe Spirit, 162
Bloor, Arthur, 12
Bluebacking Days, 71
Boat Day, 75, 178
boatbuilding, 33
boats and owners, 69, 157-164
Bordignon Masonry Ltd., 20
Brackman-Kerr Milling Co., 24
Bradshaw, George & Lorna, 179
Brazil, 96
Brazil, Tom, 33, 37, 43-51, 63, 90, 147, 166, 177, 179, 200, 201, 211
Britain River, 150
British Secret Service, 96
Brother Twelve, 74
Bruce Lake, 54, 135
Buchamer, Fred, 128
Buchanen, Guy, 32, 59
Buckley, Mr., 127
Buell, Senkler, 27
Burnett, Dr., 30, 31

CBC, 185
CPR Excursion Boat, 67
Cadboro Bay, 13
Caldwell Island, 125, 135
Calgary, Alta., 19
California, 206
Campbell, Al, 193
Campbell, Frank, 186
Campbell, Hugh, 32
Campbell, Ken, 40
cannery, 57
Cape Cockburn, 73, 77, 78, 80, 81, 90, 97, 98, 135, 136, 146, 164, 169, 170, 179, 195, 199, 200, 211
Captain Island, 131, 135
Cardero, 104
"Castle, The", 74, 93, 102
Chack Chack, 73, 74, 111, 157, 174, 177
Chack Chack Cove, 73
Chack Chack Lake, 137
Charman, A. J., 77, 78, 80
Charman's (Haven) Is., 77, 208
Chasina, 37, 55
Cherry, Art, 146
Chilco, 37, 76
Chinese immigrants, 207
Christensen, Andrew, 13
Christmas, 19, 180, 185

Christmas, E. & N., 162, 174
Church House, 179
Clarke, Geo. T., 54
Cliff-Lomond Packing Co., 115
Clio Island, 21, 94, 138, 148
Coal Harbour, 60, 97
Coast Guard, 60, 61, 195
Coast News, The, 77
Cockburn Bay, 60, 61, 83, 100, 186, 193, 198
Cockrill Bay, 54, 55
Cod Reef, 55
Colonist, 10
Columbia, 151, 159
Comox, 24, 76
Cook, Bill, 186
Cook, Clarence, 123, 186, 191
Copper Island, 201, 203
Costello, Mike, 150
cow (Henry's), 114, 116-121
Crowe, Wilf, 127
crime, 88
Cruikshank, Forbes, 61

Dainard, Agnes, 52
Daniels, Mel, 144
Dauntless, 144
Davidson Marine Freight, 130
Davis' Garden Bay Hotel, 103
Deadman's Cove, 15
De Corcy Island, 74
Deberri, Frances, 98, 99, 142, 147, 181, 208
Deberri, Slim, 44, 98, 147, 211
Deberri, Thelma, 76, 147, 148, 181, 191, 200
Deer/Game Sanctuary, 44-46
Delivery Service, 177-179
Delong, Lim, Robt. & S.S., 186
Delong's Logging, 124, 186
Deserted Bay, 66
Deserted Bay Logging, 129
diving, 211
Dominion Gov't Drydock, 19
Dragovitch, Chris, 24
D'sonoqua, 179
Dubois, Oliver, 125, 188, 191
Ducks Unlimited, 208
Duncan, deckhand, 13
Dunhill Developments, 198

Earl's Cove, 64
Easthope engine, 95
Easthope, F., 73, 94, 95, 201, 211
Eaton's, 92, 178
Edmond, S. see Wray, Sarah Jr.
Egmont, 24, 27, 65, 70, 130
Ellis Granite Co., 15
Emerson, James S., 37
Empress Jam Co., 24
England, 21
Esquimalt, 19

Fairview Logging Camp, 71
Family Herald, 102
farming, 33, 59
Farrell, Allen &/or Sharie, 112, 144, 147, 148, 157
Farrell, Keray, 144
Fathergill, Chas., 154, 155, 207
Fathergill Island, 207
Fearney Point, 21, 50, 136, 207
Fedesov, Rick, 183, 198
Fedesov, Sue, 143
Ficek, F., 94, 144, 145, 189-190
fire, 73, 130
fishing/fishermen, 27, 65, 70, 71, 94, 98, 120, 126, 127, 128, 144
Fitsgerald, 95
Fletcher, Jim, 60
'flu epidemic of 1918, 31
Follet, Ron & Lola, 123-125, 182
Follet, Chris, 124
food preservation, 30
Fordney tariff, 19
Foreman, Cliff and Sue, 211
Forresters, 72
Fox Island, 45, 137
Fox, R. I., 11, 137
Fraser Canyon, 104
Fraser family, 112
Fraser Mills, 114
Frederickson, C. J., 40, 142
Frederickson, H. &/or Florence, 192, 200, 208
Free Farmer's License, 24
Friel Falls, 135
Friel Lake, 58

"Gas-boat Bandit", 88
Gibson, E. R., 45
Gibsons and Howay, 188

216

Gibsons Landing, 64, 78, 89, 103, 143, 186, 192
Gillies Bay, Texada Is., 28
Gillis, Wm. J., 61

Gonzalves & Dames, 75, 179
Goose Lake, 181
Grafton, Vera, 185
granite, Aberdeen, 11, 15
Granite Island, 12, 32, 136
Grant, Alexander, 33, 136
Grant, A.S., 52
Green, Paul, 186
Green, Roger, 75, 125
Green, W.E., 134
Green, Mr., 58
Green Bay, 57, 104, 105, 109, 112, 123, 128, 134, 165, 177, 181, 186, 195
Green Bay Shingle Mill, 57-59
Greene, Alan, Canon, 132, 151-156, 159, 185
Greene, Rev. Heber, 151
Greene, Lorne, 89
Gregorson, Dave, 112
Grey, Tom, 119
Gua Yee, 162
Gulf Islands, 74
Gulf Lines, 117, 130, 150
Gulf Mariner, 102
Gustafson's Logging, 129

H & L Logging, 102
Ha Ha, 102, 163
Haddington Island, 12
Haggerston Castle, 12
Hallgren, Bob, 108
Halls, Clarence & Irving, 186
Hammond, Barbara, 28, 31
Hammond, Bertram, 31
Hammond, Clara, 30, 31, 52, 77, 181
Hammond, Clifford, 28, 33, 39
Hammond, Coral, 28, 31
Hammond, Dick, 37, 54
Hammond, Doris, 28
Hammond, Enid, 28, 31, 32, 40, 50
Hammond family, 25, 28-33, 40, 50, 51, 59, 137, 171, 180, 208
Hammond, Fred, 28
Hammond, Henrietta (Rita), 28
Hammond, Henry (Hal), 28, 31, 32, 33, 37, 39, 40, 52, 165, 170, 177
Hammond, Isabel, 28
Hammond, John L., 28, 30, 33, 54

Hammond, John, Jr., 158
Hammond, Mary (Minnie), 28, 59
Hammond, Mary (May) 28, 30, 32, 33, 37, 39, 170, 177, 181
Hammond, Nelson, 31, 40
Hammond, Phyllis, 31, 52
Hanna, Dora Ida (Johnstone), 63
Hanson, Gus, 94
Harding, Arlene, 98, 142
Harding, Art & Lyn, 74, 75, 85, 89, 92, 94, 100, 139, 140, 143, 156
Harding, Barbara, 98, 142
Harding, Bert & Daphne, 98, 165, 182, 187
Harding, Beverly, 98, 142
Harding, Bill Sr., 74, 75, 85, 92, 94, 156, 164, 187, 191, 211
Harding, Bill Jr. & Marj. Ann, 211, 212
Harding, David, 98, 142
Harding, Dorothy, 98
Harding, Ernie, 74, 75, 92, 94, 156
Harding, Jimmy, 98, 142
Harding, Joann, 98, 142
Harding, June, 98, 142
Harding, Margaret, 98, 142
Harding, Mary, 98, 142, 208
Harding, Paul & Agnes, 44, 50, 74, 75, 85, 92, 94, 98, 100, 142, 156, 182, 187, 201
Harding, Paul Sr., 74, 75, 83
Harding, Robert, 98, 142, 208
Harding, Steven, 98, 142
Harding, Tony & Cindy, 212
Harding, Wills, 212
Hardy Island see also Hardy Is. quarries, 21, 33-51, 63, 70, 77, 96, 135, 142, 166, 177, 188, 207
Hardy Island Developments, 188
Hardy Island Sea Farms, 212
Hardy, Sir Thos. M., 10
Harper, Mrs., 142, 143
Harris, Bob, 201
Harris, Henry, 56, 57
Harris, Sis, 162, 181, 207
Hartley, Bill, 96
Haskins, John, 96
Heid, 54
Heid, Charlie, 57
Heid, Louie, 55
Heikinnen, Otto/Captain Henry, 74, 85, 87, 88, 91, 92, 114-120, 123, 124, 156, 158

Heikinnen, Esther/Mrs. Henry, 116-121, 198
Helliar, Fred, 25, 187
Henderson, Dr., 20
Henry's cow, 117-121
Hidden Bay/Basin, 25, 28, 31, 54, 60, 61, 87, 89, 92, 93, 100, 137, 145, 146, 171, 172, 182, 185, 186, 200, 211
Hiltzes, 56
Hipp, Len, 102
Hodges, Bill, 188
Honolulu, 16
Hope, Brad & June, 172, 199
Hospital, Powell River Gen., 20
Hospital, St. Mary's, 80, 98
Hotham Sound, 56, 57, 58, 135
Howay, R.R., 188
Hughes, Tom, 90, 94, 185, 201, 208, 211
Hugo's Island see Clio Island
hunting/hunters, 24, 30, 65, 66, 72, 193, 194
Hydrographic Surveys, 9, 134

Ibey, Walter, 123
Indian history, 9, 14, 21, 65, 66, 72, 77-79, 87, 179, 195, 211
Indian place names, 134-135
influenza of 1918, 69
Irvine's Landing, 21, 26, 65, 75, 116, 178
Irving, Capt. John, 14
island ingenuity, 101, 142, 213

Jackson, W.H. & Ruth, 69
Jeffries, Grandma, 70, 71, 184
Jenkinson, Frank, 48, 150
Jervis, Jerry, 86, 88, 91, 92, 93
Jervis Express, 130
Jervis Inlet, 9, 33, 58, 63, 65, 67, 69, 72, 130, 135, 136, 164, 186, 211
Jervis Inlet water taxi, 149
Jervis Logging, 109, 111, 125, 128
John Antle, 151, 153, 154
Johnson, Frank & Irene, 203
Johnson (from Gibsons), 131, 139
Johnstone,
Alice, 69, 70, 82, 147, 150, 184
Bob, 70, 82, 144, 147, 148, 150
Bruce, 66

Catherine (Kate), 66
Charles Roscoe, 63-65
Dora Ellen (Jeffries), 48, 69, 70, 71, 82, 98, 99, 144, 147, 150, 184, 194, 197, 211
Dora L, 63, 64, 66, 70, 101
Doris, 147
Evelyn, (also Roberts/Vaughn), 43, 69, 70, 82, 98, 147, 150, 184
Forrest/Judd, 44, 46, 48, 63-72, 73, 76, 82, 94, 98, 129, 147, 150, 190, 194, 197, 201, 211
Frances, 147, 148, 150
Frank Sr., 64, 65, 69
Frank Jr., 70, 71, 82, 145, 146, 147, 148, 150
Grace, 69, 70, 82, 98, 150, 184
Ivan, 66, 69
Jack, 66
Patrick, 64
Ruth, 64
Steve, 64, 197
Thelma, 69, 70, 82, 89, 98, 150, 184, 197
Thomas Forrest, 148
Jorgenson, Ivor, 88
Jorgensons, 186

Keast and Allen, 15
Keefer, Hugh E., 15
Kelly and Murray, 19
Kelly Island, 37, 135, 178, 207
Klaussens, 72, 73
Klein, Charlie, 103, 186
Klein, Pete, 94, 186
Kokomo Lake, 124
Krentz, Dorothy, 99, 142, 147
Krentz, Richard, 98, 148, 198
Krentz, Richard Jr., 98, 99, 142

L & J Timber, 129, 133, 186
L M & N Logging, 124
Lady Cecilia, 159, 178
Lady Cynthia, 159, 178
Lambert, Fran see Deberri
Laughlins, 186
Larson, George & Alice, 144, 148, 191, 203
Lasqueti Island, 157
Lauson, Oliver, 186
Lawrey, Captain, 31
Lee Lake, 137
Lees, Samual J. & Mrs., 52
Lewises, 32
Leyland, Christopher D., 43, 45
Leyland, Christopher J., 43

limerock, 10
Linber, Mr., 56
Lipp, Ray, 211
Lloyd, Al & Queenie, 100, 204
Lloyd's Store, 179, 181
Log The, 152
logging, 33, 65, 71, 85, 94, 108, 111, 120, 124, 125, 128-133, 180
Lombes, Magnus, 19
Loutitt, Hubert & Bunny, 167, 172, 192-194, 198
Lyle, John, 21

McKay, Jock, 15
Macomber, LeRoy and/or Marion, 43, 44, 45, 46, 70, 71, 138, 168, 188
McConnell, Geo., 114
McDougall, Don, 205, 206
McEwen, Marj. (Roberts), 144, 157, 182, 192, 197, 211
McIntyre, Allen, 88
McIntyre, Marg., 86, 88, 91, 92, 93, 194
McKechnie, Ian, 114
McKenzie, Don & mother, 179
McKenzie Lake, 136
MacKinnon, John & J., 37, 43, 188
McLaughlin, John, 72
MacMillan Bloedel, 199
McDairmid, J. & Co., 15
McDonald, Jack, 40
McIntyre, Bat, 44
McMinnville, Oregon, 19
McNutt Dave & Ethel, 75-76, 186
McNutt Bros., 138, 139, 146, 147, 167, 185, 191, 211
Mack Truck Dealership, 104
Madiera Park, 103
Mahood, Ian, 188
Mahood's Logging, 188
mail service, 37, 48, 69, 130, 137, 138, 144, 192
Malahat, 60
Malibu, 69
Manley, Jack, 205, 206
Manzanita/Senkler's Is., 27, 205
Marian, John & Australia, 195
Markowski, Count, 44
Marshall, Art, 186
Maud, 14
May, Linda & Tom, 211
Maynard, Carole, 83, 84, 87, 98, 100, 142, 147, 185, 191

Maynard, John, 98, 142, 185, 208
Maynard, Lorne, 83, 84, 87, 91, 98, 136, 138, 139, 146, 147, 167, 185, 191, 211
Maynard, Royal, 98, 100, 142, 185
medical help, 30, 60, 80, 98, 149
Mermaid, 64
Merrick, Betty, 192
Merrick, Paul, 199
Millard, Sandy &/or Grace, 146, 147, 184
Miller, George, 21
Milligan, Bill, 129
Milligan, Blair, 132, 133, 143
Milligan, Doug, 129, 131, 139, 140, 141, 143, 158
Milligan, John, 129, 140, 142 Brenda, 131
Milligan, Kathy, 129, 139, 140, 141, 143, 171, 183
Milligan, Lew & Joan, 44, 129-133, 142, 148, 167, 171, 191, 215
Milligan, Rick, 140
Milligan, Sue, 129, 132, 133, 140-143, 171, 172, 183, 185, 201-204
Mitchell, J. & B., 168, 174
Morien II, 123, 192
Morrice and Abel, 15
Mortenson, Yolana see Roberts
Murdock, Royal, 105, 111
Murdock's Store, 119, 179

National Geographic, 211
Navy boys, 98, 212
Naylor, John Murray, 43
Neilson, Chris, 129
Nelson, Sir Horatio, 10, 135
Nelson Is. Contracting, 133
Nelson Is. Sand & Gravel, 212
Neville Rock, 135
New Westminster bridge, 15
Nile Point, 136
Nixon, C.T.R., 33, 37
Northern Developments Ltd., 188
Nuotio, Allen, 88, 89, 93
Nuotio, Geo. & Cecilia, 88, 89, 93
Nuotio, James, 98
Nutria, 176

Ocean-Lake Estates, 198
Onassis, Aristotle, 199
orchids, 174
Orpana, Oscar, 131

Osborne, Dod, 96
Oswald family, 206
oysters/oyster farm, 70, 211, 213

Parliament Buildings, 10
Partington, Geoff, 96-98, 144, 152-156, 202, 212
Partington, Rob, 97, 154
Patrick, Walter, 162
Paulus, Vern, 198
Pearson, Harold, 108
Peddie, Tom, 131
Pender Harbour, 24, 48, 50, 64, 69, 75, 80, 84, 94, 97, 100, 102, 103, 105, 107, 108, 110, 112, 115-117, 125, 130, 143, 146, 167, 179, 180, 181, 186, 208
Peters, Mrs., 142
Peterson, Lester, 77, 134
Pettigrew, Ann, 94, 101, 102, 147, 151, 154, 170, 172, 201, 207, 212
Pettigrew, Jacqueline, 101, 102, 166, 169-171, 177, 212
Pettigrew, Marjorie-Ann, 212
Phelan, 166
Philip, Charlie, 104
Phillips, Rae, 186
Picken, Frances, 150, 211, 213
Picken, John, 144, 150, 158, 160, 168, 172, 211, 213
Picken, Simon, 170, 213
Picken, Sue, 168, 213
Picken, Stan, 213
Pilot, 12, 13
Place of Quiet Waters, 194
place names, 134-137
Plumper, 9, 135
Point Grey, 19, 167
Porter, Digby, 188
Powell Lake Contracting, 133
Powell River, 180, 208
Powell River Co., 188
Prepontaine, Claire, 52
prices, 64, 75
Princess Louisa Inlet, 66
Principia, 44
Prior, Cam, 108
Pritchard, 21
Prohibition, 60
prospecting, 66, 72
Province, The, 32, 77

Quadra, 60
Quadra Island, 71
Quarries, 11, 14-20, 72, 207
Blind Bay, 82, 182

Fox Island, 19
Granite Island, 19, 75, 94
Hardy Island, 19, 37, 40, 43, 52
(Sechelt Granite Quarries)
Quarry Bay, 12, 14-20, 21, 78, 84, 94, 135, 212
Quarry workers, 14-20
Quillayute, 150, 196

radio, 76
Rat Portage Logging, 30, 54
Read, George, 125
Read, Jim & Lou, 125, 191
reports, Min. of Mines, 11
Richards, Capt. Geo., 9
Rittenhaus, Minnie, 59
road to Vancouver, 150, 191
robbery, 88
Roberts Creek, 74, 102, 103, 139, 191, 199
Roberts, Cherry, 73, 74, 79, 80
Roberts, Harry, 45, 73, 74, 76, 77, 79, 80, 81, 84, 89, 95, 97, 99, 100, 101, 103, 137, 144, 157, 160, 164, 165, 170, 174, 177, 191, 199, 200, 201, 211, 212
Roberts, Lee, 77, 79, 102, 103, 158, 169, 171, 177, 186, 191, 204
Roberts, Yolana, 73, 74, 78, 79, 93, 94, 101-103, 154, 165, 169-176, 191
Roberts, Zoe, 83, 94, 102, 103, 169-172, 177, 204
Robinson, Charlie, 32

St. Mary's Hospital, 98, 146
St. Vincent's Bay, 131, 135
Saltery Bay, 48, 70, 130, 135, 143, 150, 179
Sakinaw Lake, 97
Samson, Mr., 109
Sandvold, Cherry, 50, 130, 142, 147, 200 see also Roberts
Sandvold, Chris, 158
Sandy Cape, 207
Sansen, 114
Santa Maria, 31, 37
School District #46, 139
schools, 65, 71
Ballet Bay, 133, 139-143, 185
Brooks, 133
correspondence, 143, 213
Hardy Island, 40
Henderson, 133
Max Cameron, 133

218

Nelson Island, 52
St. George's, 131
St. Vincent's, 131, 135
Schutts, 72, 89
Seattle, 11, 18, 19, 64
Secco, Mary, 40
Sechelt/Sechelt Inlet, 124, 211
Sechelt Health Unit, 149
Selma, 37, 161
Senkler, Harry & Marg., 27, 205
Shamrock Lumber Co., 186
Shannon, John, 186
Shearer, Jean & David, 211
Sherry, Jessie, 139, 142
Shipbuilding, 89
Shipwreck, 12
Shuck, Raymond M., 144, 190
Simon Fraser Univ., 108
Sinclair, Bertram & Ora, 32, 137, 163
Skookumchuck, 124
Skwalt, 135
Sladey, Olli, 186
Slaven, Sam, 32
Sliammon, 87, 129
Slide, Saltery Bay, 70
Smith, Grace, 52
Smith, George Y. & Mrs., 31, 156
Smith, Ruth, 40
Smith, "Smitty", 97
Smith, Wm., 32
Social Credit Gov't., 122
Soldier settlement, 59
Spartan, 162, 179
Spence, Jack, 118
Spencer, Victor, 32
Spencer's Dept. Store, 32
Spilsbury, Jim & Win, 44, 50, 87, 90
Stager, Frank, 162
Stevens, Kenny, 203
stores, 37
storms, 165-166
Stillwater, 75
Strawberry Island, 136
Stringer, Rev., 146, 147
Sunray, 68, 79, 146, 175

surveying, 91, 92
Swanson, Frank & Anna, 186
Sweeny, Michael, 54

T & S Logging, 188
Talbot-Lehmann, 92
Tait, Bob, 99
Tarbuck, Edith, 52
Tegg, Harry, 21, 33, 34
telephone, 50, 143, 167, 168
Telescope Passage, 10, 46, 66, 135, 144, 201, 203
television, 148, 171
Texada Island, 48, 80
Thema, 83, 164
Thomas, Harry & Margery, 90, 91, 100, 136, 179, 191
Thomas, Audrey, 90, 136
Tidalrush Farms, 211, 212
Tidewater Navigation, 130
Tom's Island, 212
Tough, George, 21
trapping, 33, 65, 70, 71
Traynor, J. Alan, 206
Trebett, Charlie, 109
Trevor, R. Dan, 177
Trial Islands, 102
Triton, 95
Tyee Airways, 193, 197

UBC Extension Dept., 102
Underwood, Rowena, 190
Union Steamships, 37, 75, 76, 137, 180, 211
United States, 10, 19
Union Tidewater, 130

Valdez Island, 74
Vancouver, 10, 19, 20, 21, 26, 27, 30, 37, 52, 75, 89, 91, 95, 102, 126
Vancouver, Capt. Geo., 9
Vancouver Bay, 66, 188
Vancouver Granite Co., 15
Vancouver Island, 74
Vancouver Sun, 95
Vanguard, 129, 164

Vanguard Bay, 88, 128-133, 135, 156, 164, 167, 169, 171, 201, 207
Vaughn, Gary, 99, 142
Vaughn, John, 98, 198
Vaughn, Evelyn see Johnstone
Velos, 12-14
Vicars Island, 205
Vickers, Jack, 21
Victoria, 10, 12, 15, 19, 102, 212
Victoria Harbour Seawall, 10
Victory, 10
View Pt. Lodge, 74, 83, 98, 126, 128
Viitanen, Ken, 123, 174
Viking Prince, 123

wages, 71, 72
Washington, Lake, 11
water rights, 92
Warnock, Martha & Martin, 35
Waterman, Miss, 142
Wehner, Edward, 94-97, 174, 208
Wehner, Madam Lotte, 95, 147, 174, 185, 200
Welcome Pass, 78, 101
West, George, 25, 26, 167
West, John, Jr., 26, 73
West, John, Sr. & Mrs., 25-28, 153, 155
West, Mrs. Sr., 25
West, Pansy, 26, 43, 73, 206
West, Robin, 26, 73
West Coast Granite Co., 19
West Lake, 73, 128, 130, 136, 198, 205-207
Westbrook, Bill & Mrs., 182, 183
Westmere, 26, 27, 90, 126, 127, 128, 152
Whalley, Graham, 108
Wheatly, Andy, 213
Wheeler, Lilian, 52
White, Cindy, 105, 106, 108, 110

White, Frank, 104, 110, 123, 188
White, Howard, 104, 105, 110, 171
White, Kathleen, 104, 105, 106, 110
White, Marilyn, 105, 106, 108, 110
White Arrow I, 164
Williams, Ralph, 186
Wilson, Frances, 146
Wilson, Jim, 213
Wilson, John (Brother 12), 74
Windsor Cannery, 115
Wood, W., 37
woodcutters, 64
Woodfibre, 83
Woodward, Billy, 32
Woodward's Dept. Store, 32, 101, 178, 193
World, The Vancouver Daily, 32, 178
Wray,
  Charles & Mrs., 20, 21
  Emily, 21, 209
Wray family (John), 20-26, 37, 65, 166, 208
  Harold, 21
  Harriett, 21, 209
  John, Jr., 21, 50
  Ruth, 21, 209
  Sarah, Sr., 20
  Sarah, Jr., 21, 37, 209
  Wilford (Tiff), 20
Wray, Lawrence & Kay 90, 126-128, 155, 166, 191, 206, 207
  Alec, 128
  Betty, 126, 128
Wyoming, 63

Yates, 105, 112, 123, 182
Yates, Frank, 105
Yates, Harry & Lorene, 123-125
Yates house, 106, 108
Yolana Lake, 137
Young, Jim, 32

Zoe Lake, 137

Author Karen Southern, left, shares an island moment with good friends Joan and Lew Milligan.

ABOUT THE AUTHOR

Karen Southern was born and raised in Powell River, B.C., less than 25 miles (40 km) from Nelson Island. Her association with the island residents began in 1975 with an introduction to the Pickens of Blind Bay. She is co-archivist for the Powell River Historical Museum Association and the current president of the Powell River Heritage Research Association. As well as free lance writing, she is a part-time piano teacher, teaching beginning students.